In Defense of Negativity

STUDIES IN COMMUNICATION, MEDIA, AND PUBLIC OPINION

A series edited by Susan Herbst and Benjamin I. Page

In Defense of Negativity

ATTACK ADS IN PRESIDENTIAL CAMPAIGNS

John G. Geer

The University of Chicago Press

Chicago and London

JOHN G. GEER is professor of political science at Vanderbilt University.

The University of Chicago Press, Chicago 60637
The University of Chicago Press, Ltd., London
© 2006 by The University of Chicago
All rights reserved. Published 2006
Printed in the United States of America

15 14 13 12 11 10 09 08 07 06   1 2 3 4 5

ISBN: 0-226-28498-0   (cloth)
ISBN: 0-226-28499-9   (paper)

Library of Congress Cataloging-in-Publication Data
Geer, John Gray.
 In defense of negativity : attack ads in presidential campaigns / John. G. Geer.
   p. cm. — (Studies in communication, media, and public opinion)
 Includes bibliographical references and index.
 ISBN 0-226-28498-0 (cloth : alk. paper) — ISBN 0-226-28499-9 (pbk. : alk. paper)
 1. Campaign management—United States. 2. Advertising, Political—United States.
3. Political campaigns—United States. 4. Presidents—United States—Election—History.
5. Negativism. I. Title. II. Series.
JK2281.G44 2006

324.7'3'0973–dc22

2005015164

⊚ The paper used in this publication meets the minimum requirements of the American
National Standard for Information Sciences—Permanence of Paper for Printed Library
Materials, ANSI Z39.48-1992.

To my brother, David F. Geer

Truth . . . has to be made by the rough process of a struggle
between combatants fighting under hostile banners.

JOHN STUART MILL, *On Liberty*

Contents

Illustrations

TABLES

Acknowledgments

As the title of this book indicates, I offer a defense of negative advertising in presidential campaigns. My core argument is that negativity has far more merit than conventional wisdom would lead us to believe. Criticisms, even harsh ones, enrich the prospects for democratic governance. I develop this argument from theoretical, normative, and empirical perspectives. The value of negativity, however, extends beyond the electoral arena. It also improves our scholarship and helps to invigorate our research communities. We often do not think of it in these terms, but I am truly grateful for the "negativity" of friends, family, and colleagues. Without their criticisms, this book would not have been possible. I benefited tremendously from these thoughtful "attacks" and I am pleased now to thank all of those who have been so integral to this project.

To begin, let me extend my deep appreciation to colleagues and friends with ties to Vanderbilt University. Brad Palmquist, who has moved to sunny California to conquer internet polling, provided helpful feedback on a number of issues, including some thorny methodological questions. Ben Radcliff, who went back to Notre Dame in search of good beer, gave me thoughtful and detailed reactions to key parts of my argument. Geoff Layman, who now enjoys Terrapin basketball, graciously read a draft of the manuscript and offered many helpful suggestions. He also was always willing to discuss my project at any time, which was invaluable to me. Marc Hetherington, now a content Red Sox fan, provided excellent assistance with the last few chapters of the manuscript. In addition, I owe many thanks to the students from my two seminars on negative advertising in 2002 and 2004. These courses provided me a chance to think more about my arguments, especially as these very talented undergraduates prodded and pushed me on various fronts. I must also thank Caitlin Sause, a member of one of those seminars, for generously sharing some of her data from the 2004 election.

I would be remiss not to offer special thanks to Bruce Oppenheimer, who inexplicably thinks congressional elections are more interesting than presidential elections. Despite this questionable judgment, Bruce read the entire manuscript and supplied many good ideas. Moreover, we had numerous conversations about the project and Bruce always offered sound advice. Bruce is both a superb critic and a good friend.

There are two other people that warrant special mention. First, my father (and one-time coauthor), James Geer, commented on an earlier draft, giving me suggestions about how to clarify some arguments. Having a father who is also a coauthor provides a special kind of collaboration that I appreciate more each and every day. Second, I want to express my appreciation to Katherine Barbieri. Kathy read rough drafts of early chapters and gave me timely and thoughtful comments. She would often read a chapter before any one else, which meant she had to deal with lots of typos and incomplete arguments. She carried out this task with much cheer and good humor.

I owe particular thanks to the Center for the Study of Democratic Politics (CSDP) at Princeton University. The CSDP provided the support that allowed me to take a full year off from teaching, while offering an ideal setting to write and to think. It is an absolutely wonderful place that I recommend to all scholars. In particular, I thank Doug Arnold, Jason Casellas, Patrick Deneen, Amy Gershkoff, Fred Greenstein, Stan Kelley, Shana Kushner, Jonathan Ladd, Rick Lau, Gabe Lenz, Dave Lewis, Nolan McCarty, Adam Meirowitz, Tali Mendelberg, Diane Price, Tom Romer, and Keith Whittington. I also must thank my fellow visiting scholars at the CSDP: John Huber, Valerie Hunt, David Karol, Markus Prior, and Ken Shotts. They helped to create a wonderful social and intellectual environment, whether we were going out for drinks or talking about each other's work in the hallway. Our year together was great fun and I learned a tremendous amount. John Huber deserves an extra note of thanks since he kindly read the full manuscript and offered many helpful suggestions. Last, but not least, I must express my heart felt appreciation to Larry Bartels. Larry is not only a valued friend, but he is always willing to provide help with any research question. Larry is someone who truly believes in the collective good. He runs the CSDP with the idea of creating an environment where everyone works together to improve each other's scholarship. As evidence of this, I could stop by his office any time and pick his brain about some puzzle or problem. It was usually not a long conversation, since Larry's mind is sharp enough to develop sound solutions very quickly. His willingness to discuss any subject at a moment's notice was exceptionally generous and the quality of the help was off the charts. This kind of attitude was shared by everyone with ties to the center. I owe the CSDP and all these people a great deal. This book, simply put, would not have been written without their support.

It is now important to mention Julian Kanter. Julian is an unsung hero in this project and other projects which have made use of the Julian P. Kanter Political Commercial Archive at the University of Oklahoma. Julian had the foresight to realize that television advertising was important and needed to be collected for the historical record. He came to this realization in the late 1950s—long before anyone else did. Because of his instincts, he collected an amazing array of material for scholars and other interested parties. I think it only fair to acknowledge his important role in this book and the larger scholarly process. The following term is often overused, but it is entirely appropriate here: Julian P. Kanter is a *pioneer* in the field and he deserves recognition for his many efforts. I hope these few sentences let Julian know how much I appreciate all he has done for me, and more importantly, for the study of political communication.

My thinking about this subject has also profited tremendously from interviews and conversations with Alex Castellanos, Carter Eskew, Bill Fletcher, Mike Murphy, Roy Neel, Greg Stevens, Jennifer Tierney, and Vin Weber. These individuals all possessed outstanding insights about negativity, elections, and campaigns. It was not only fun to talk with each of them, but I learned a great deal about the political process and how practitioners think about negative campaigning. I have been particularly lucky to have had the chance to teach with Roy Neel, who has been and continues to be a close advisor to President Clinton, Vice President Gore, and Governor Dean. Our interactions have given me better insight into the political process. I am truly fortunate, both personally and professionally, to have had the chance to work with Roy.

My experience with University of Chicago Press has been wonderful. Susan Hersbt, the series editor, offered a set of criticisms of the manuscript that were on target and truly allowed me to improve it. How she manages to be an insightful critic and dean of a major college all at the same time is more than amazing. In fact, it is down right intimidating. The other reviewers also provided insightful suggestions that allowed me to clarify key ideas and arguments. John Tryneski, the editor at the University of Chicago Press, has provided encouragement and support for this project, and has been a delight to work with. Any one who has a chance to work with these fine people should not hesitate for a moment and seize the opportunity.

As with any book, my appreciation extends beyond those who had any direct contact with writing of the manuscript. In particular, I benefited from a great circle of friends and family. Friends, such as Randy Sharber, helped me keep things in perspective, especially as we coached our kids' baseball teams over the years. David Bader, a "real" scientist, was (and is) always willing to have a beer and a few laughs. My mother, Jean Geer, makes sure I know that she can and will help me in any way possible *and* at a moment's notice. My children, Megan and James, saw the importance of my spending time at the CSDP. Though they knew during the course of that year that I would be only able to see them every other weekend, they understood the benefits of my having the full year off from teaching to complete this book and were extremely supportive of me during this time. They are the true joys in my life and I appreciate them more than they will ever know.

To put the finishing touches on this manuscript, I locked myself away at my summer home on Joe's Pond in West Danville, Vermont. This is a place of great beauty, charm, and personal comfort for me, having spent lots of time as a child at this "camp" and on this lake. It is also a place where I can (and did) get a lot of work done and watch the loons all at the same time. I had the good luck in 2003 to be able to purchase this home with my brother, David Geer. It had been owned by our uncle Jim years earlier. "Uncle Jim's Camp" will be a great place to get work done over the coming years. But more important, it will be a place where friends and family can gather to spend time with one another as we water ski, tube, fish, or just cruise the lake on our pontoon boat, the *Jenal III*. I want to thank Jane Milne, my cousin, who helped make Joe's Pond a second home to me and my children. It is a special place and all the more special because of people like Jane. I hope she understands what a warm and open heart she has and how her generosity and love makes Joe's Pond so special to so many people.

Now, mere words cannot convey fully or properly my feelings towards my brother, David Geer. I owe him far more than just "thanks." He and I are a team in many ways, whether we are buying various "toys" for the summer home or figuring out the best way to flip someone on a tube as we pull them at high speeds with our ski boat. But rather than offering a few sentences that would inevitably fall short of expressing my thoughts, I have simply dedicated this book to him. I hope and trust that this dedication will convey my feelings toward him and my personal debt to him for being such a great and supportive brother. I am indeed lucky on this front.

With all the help of these kind and knowledgeable people, I have no excuses. Whatever is of value in the pages is due to their generous assistance and support. The problems are all my responsibility.

So, now with the book complete, I must await the negativity of my colleagues as they read and evaluate the ideas, arguments, and evidence presented in these pages. As a defender of negativity, I am ready not only to accept the slings and arrows of my fellow social scientists around the country, but to acknowledge that this process is in and of itself a good thing. It may not always be pretty or fun, but criticism is essential for improving any undertaking we are engaged in, whether it be advancing a program of research or electing a president. I look forward to these exchanges and hope that observers of all stripes will better appreciate the many payoffs from negativity in our free, open, and democratic society.

John G. Geer
Joe's Pond, Vermont

CHAPTER ONE

The Need for Negativity:
An Introduction

Negative advertising is the crack cocaine of politics.

SENATOR TOM DASCHLE

Senator Daschle's comment is more colorful than most, but its basic conclusion is not unique.[1] There is a consensus among policy-makers and political elites that attack advertising in campaigns, like crack cocaine, is dangerous to the well-being of our society. Hardly a day goes by during an election season without some discussion of "negativity" and its adverse impact on our electoral process. We are, in effect, awash in a sea of negativity about negativity. David Broder, the dean of political journalists, claims that "trivial is too kind a word" for the content of today's campaigns, arguing that "the ads people are seeing are relentlessly negative: loaded words and nasty implications about the opposition candidates; often never a hint as to why a voter should support the person paying for the TV spot."[2] Another observer, Victor Kamber (1997, xiii), argues that negativity poisons the political debate by presenting arguments that are "ridiculous, irrelevant, and irresponsible," dragging down the discussion "to the level of tabloid scandal."

These types of concerns are commonplace. The title of Kathleen Jamieson's (1992) book represents the typical sentiment of pundits: *Dirty Politics: Deception, Distraction, and Democracy*.[3] There is an unusually strong association between negativity and deception. Consider the fact that we rarely label negativity as "tough, competitive politics" or "heated exchanges" between combatants. Instead, it is almost always equated with being "dirty"—something that is "not fair," "below the belt," and in need of a good "cleaning."

The public shares this distaste for negative advertising. As Larry Bartels (2000, 1) notes, the "ordinary citizen's perception of the electoral process is marked by cynicism and dissatisfaction with the nature and tone of the contemporary campaign discourse." In poll after poll, data confirm Bartels's observation. In July 2000, nearly 60% of the public, according to a Gallup Poll, was dissatisfied with how candidates conduct their campaigns (Brooks 2000a). A major part of the public's unhappiness with elections was tied to negativity. Only 19% of the public felt that negative advertisements even had "a place in campaigns." The vast majority of citizens do not even think you can learn anything of value from negative advertisements. In the 2000 Vanishing Voter survey, 75% of the public thought that "candidates [were] more concerned with fighting each other than solving the nation's problems" (Patterson 2002, 51). Two years later, a different poll found that "eight in ten voters say negative, attack oriented campaigning is unethical and damaging our democracy."[4] In February 2004, 81% of the public in a poll sponsored by the Pew Research Center indicated that negative campaigns bothered them "somewhat" (20%) or "very much" (61%).[5] Headlines, such as the one in *USA Today* on October 22, 2002, capture the electorate's general sentiment quite well: " Orgy of Negativity Has Many Voters Disgusted."

Scholars often join the fray, arguing that negativity has detrimental effects on the political process. Perhaps the most important of these concerns involves the so-called demobilization hypothesis. Stephen Ansolabehere and Shanto Iyengar (1995) contend that negative advertising disenfranchises voters by turning them off from the political process.[6] Ansolabehere and Iyengar are sufficiently worried about the pernicious effects of negativity that they offer recommendations designed to decrease the use of attack ads in political campaigns. Thomas Patterson (2002, 51) shares this basic concern when he observes that "negative politics appears to wear some people down to the point where they simply want less of politics." Bruce Buchanan (2000, 364) too complains about negativity, arguing that candidates "should emphasize their own plans and qualifications and strike tones much more likely to inspire than alienate."

In short, worries about negativity lie at the very center of concerns about the health of our electoral system and whether that system promotes a process that can be thought of as democratic. These are serious concerns that warrant serious attention. The problem is that we are all too quick to criticize the system and wring our hands over the ill-effects of negativity. We need to pause, reconsider starting assumptions, and marshal systematic data that will allow us to assess more fully these fears and concerns. For example, why are political commentators so troubled by negativity? Any deliberative process usually benefits from having criticism and debate. Why would attacks in campaigns be so problematic? Why do they not advance the debate? Politics is often rough and tumble; why isn't attack advertising thought of in those terms? Why are we so worried about "civility" in campaigns? If some aspect of a candidate's record is alarming, is it not important to raise that concern in an attention grabbing fashion? Shouldn't the public understand the seriousness of the problem?

Campaigns are not feel-good exercises; they are pitched battles for control of the government. The stakes are often high and the competition is usually fierce. The real issue should be whether or not candidates present the information in campaigns that is useful to voters. The tone of that information should be a secondary issue, at best.

This book seeks to advance our understanding of negativity in campaigns, in general, and attack advertising, in particular. My focus is on the ads presidential candidates' have aired on television over the last the last five decades and the quality of information contained in those commercials. I shall tackle the topic of negativity from normative, empirical, and theoretical perspectives. The end result will be a set of ideas and evidence that I hope will help to stem this tide of disgust and help to forge a reevaluation of the merits of negativity in political campaigns.

PROPAGANDA AND NEGATIVITY

We can all recall attack ads that have rubbed us the wrong way. One of the most cited examples of an unfair attack is the so-called Daisy spot President Johnson's campaign ran during the 1964 presidential election. In this famous ad, a small girl is picking petals off a flower and counting the number pulled off. As she does, an ominous voice begins a countdown—"ten, nine, eight, seven, six . . ." At the end of the countdown, the screen is filled with a nuclear blast, followed by Lyndon Johnson saying: "These are the stakes—to make a world in which all of God's children can live or to go into the dark. We must either love each other or we must die. Vote for President Johnson on November 3rd. The stakes are too high for you to stay home." This ad was called "vicious,"[7] "disgusting,"[8] and "a lie."[9] Barry Goldwater, the implicit target of the ad, responded angrily by saying, "The homes of America are horrified and intelligence of Americans insulted by weird television advertising by which this administration threatens the end of the world unless all-wise Lyndon is given the nation for his very own."[10] Yet, defenders of the ad point out that the spot was addressing the most important issue of the time: nuclear war. It was presenting that theme against the backdrop of Goldwater's own statements about the possible use of nuclear weapons.[11] So why should it be so unreasonable to raise an issue that was most threatening to the lives of the American people and alert voters to what candidates have said about such an important matter?

Over two decades later the Tank ad, in which George Bush criticized Michael Dukakis's views on defense, drew criticism from many quarters. For those who may not remember, this spot made use of news footage the Dukakis campaign hoped would make their candidate look tough on defense. The Governor was driving in a tank, wearing the appropriate head gear that his advisors thought would convey the pro-military image they sought. But the camera was not kind to Dukakis and the Republicans seized on the opportunity. As the tank made its turns with Dukakis giving directions and waving to the crowd, the Bush ad listed all the defense programs Dukakis opposed. To add a little spice to the attack, the Republicans inserted the sound of grinding gears to the audio, suggesting that Dukakis could not even make the tank run smoothly.[12]

Kathleen Jamieson (1992, 6), when assessing the ad, observed that it "suffers from the weakness that pervades contemporary campaigning: It tells us what Dukakis is against but not what Bush is for." But why should that be a "weakness"? Shouldn't the public have known that Dukakis had a record of opposing various defense programs, especially with the cold war still raging? Moreover, given that Dukakis was claiming that he was strong on defense, was it not fair that the Bush campaign comment on the accuracy of that claim? Jamieson pushed further, claiming that the real problem was that the ad misrepresented Dukakis's position on the various defense programs mentioned in the spot. For example, she questions the claim in the ad that the Democrat from Massachusetts opposed "virtually every weapon system we developed,"[13] noting that Dukakis "did not oppose the Stealth Bomber but favored using it as a bargaining chip if conditions with the Soviets warranted" (1992, 7). Jamieson's complaint has some merit. Even so, the basic point remains: Dukakis was not an advocate for the Stealth Bomber.[14]

I am reluctant to judge definitely whether the ad was "misleading" or not. The claims were surely exaggerated. But were they misleading? I am not sure. In the end, one's answer is highly dependent on one's conception of "misleading." It is probably fair to say that, on average, Bush did have a stronger record of supporting weapons systems than Dukakis. This point that may be the most relevant, since it makes the ad at least defensible and surely underscores why the ad appeared so effective (or at least drew so much commentary).

Even so, critics of attack advertising can still label these ads as misleading. Barry Goldwater, despite all the rhetoric, was not in favor of nuclear war, nor was Michael Dukakis actually a supporter of a "weak" national defense. But herein lies the central problem: propaganda, by its very nature, exaggerates. It always puts the best possible spin on an issue. No candidate can be expected to be a neutral observer, judiciously weighing the key points of contention. They are highly motivated partisans seeking control of the government, making their best case for holding that office.

What seems to go largely unnoticed by many critics of negativity is that exaggeration applies to positive propaganda as well. When Ronald Reagan touted his tax cuts in his 1984 advertisements as he sought reelection, he left out references to the large tax increase he signed into law in the middle of his first term. That should come as no surprise, but few observers label those ads as misleading. In 1988, Michael Dukakis's spots stressed the fact that he had balanced the budget in his own state of Massachusetts ten times.[15] While the claim was technically accurate, it ignored the fact that the state's constitution required a balanced budget. Voters were encouraged to believe that Dukakis was a fiscal conservative. Was that an unfair inference? We tend to evaluate the content of attack ads and assume positive advertising is reasonable and accurate. Perhaps this inconsistency helps explain why Bob Squire once said, "most lies in politics are told in positive ads."[16]

The underlying point here is that it is difficult, and perhaps impossible, to assess with any precision whether any ad is truly misleading. By some standards, all ads are misleading in the sense they stretch the truth. The core problem is that one has to decide when exaggeration crosses the line. There are times when it is clear. But, for the most part, the issue is at best murky, because by definition the objective of propaganda is to present biased information on behalf of a candidate (or a cause). While I will address this topic in concluding chapters of this book, I will leave the assessment of whether political advertising is misleading to pundits and other scholars.

I seek, instead, to develop a general and systematic understanding of how negativity works in presidential campaigns and whether it promotes or hinders political debate. My goal is to see how negative ads affect the information environment[17] available to voters during a campaign. Do negative ads undermine or advance the quality of information available to voters as they choose candidates?[18] As a result, I do *not* examine how negativity influences voters, as it has been and continues to be ably investigated by a number of scholars (for example, Freedman and Goldstein 1999; Lau and Pomper 2002; Kahn and Kenney 1999). I am interested in the content of the ads themselves. In an important way, this project is a necessary first step in understanding the impact of negativity on the electorate. Scholars and observers need to know its shape and contours. With that empirical base, we can then build more effective research designs that will generate data that should be able to offer even sounder generalizations about the workings of attack advertising on the public.

A PLAN OF ATTACK

To advance our understanding of negativity in political campaigns, we need to accomplish a number of goals. First, we must jettison the assumption that negativity undermines democratic politics. Scholars and observers all too often start from the belief that attacks breed incivility and prevent citizens from learning about candidates' true personalities and their real plans for governing. As Kathleen Jamieson (1992, 216) reminds us, the real fear is that negativity will breed such passions that "the public will embrace a course of action not in its own interest." This starting point, as I will explain below, is problematic. Negativity plays an important and underappreciated role in democracies.[19] In fact, I will argue that the practice of democracy *requires* negativity by candidates. In other words, the give and take of democratic politics demands that we know both the good and bad points of candidates and their policy goals. The opposition is well-suited to discussing the weaknesses of the other side. Therefore, in order to learn about the risks and problems associated with potential office holders, we need the opposition, in effect, to "go negative." When going negative, candidates can actually advance the debate, not undermine it. This simple point seems forgotten in many of the discussions about the subject.

As part of this effort to reassess negativity in campaigns, I seek to develop a better theoretical understanding of this type of appeal. In the third chapter, I offer such a framework. As a preview, I posit that there is an *asymmetry* between negative and positive campaign appeals. For a negative appeal to be effective, the sponsor of that appeal must marshal more evidence, on average, than for positive appeals. The public, like our legal system, operates on the assumption of "innocent until proven guilty." A candidate cannot, I will show, simply assert that their opposition favors a tax increase. They must provide some evidence for that claim or it does not work and may in fact backfire on the sponsor of the attack. By contrast, that same candidate can claim he or she favors a tax cut, with far less documentation. Attacks, in short, place different demands on politicians and their staffs than do self-promotional propaganda. This asymmetry leads to a number of testable hypotheses about the differences between negative and positive appeals.

The second major thrust of this project involves gathering systematic evidence about negativity in campaigns. There have been few data collected concerning the appeals candidates make to the public during campaigns. We need such evidence so we can move past the interesting, but often incomplete, narratives about the workings of political advertising, in general, and negativity, in particular.[20] I am not the first to complain about the lack of evidence. William Riker (1996), for example, observed that "we have very little knowledge about the rhetorical content of campaigns." To fill this void, I have collected an extensive data set that seeks to measure systematically the appeals candidates have made over a sizable number of campaigns.[21] Specifically, I have undertaken a thorough content analysis of presidential ads aired on television from 1960 to 2000. These data are unique for their *detailed* reading of so many political ads. For instance, I know from these data not only whether an economic issue was mentioned in an ad, but whether it was a statement about unemployment or an attack on the opposition for supporting a tax increase. I also have measures of the personal traits discussed in these political spots, along with references to what I term values—general appeals about broad themes such as neighborhood and freedom.[22] I have also supplemented these data with interviews with political consultants, conducted some additional content analyses of the news media's coverage of negativity, and collected relevant aggregate data. These additional pieces of evidence help to flesh out my general argument about negativity.

The third part of this undertaking is to develop clear and explicit standards for evaluating negativity. An attack spot hits the airwaves and political commentators decide essentially on an ad hoc basis whether it is "fair" or "unfair." The Daisy spot and the Tank ad, which I mentioned earlier, were judged by many commentators as unfair and misleading, while others defended the ads as reasonable and fair. This seat of the pants approach tends to yield evaluations that are inconsistent and do not develop an accumulation of knowledge. The end result, frankly, is confusion. I will develop a set of standards to judge the appeals, both positive and negative, that candidates make in their television advertising. These guidelines will help to clarify the debate and ensure that we are all working from a similar analytical framework.[23] One may take issue with aspects of my benchmarks, but, for the most part, readers should find much merit in them.

In remaining parts of this introductory chapter, I will provide reasons why we need to rethink our opposition to negativity in campaigns. This effort will include some historical context that underscores the underappreciated role of attacks in American politics. Additionally, I will develop an argument about the importance of negativity in democratic politics. That discussion will serve as the springboard for the upcoming chapters.

WHY NEGATIVITY PROMOTES DEMOCRACY

Whether one starts from the premise that negativity in politics is good, bad, or mixed, attacks have been a staple of political life for as long as there have been politics. Politics is about conflict, deciding who gets what share of limited resources. The result is disagreement about the distribution of those resources, which inevitably breeds negativity. At one level, everyone understands that conflict is part and parcel of politics. But at another level, there is a desire to sweep such disagreements under the rug and talk instead about "points of agreement." It may be more civil and even understandable to downplay the core disagreements we all have. The problem with this approach, however, is that we often fail to appreciate the important role negativity can play in democratic government. Certainly the advocates of responsible party government understood the role of criticism and attack in a competitive party system (Schattschneider 1942; APSA Report 1950; Ranney 1962; Epstein 1986). Their conception of democratic government rested heavily on having an effective and *vocal* opposition.

We rarely think of it in these terms, but this country was founded in large part through political attack. The Declaration of Independence— one of our most honored documents—was largely a set of negative appeals. The founders were unhappy with King George, and they expressed their unhappiness in this highly critical tract. In fact, by my count, about 70% of the statements in that famed document were criticisms of the British government.[24] That is a high rate of negativity and it certainly outstrips modern presidential campaigns in the sheer frequency of attack (see the next chapter for specifics). It was these criticisms that provided the basis for thinking about abuses of power and the centrality of certain basic human rights. Without such negativity, the argument for establishing a new nation that derived its "just powers from the consent of the government" would not have been possible.

The debate over the ratification of the Constitution is another example of negativity. William Riker (1996) demonstrated this fact clearly by documenting the nasty tone that characterized the struggle between the Federalists and Anti-Federalists as they debated the merits of the new Constitution. Nearly all of the arguments the Anti-Federalists offered were negative. The Federalists also frequently attacked the Anti-Federalists, although less often. This negativity not only provided the public and relevant elites a chance to evaluate the merits of a new Constitution, it led the founders to adopt the Bill of Rights—an invaluable set of reforms that assured important liberties.

As one flips the pages of American history, there are many other examples of negativity. A number of historians have called attention to the harsh partisan rhetoric of the 1790s and early 1800s (see Silbey 1999; Altschuler and Blumin 2001; Robertson 1995; Cmiel 1990; Weisberger 2000; Ellis 2002). The Jackson-Adams election in 1828, for example, was exceptionally divisive. The former general was called, among other things, a murderer and a cannibal,[25] while his wife was accused of being a whore.[26] There are many examples of this highly caustic tone from the political battles of that era. Adams and Jefferson faced unheard of attacks in their famous battle in 1800 (Ellis 2002). After culling through an impressive array of party documents, Joel Silbey (1999) offered the following observation:

> The pamphlets contained extravagant overstatement, heated defamation, polarizing excess, and threatening and divisive imagery. Their tone was unremittingly negative, harsh, and hostile, filled with fearful images. Their authors conjured monsters, the avaricious bank, the uncontrolled despot, and later the aggressive slavocracy and the rampaging abolitionist. (xvii)

Despite the harshness of the rhetoric, our nation did not collapse. The experiment conducted by our founding fathers was far from a sure thing. No one knew if this republican form of government would endure. Yet even in its infancy, the nation survived the charges and counter-charges hurled by the various combatants. Perhaps that should have been expected, since the rise of the nation was fueled in and of itself by criticism.

One might counter, however, that today's attacks are different and more destructive than those in the past. Some believe we have entered a new divisive era of politics that is more about tearing people down than passing legislation that will improve the lives of our citizens. Thomas Patterson for example, acknowledges that

> Negative campaigns are as old as the Jefferson-Adams race of 1800, but today's version has no historical parallel. The volume is unlike anything that has gone before. "You can't compare a nasty quote about Thomas Jefferson," says former presidential speechwriter Richard Goodwin, "with the intensity and penetration [of today's attacks]." (2002, 50)

Or as David Doak, Democratic political consultant, noted: "There were always negative things said on the stump, but not . . . in your living room while you were eating popcorn."[27] There appears to be genuine concern that the ability of the thirty-second attack ad to reach nearly all average voters represents a real threat to this nation's political system.

But these kinds of concerns seem at best premature and at worst, simply wrong. To begin with, we do not know enough about negativity in campaigns, current or past, to make any generalization with much confidence. For example, the electorate in the early 1800s was much, much smaller than it is now (see Kelley 1983), so it may have been easier to reach eligible voters than scholars often assume. We also have no clear sense of the distribution of pamphlets and other pieces of propaganda. Word of mouth may have provided a way to distribute such information. It is pretty clear that the goal behind the publication of these pamphlets was to reach the mass public. In writing about these pieces of propaganda, Silbey notes that the parties sought to link "their messages to a general audience" and "tried to touch the texture of personal experience" (1999, xvii). The problem is that we do not know the "market penetration" of that era.

I cannot provide an answer to whether politics is more or less negative now than in the past. But this discussion highlights two important points. First, there is a tendency for political observers to leap to conclusions that the available data do not support. Second, real or not, there is a widespread belief that negativity is a problem in today's electoral process with little historical precedent, and that "reality" is leading the problem to draw more and more attention. Just consider that in the 2000 elections (from September to November) the Associated Press had ninety-five stories, according to Lexis-Nexis, that dealt with the negative campaigning. In 1980, there was just one story written by the AP on the same subject.[28] Yet in that same year Reagan ran a more negative campaign than George W. Bush (Geer 2003). Such data show that pundits, journalists, and political observers of all stripes are writing and talking more about the subject than just two decades ago. That change in the level of interest in and of itself justifies the kind of investigation I am undertaking here. But it also suggests that perception and reality are out of synch.

But I want to say more than just that democracy can survive negativity. I'm making a bolder claim: negativity can advance and improve the prospects for democracy. Without negativity, no nation can credibly think of itself as democratic. Just consider all the concern expressed during the 2004 Russian elections once the serious competition evaporated and Vladimir Putin was left effectively unchallenged. Observers viewed this as a bad development for the democratic process, because no one was around to criticize Putin and his record. Attacks may be painful to some, but they are essential for change to take place and for any nation to prosper. It is important to realize that the agents of change (e.g., candidates or parties) must first demonstrate the reasons why change in needed. That is, they need to go negative before they can go positive. In short, attacks can enrich the quality of democratic life.

One of the hallmarks of a democracy is the chance for open and free expression. There has been a long-standing belief that for the best ideas and policies to surface, citizens and elites need an opportunity to criticize government and to debate the best course of action. In many ways, progress is the offspring of criticism, attacks, and negativity. Over 350 years ago, John Milton (1644–45) in *Areopagitica* argued that it was best to "let truth and falsehood grapple . . . in a free and open exchange." In this particular case, Milton was concerned about censorship by the British government, fearing that the curtailing of criticism would weaken society. John Stuart Mill (1859) some 200 years later went even further, contending that an opinion gains legitimacy and credibility if it faces criticism:

> If the (dissenting) opinion is right, they are deprived of the opportunity of exchanging error for truth: if wrong, they lose, what is almost as great a bene-fit, the clearer perception and livelier impression of the truth, produced by its collision with error. (*On Liberty*, 79)

Just consider how history judges Presidents John Adams and Woodrow Wilson for suppressing public criticism. In the first case, Adams and the Federalist controlled Congress passed the Alien and Sedition Acts (1798), which prohibited spoken or written criticism of the government, Congress, or the President.[29] In the case of World War I, Wilson's Postmaster General blocked the magazine *The Masses* from the mail because it contained criticism of the U.S. war effort. The *Nation* was also included in this ban, because it too expressed antiwar sentiment. Both of these instances are viewed as dark clouds over the records of these two men, as well as the country.

It is now widely accepted that the ability of citizens, activists, and leaders to criticize government is an essential part of a democratic regime and any effort to block it is viewed as undermining the very freedoms we associate with such regimes. The Supreme Court has made this point quite clear. In *New York Times Co. v. Sullivan* (1964), the court ruled that the value of a free debate trumps any possible damage to the reputations of public officials. In that decision, Justice Brennan wrote, "we consider this case against the background of a profound national commitment to the principle that debate on public issues should be uninhibited, robust, and wide-open, and that it may well include vehement, caustic, and sometimes unpleasantly sharp attacks on government and public officials."[30]

Most of these arguments hinge on having a free and vibrant press. It is journalists who have the responsibility to evaluate the actions of those in power and of those who want power. Those judgments and information are essential to informing the public.

While it is true that a free press is an essential part of any regime that purports to be democratic, that is only part of the story. We also need the criticisms from competing candidates to ensure that we more fully vet the respective plans and qualifications of these politicians. My logic here is two-fold. First, parties and candidates have a clearer incentive to be "effective" critics than journalists. Office seekers (and holders) want to put the opposition's policies under a microscope, since any problems and weaknesses can serve as a wedge for attracting votes in the upcoming election. Journalists have incentives to investigate and to subject the parties and candidates to scrutiny. As Zaller (1999) points out, such stories can give them prestige and influence in their business. While it is also part of general job satisfaction, journalists are really looking for a good story, perhaps for a new angle on the campaign. Jamieson and Waldman (2002) concur, arguing that reporters develop "frames" as they cover particular stories. These frames allow them to be "storytellers," but they also keep them from informing the public about all the relevant facts (see also Fallows 1996; Patterson 1993). Journalists are not asking as pointedly as the candidates about what is wrong with the opposition's plans for government and their personal style. These questions drive the competing candidate's campaign as they march toward election day. Now, of course, that incentive for candidates does not mean they are objective critics, but it does mean that they should be engaged critics and ensure that policies are subject to close inspection.

There is a second advantage of "candidate negativity" as opposed to "press negativity." The press appears interested in being critical (see Patterson 1993), but its coverage of campaigns, for example, tends to be more about the horserace and campaign strategy than about the relative merits of the contender's policy views or about the respective leadership traits (Robinson and Sheehan 1983; Farnsworth and Lichter 2002). Even their coverage of politicians in office seems not particularly aimed at evaluating performance. It tends, instead, to be more descriptive (Arnold 2004). Bennett (1996) and others bemoan the decline in "hard news," which inevitably weakens the ability of the press to perform its role as critic. Candidates, by contrast, rarely talk about the opposition's campaign strategy or their prospects of winning and instead aim their fire on their plans for government and personal competence.[31]

Democratic theory stresses the importance of the opposition, in a way that is almost (but, of course, not quite) like the two sides in a trial. The opposition has a duty to be critical and we only have effective democracy when the opposition actively opposes what the current set of office holders want to accomplish. The vital role of the opposition is institutionalized in most parliamentary systems with strong parties; there are usually entire shadow governments and shadow cabinets, whose entire purpose is to criticize and go negative on a day to day basis. Just consider that the prime minister of Great Britain faces questions from the opposition on a frequent basis. It is a ritual designed to keep the party in power honest and ensure that they can defend their actions.[32] Negativity, in short, is essential for a thriving democracy.

There are additional payoffs for democratic life from the ability of candidates to "go negative." First, the threat of criticism provides politicians incentive to adopt sound policies and to be the type of individuals who will attract votes. The irony here is that we cannot observe these payoffs from negativity—what we might call the latent consequences of negativity. Nevertheless, we all should appreciate that the *threat* of criticism creates additional reasons for politicians to be as responsive as possible.

Second, criticism can increase the quality of information available to voters as they make choices in elections. To make good decisions, they need to know the past record of candidates and what they propose to do in the future. A central part of that information involves understanding the *shortcomings* of candidates. As Alex Castellanos, George W. Bush's media consultant in 2000 and 2004, observed, negative ads "inform the people about the consequences of the wrong choice."[33] If a candidate has done a poor job in a current or previous elected office, it is important for voters to know that. If the contender has a tendency to support questionable legislation, voters too would profit from learning about such problems. If a candidate has not been truthful with the public, that information is of obvious relevance. Citizens benefit from as much information as possible, which includes the good and the bad—the positive and the negative.

Negativity (and the threat of it) makes accountability possible. Without accountability, democracy falters. If an incumbent does a poor job in office, it is very unlikely that that person will be (publicly) self-critical. The opposition party, therefore, needs to serve "as a critic of the party in power, developing, defining, and presenting policy alternatives which are necessary for a true choice in reaching public decisions."[34] Of course, challengers are likely to raise more problems than may actually exist. Hence, the incumbent needs to respond. The elected official needs not only to set the record straight, but also to point out potential weaknesses of the opposition. Negativity, therefore, creates a competitive dynamic that should yield a richer information environment than if candidates just talked about their own plans for government. In many ways, it is negativity that will draw candidates into the center of the ring.

These exchanges have additional benefits. Assume Candidate 1 has adopted positions on two issues, A and B, which the majority of voters support. Also assume Candidate 2 has offered views on two different issues, C and D, which the majority of voters support. With only positive campaigning, Candidate 1 would stress A and B, while Candidate 2 would talk about C and D. Voters would have noncomparable information about the two candidates—hardly an ideal way to choose between the two contenders. To make matter worse, there would not be any vetting of the two candidate's views on these issues. While Candidate 1 claims to hold a position on Issue A that the majority of the public backs, is it a fair representation of his or her true opinions? Has this candidate always held that position? What does the record indicate? The opposition, by attacking, could spur more discussion about the issue and raise doubts about Candidate 1's real position on Issue A. It is through negative appeals that voters can learn about the respective positions of candidates on all four issues. Candidates will be less able to duck issues and their stated views on other issues will be subjected to scrutiny. The end result should be an enriched information environment, leading to more rational decisions by the voting public.[35]

My point that negativity can improve the information environment for voters is hardly new. Consider that James Madison, when criticizing the Alien and Sedition Acts, argued that to have "a free and responsible government," the public needed to know the "comparative merits and demerits of the candidates for public trust."[36] Scholars over the years have shared Madison's observation. Stanley Kelley (1960, 10) once observed that voters need "to know what it is that distinguishes the candidates for a particular office." Kelley (1960, 16) goes on to argue that voters need "to be exposed to the arguments of both sides." Dennis Thompson (1970, 106) concurs, calling for "confrontations" in campaigns to check the tendency of one side to oversell itself. R. Douglas Arnold (2004, 12–13) puts the matter quite simply: "an environment in which incumbent representatives and their supporters emphasize their accomplishments while challengers and other critics emphasize representatives' shortcomings can be an informative one for citizens."

There is also an impressive line of empirical research that shows the quality of decision making *increases* when one is exposed to criticisms of relevant arguments. Over fifty years ago, Hovland and colleagues (1953, 110) provided experimental data consistent with this claim. When discussing elite decision making, Alexander George (1972) contends that better decisions are made when participants disagree. These disagreements (i.e., "multiple advocacy") allow presidents to learn about competing perspectives and render more informed decisions.[37] More recently, Diana Mutz (2002, 118) has shown that when citizens are exposed to "cross-cutting" information, they learn more about the "rationales for opposing views."

The bottom line is that criticism is important because those out of power must have the right and ability to raise doubts about those in power (and vice versa). Otherwise, the public does not have access to full information "about the relevant alternative policies and their likely consequences" (Dahl 1998, 37).

CONCERNS THAT NEGATIVITY
UNDERMINES DEMOCRACY

Democracy can benefit from criticism and the chance for people to learn about problems with various proposals for government. I suspect that most commentators would agree with this claim *in the abstract*. Where disagreement is likely to arise is my association of negativity with criticism. Skeptics would argue that negativity is not equivalent to criticism. Rather, negativity is best thought of as unfair or excessive criticism. The concern is that these attacks will undermine the opportunities for voters to learn about politics, to hold elected officials accountable, and to make good decisions.

Such worries about negativity tie to larger issues that scholars have been writing and talking about when discussing the need for "civility" and "deliberation" (see Gutmann and Thompson 1996; Sapiro 1999; Macedo 1999; Mansbridge 1980). Negative ads often strike people as uncivil, scurrilous, and nasty. As Lynn Sanders (1997, 348) points out, deliberation requires mutual respect among participants. How can the nasty personal attacks leveled by candidates against each other foster mutual respect? How can people reason together when candidates are slinging mud at each other? Attack ads, according to this perspective, undermine the political debate and serve as obstacles to informing voters about which candidate deserves their support. If so, then negativity blocks the ability of the public to perform properly their task in a democracy—just the opposite of what I argue above.[38]

There is an additional dimension to these concerns. Negativity will play to the emotions of citizens, weakening their ability to reason (see Brader 2005). There is a long-standing belief that "aroused publics might . . . be vulnerable to demagoguery. They might be stirred up to invade the rights or trample on the essential interests of minorities" (Fishkin 1991, 21). Negativity, in effect, lessens the ability of citizens to act rationally and to act in their best interests (see also Jamieson 1992). Power-hungry politicians, it is feared, use scare tactics and misleading claims to keep people from supporting a particular candidate. Such emotional and misleading claims weaken democracy because they will manipulate voters.

One key assumption underlying this counterperspective involves whether voters have the skills necessary to weather a storm of negativity. Those who worry about the ill-effects of attacks tend to think of voters as inattentive and easily manipulated. In contrast, those who see potential benefits from negativity will usually have more faith in the public's ability to handle the onslaught of thirty-second attack ads.

The competence of the electorate has been discussed by a number of scholars. In the final analysis, the answer usually hinges on the standards one uses. Kelley (1983), for example, offers a set of standards that suggests the weakly committed (i.e., poorly informed) do a good job of understanding the candidates' positions on issues they *care* about. Popkin (1991) pushes this line of argument further, advancing the notion of low information rationality. Voters can make use of visible events to cast a credible and defensible vote. Lupia and McCubbins (1998, 4) continue this general theme by noting that "limited information need not prevent people from making reasoned choices." Most recently, Zaller (2004) shows that the "floating voters" (i.e., the nonpartisan and not very well informed voters) cast ballots in sensible ways. Their choices are driven by the state of the economy, the respective moderation of the candidates, and whether any big foreign policy successes have happened lately. Of course, one can invoke different standards and paint a far less favorable portrait of voters (Keeter and Delli Carpini 1996; Converse 1964). It is clear that sizable numbers of citizens simply lack information about the basic workings of government and the key players who hold important positions.[39] This lack of information is always buttressed by the nagging concern that Downs (1957) pointed out long ago—that it is in the self-interest of voters to be poorly informed.

A second issue in this debate involves how much we value "rational" citizens. Do we want citizens to engage in constructive dialogue during campaigns, which allows them to reason about their choices in a systematic fashion? Academics find much merit in the idea that voters should think carefully about their choices, weighing the relevant costs and benefits in some rational, self-interested fashion. But while that ideal may be attractive for many, it ignores the possible benefits of injecting emotion into the political debate. It may be best to get voters' attention through strong partisan appeals. Party activists apparently held such views in the 1800s (Altschuler and Blumin 2000). Or consider the rise of the Dean candidacy during 2003. It was based on the excitement the former governor generated by attacking the Bush administration's policies. Howard Dean tapped into the anger that key parts of the electorate felt toward President Bush. It seems reasonable to believe that emotional appeals will be more interesting to at least some voters, stimulating more interest in politics. People do enjoy a good fight; witness the interest in boxing, hockey, or football. So the competition that is part and parcel of negativity may possess some real benefits as the public may become more engaged by these electoral duals.

This general argument has been advanced in a thoughtful book by George Marcus (2002). He, in fact, makes the unorthodox argument that "people are able to be rational because they are emotional; emotions enable rationality." Marcus's earlier work with Neumann and MacKuen (2000, 1) further reinforces this point by contending that "emotion and reason interact to produce a thoughtful and attentive citizenry." They point out that negative events can stimulate attention and give people incentive to learn about what is going on in the world. In fact, these scholars (1993, 681) suggest that negative campaigns might "spur concern about the current state of affairs," which might "motivate people to pay closer attention to public affairs, to engage their full capacities, and to make rational decisions."

But even if one thinks voters are sensible and that emotion can be a good thing, one still might view negativity as undermining democracy. If negativity "crosses the line," it can weaken the quality of information available to voters. The idea is that in the effort to win, candidates become so critical of each other that they undermine the legitimacy of their respective candidacies. This is the electoral equivalent of nuclear war— contenders fight so hard that neither side is left standing.

This basic concern about the balance between criticism and excessive criticism is long-standing. John Stuart Mill (1859, 112) noted that "some of those who say that the free expression of all opinions should be permitted, on the condition that the manner be temperate, and do not pass the bounds of fair discussion." In other words, we need to have "civil" exchanges and "fair" discussion. The general point is sound. If candidates get into such fierce name-calling that the debate degenerates into a pointless exchange, then perhaps negativity does the damage its detractors fear.

But when is this line crossed? It is not clear. Reasonable people will disagree on where the line is and when it might be crossed. As suggested earlier, these kinds of judgments are difficult to make in an objective fashion. We tend to view these partisan exchanges with our own partisan lens.

Nevertheless, the central point of this discussion is that criticism *can* be essential to democratic politics. Do attacks in campaigns constitute a useful form of criticism that allows the public to hold officials accountable? That is, does negativity increase the quality of the information environment available to the public? Or is negativity too harsh? Is it too often unjustified personal slander? Does it deal with issues that are little more than red herrings? We can all cite some examples of negative ads that have gone too far. But, we can also cite examples of ads where candidates talked about issues and traits in sensible ways. The key here is not to assess these questions in an ad hoc fashion referring to a handful of ads that may have caught our attention. Instead, we need to undertake a careful and systematic reading of a representative sample of ads—both negative and positive—that will permit us to make some sound generalizations about the workings of propaganda, in general, and negativity, in particular. To make those generalizations, we will also need to establish clear and defensible standards to judge these matters.

It is these central tasks that will serve as the central motivation behind the rest of this book.

A ROAD MAP

In an effort to provide a road map for the upcoming chapters, I will briefly talk about each of them in the order they appear in the text.

Chapter 2 describes, with some care, the data I have collected to undertake this investigation. Since so much of my argument hinges on the value of my evidence, it is essential that I spell out the relevant details. Once that task is complete, I then show that negativity is on the rise in presidential elections—a result that confirms the fears of its many critics and further speaks to the need to address this general topic.

The third chapter serves two critical goals. First, I will establish a set of normative standards for assessing the quality of information in campaign appeals. These standards allow us to judge the relative informative potential of negative and positive appeals. Second, I will contend that there is an *asymmetry* between negative and positive appeals. Namely, that negative appeals are more likely to have documentation supporting them than positive appeals. I will provide considerable evidence to support this claim. This asymmetry, in turn, affects how candidates frame their attacks and self-promotional arguments, which produces a series of important and testable hypotheses about the differences between negative and positive campaign rhetoric.

Chapter 4 assesses the merits of personal attacks. I begin by arguing that personal attacks are not excessive in presidential campaigns and showing that they are *not* on the rise. So, despite all the common assumptions that modern campaigns are increasingly fueled by harsh personal criticism, the evidence simply does not support such a view. Even so, about a quarter of all attacks involve some reference to the traits of presidential candidates. The question becomes, then, are these attacks inflammatory or do they deal with reasonable concerns that any informed voter should think about? Given my benchmarks, it appears that these attacks are defensible and are usually not a subject of concern.

Chapter 5 evaluates the merits of issue-based attacks. To begin, I ask whether these attacks are about legitimate issues. Are they about important and real problems? My core argument hypothesizes that the answer should be yes; yet conventional wisdom suggests that policy attacks tend to focus on frivolous issues. Which view is correct? I will develop a set of standards to answer these questions. The findings again suggest that negativity better deals with issues of importance to the public than positive appeals. In the second part, I show theoretically why issue attacks will be more likely to spell out the policy differences between candidates, presenting evidence consistent with this insight.

The preceding three chapters offer a compelling defense of negativity in presidential campaigns. Chapter 6 seeks to push this matter further by evaluating one of the most controversial presidential campaigns in modern times: the much discussed Bush-Dukakis battle in 1988. It is clear that something happened in 1988 that warrants close inspection. In recent years, the news media have devoted much attention to attack advertising. This strong interest began quite suddenly in 1988. What happened? Is there something different about 1988 that justifies this attention? To answer these kinds of questions, I make use of my content analysis of ads, but I also include other sorts of evidence to make more nuanced judgments about the negative and positive appeals in that campaign. Most of the conventional explanations of what happened in 1988 do not hold up under scrutiny. It appears that much of the explanation lies with the behavior of the news media, not the candidates.

I will conclude by evaluating some broader questions about negativity and the electoral system. While negative appeals contain useful information, perhaps negativity still has a pernicious effect on the citizenry. To test for these possible macroeffects, I examine whether this rise helps explain the public's declining trust in institutions, their loss of faith in elections, and the often discussed decline in turnout. Negativity does not appear to be the culprit. Next, I consider why negativity has been increasing over the last forty years. My basic thesis is simple: negativity is on the rise because parties have more about which to disagree. One of the fundamental developments in recent years has been a growing polarization of the parties (e.g., Poole and Rosenthal 1996). With more polarized parties, there are more grounds for attack. The data support this hypothesis. The second to last section of this chapter addresses the kind of democracy advanced by negativity. I argue that negativity is far more tied to promoting retrospective notions of democracy than prospective ones. At the end, I tackle the relationship between negativity and civility in the democratic enterprise, contending that there is no causal connection between these two forces while raising doubts about the ill-effects of incivility in democratic societies.

CHAPTER TWO

Assessing Negativity

Campaigns are important *democratic* institutions, because they link politicians and voters. In the weeks and months prior to an election, candidates send messages to the public about why they deserve their support. The public, in turn, considers these messages when voting. The ability of campaigns to be democratic, therefore, depends heavily on the quality of information available to voters as they cast their ballots. This "information environment" is more, of course, than just the messages politicians send to voters. Arnold (2004, 12–13) reminds us that journalists and interest groups are key actors as well. This book, however, is about assessing this democratic connection between politicians and voters and whether negativity has undermined it. So while these other actors are important, I am limiting my attention to how well politicians forge this democratic link between themselves and voters during the campaign.[1]

Candidates, of course, engage in many forms of persuasion as they seek the support of the mass public. They give speeches, conduct meetings, hold interviews with journalists, take questions from the press, and participate in debates—to name a just few. Most of these efforts contribute to the *information environment* available to voters, usually indirectly through the filter of the news media. The public rarely watches a complete speech, but small excerpts may well appear on the local or national news. The same would be true for press conferences. However, televised debates, especially in the presidential arena, do draw a large audience. Even so, journalists' questions structure debates, influencing the agenda and shaping the kinds of messages candidates can send to the electorate in these forums. As a result, most propaganda efforts do *not* directly speak to this democratic link between the public and candidates. There is, however, one mode of communication that taps directly (and in an unfiltered fashion) the information candidates convey to the mass public: paid political advertising on television.[2]

At this point in time, paid advertising on television is clearly the most important mechanism presidential candidates can use to send messages *directly* and *unfiltered* to the public. Candidates can literally reach millions of voters with each paid spot. Obviously, the information that the news media provide about the campaign matters greatly, but contenders cannot control the content of what journalists say and write. With advertising, candidates shape and mold the themes they want to convey to voters. These simple realities led Kathleen Jamieson (1996, 17) to observe "political advertising is now the major means by which candidates for the presidency communicate their messages to voters." Marion Just and colleagues (1996, 15) second this view, noting that advertisements on televisions are "one of the most effective ways for candidates to present themselves . . . a wide audience." Stephen Ansolabehere and Shanto Iyengar (1995, 3) cast an even broader net by arguing that advertising on television "has become the main means of political communication in the United States." Presidential nominees pour money and resources into the creation and airing of these spots (e.g., West 2001; Luntz 1988). Lynn Vavreck (2001), for example, reports that of the $343 million spent on the 2000 presidential campaign, paid advertising consumed $213 million of it (62%).

Even with continuing technological change, especially the growth of the World Wide Web, there is little sign of a decline in the importance of televised spots. Ken Goldstein and Paul Freedman (2002) found that the amount of paid advertising in presidential elections increased between 1996 and 2000. Using an impressive data set about TV advertisements, they report that presidential aspirants aired 52% more ads in the general election in 2000 than four years earlier. The actual number of ads aired is quite daunting. In 1996, Dole and Clinton aired 162,160 spots. Four years later the candidates aired 247,224.[3] These data highlight the central role television advertising plays in American presidential elections. The 2004 campaign further underscored the importance of television advertising. Not only did Senator Kerry and President Bush begin their advertising campaigns in March, the two parties spent nearly $500 million on radio and TV commercials.[4] It was more than twice the amount of money the candidates spent in 2000 (Sidoti 2004).

There is yet another development that makes this attention to paid advertising even more important in our effort to understand this information environment created during campaigns. Over the last twenty-five years, the sheer growth in the number and kinds of different programming on television is staggering. With the rise of cable and satellite networks, the public now has a wide choice in what programs to watch. This choice has important political consequences. Markus Prior (2002, 2003, 2005) has documented quite nicely that citizens are now able to move away from traditional news programming and watch instead reruns of *Seinfeld*, *SportsCenter*, *West Wing*, or other shows of interest. So whereas in the 1960s families had limited choice about what programs to watch—the evening news was the only option during the dinner hour—now they are flooded with choices. The end result is that the audience share for network news is declining (see Prior 2003, 2005). People are simply opting out of the evening news. That means for more and more Americans a main point of contact with political information is the televised spot, which can air during the shows they are watching. This development further underscores the need to understand how politicians communicate with the public through the televised spot.

Given the importance of television advertising, it is of little surprise that scholars have sought to assess its characteristics. At the presidential level alone,[5] there are a number of recent efforts to measure the content of ads (e.g., Vavreck 2001; Jamieson 1996; Jamieson, Waldman, and Sheer 2000; Goldstein and Freedman 2002; West 2001; Benoit 1999; Kaid and Johnston 2000).[6] For this book, I focus largely on the content of presidential ads aired on television from 1960 to 2000.[7] These data are unique in that they provide a detailed reading over time of the messages presidential nominees send to voters in their effort to capture the White House.

This chapter provides a blueprint to understand these data. I start by defining "negativity." This is a concept of obvious importance to this study. It is also a term that has a good deal of conceptual ambiguity associated with it. By defining the term explicitly at the outset, I will lessen the chance for miscommunication.

DEFINING NEGATIVITY

Negative advertising is a concept that has a long history—or at least longer than I had initially thought. In combing through research on the general subject, I stumbled across an essay titled: "The Historical Trend of Negative Appeals in Advertising." That title was in and of itself interesting, but my interest soared when I realized the essay had been published in 1929 in the *Journal of Applied Psychology*. Lucas and Benson (1929, 346) begin by stating that the "controversy over the use of negative appeals in advertising is one of long standing." In particular, they were interested in sorting out the relative effectiveness of "positive" and "negative" appeals. However, Lucas and Benson (1929, 347) employ a definition of negativity that differs in important ways from today's connotation:

> Any appeal to human motivation involves either a desire for attainment or an impulse to avoid. All appeals to attainment may be called positive, while appeals to avoidance are negative. A negative advertising appeal is then an attempt to stimulate the reader to the avoidance of a repulsive situation.

For them, a positive appeal in a political campaign would be "if you want a peaceful and secure nation, vote for George Bush." By contrast, a negative appeal would be "if you want to avoid another terrorist attack like 9/11, vote for George Bush." Negativity did not involve a direct attack on the competition. It involved how the appeal was framed. Namely, does it stress the payoffs of a particular candidate or the costs of not choosing that candidate?[8]

The point of this discussion is more than just intellectual curiosity. We need to be clear about the definition of key concepts. The clarity is of particular importance in light of the tendency of pundits and observers to be imprecise. Mary Matalin, for example, argued in 2004 that two Bush attack ads, which questioned Senator Kerry's views on taxes and defense, were not negative ads, but "ready-to-engage-on-the-issues ads."[9] Sixteen years earlier, Vice President Bush stated "it isn't negative campaigning to try to help the American people understand the differences" (Blumenthal 1991, 292). These kinds of statements do not clarify matters. As Darrell West (2001, 64) comments, "critics have widely condemned the advertising style in recent elections, but few have defined what they mean by *negativity*. Observers often define negativity as anything they do not like about campaigns."[10] Glenn Richardson (2001, 776) goes further, arguing "the use of 'negative' to describe political advertising may have become so commonplace, even among scholars, that it has become an umbrella under which several distinguishable attributes have been vexatiously subsumed."

My definition of negativity seeks to avoid some of these problems. It is simple and straightforward: *negativity is any criticism leveled by one candidate against another during a campaign*. Under this definition, there is no gray area. An appeal in a campaign either raises doubts about the opposition (i.e., negative) or states why the candidate is worthy of your vote (i.e., positive). There is no middle category. Note that this definition does not speak to whether the criticism is about policy or about traits. Any type of criticism counts as negativity. There is an association, especially among the public, that negative appeals are only personal attacks

(Brooks 2000a; Freedman, Wood, and Lawton 1999; Sigelman and Kugler 2003). This definition does not distinguish the substantive nature of the attack. Additionally, my definition does not contain any evaluative judgment of the merits of an appeal. I make, for example, no distinction to account for the harshness of the tone. Kim Kahn and Patrick Kenney (1999, 878) write about "mudslinging," which refers to attacks that are "inappropriate" or "when the messages are presented harshly." Similarly, I do not try, when measuring negativity, to judge whether the attack is "fair" or "unfair" (Freedman and Lawton 2001). Such themes, however, are not absent from this book. Chapter 6 takes a closer look at the appeals from some of the most controversial ads from the 1988 presidential campaign.

Because the term "negativity" has become entangled with various normative judgments about the merits of different types of criticism, much confusion has resulted. This confusion has led some scholars to use a different nomenclature in an effort to avoid those problems. Perhaps most notable is Kathleen Jamieson's suggestion that scholars and pundits talk about "attacks" or "contrast" rather than "negativity," since the latter is all too often associated with dirty politics.[11] While I agree with Jamieson and others that the concept of negativity is tainted in many quarters, I prefer not to jettison the term.[12] It is a key part of the discourse used to assess political campaigns. If we introduce new terms and concepts, we may only be muddying the waters. Instead, I will employ a simple and clear definition.[13]

THE GOAL OF DATA COLLECTION

In my effort to define, measure, and ultimately understand negativity in presidential campaigns, I need to adopt an approach to collecting the data that matches my goals. Candidates air TV ads, whether positive or negative in tone, that offer reasons for the public to support them. I want to tap those reasons. As a result, I am not interested in characterizing each spot per se, but capturing the appeals (i.e., reasons) contained within each advertisement.

A good deal of previous work has sought to capture the meaning of the full spot, treating it, for instance, as an "issue" or a "trait" ad (e.g., Joslyn 1980; Kaid and Johnston 1991; 2000; Johnston and Kaid 2002). While that tactic makes good sense when the questions motivating the analysis are about the ads themselves, my objectives are different. I seek to capture the messages politicians send to voters via the medium of the paid television advertisement. This goal requires that I take a careful look at the component parts of each ad.

Jamieson, Waldman, and Sheer (2000) have adopted a similar perspective to mine, examining the content of ads by evaluating the argument or idea.[14] Benoit (1999) too implements a comparable strategy. I am, however, interested in breaking down the arguments even further into their components parts. Politicians send multiple messages to voters through advertising, and my content analysis seeks to capture them. In so doing, I map the information environment candidates make available to the larger public. I should note that this focus does not prevent me from presenting results by the type of ad. I have collected such information and use it with some frequency.

THE SAMPLE

The vast majority of the political advertisements used in this project come from the Julian P. Kanter Political Commercial Archive at the University of Oklahoma. For presidential ads from 1960 to 1996, I relied heavily on this archive.[15] For the 2000 campaign, I made use of the spots collected by Shanto Iyengar and made available through the CD-ROM *In Their Own Words*.[16] There are other sources one can use for political advertisements, such as the Annenberg School[17] and now various websites (e.g., http://livingroomcandidate.movingimage.us/). Websites usually provide examples of some of the more famous ads, but these collections are not nearly as comprehensive as the Kanter or Annenberg archives.

While there is some disagreement (see Jamieson, Waldman, and Sheer 2000), upon close inspection the Kanter Archive holds the most complete set of advertisements for presidential elections over the last forty years. The Annenberg CD contains about 86 ads per election from 1960 to 1996.[18] The Kanter Archive has, on average, 113 ads for each of these presidential contests.[19] In particular cases, such as Kennedy's campaign in 1960, the Annenberg Archive does possess more spots. But that is the exception rather than the rule. For Reagan's 1980 bid for the White House and Dukakis's run, the Kanter Archive has far more ads (136 to 17 in 1980 and 126 to 46 in 1988) than what is available on the Annenberg CD.[20]

It is not possible to reconstruct the full set of advertisements created by the candidates. The campaigns did not always keep good records and often a number of different firms created spots making bookkeeping even more difficult. As a result, it is easy to see why scholars have ended up using differing samples. But, frankly, the issue is not which source is superior to the other. Each represents important opportunities to learn about the workings of political campaigns. And as I will show, even with different samples, the results all appear quite comparable. So although the numbers of ads may vary slightly, scholars have collected a sample that is good enough to yield robust findings.

Even though I have had access to over 1100 ads from presidential campaigns,[21] I did not include every ad available at the Kanter Archive. Recall that my goal in this data collection was to assess the kinds of appeals made by presidential candidates in their fight to win the election. As a result, when drawing my sample of ads, I employed a number of criteria that screened out some ads. I shall list them here and then comment on them in turn:

1. The ad had to be sixty seconds or shorter in length.[22]
2. The ad had to be aired on television.
3. The ad had to be sponsored or authorized by the candidate's campaign.[23]
4. I included only unique spots, not duplicates or near duplicates.
5. I did not code an ad with a specific message to a single state.
6. I did not code Spanish language ads.

I limited the sample to ads that were sixty seconds or shorter because they constitute the bulk of the contenders' advertising campaigns. At the Kanter Archive, usually 90% or more of all ads are one minute or less in duration. This focus should allow me to capture the major campaign themes of the nominees. Moreover, in recent years there has been a greater emphasis on the shorter spot, making this choice even more reasonable. In the 1960s, 75% of the spots in my sample were sixty seconds long.[24] In the last three presidential elections, only 6% were a minute, with over 90% being thirty seconds in length. Thirty second (and shorter) spots now dominate the airwaves.

I coded only those ads that actually appeared on television. The archive possessed a handful of spots that the candidates' campaigns created, but decided not to run. For example, Tony Schwartz created a very hard-hitting and graphic spot in 1972 for George McGovern showing a Vietnamese woman running with a dead child in her arms. A child's voice (actually Schwartz's young son) posed the question: "do presidents know that bombs kill people?"[25] Since I am interested in only those appeals presented to the electorate, I did not include these unaired ads in the analysis. In recent years, it has been far easier to determine if a spot has been aired or not. Data, like those now available through the University of Wisconsin's Advertising Project, make it possible to track whether an ad aired on television or not. For the early years, the records are not nearly as good. I cannot, as a result, claim with complete confidence that all spots included in my sample were aired. But I am quite sure that the ads in my sample meet this criterion, largely because of my confidence in the personal records of Julian Kanter. He kept close tabs on whether or not the spot appeared on television as he built his collection of ads. If mistakes were made, they were rare, and given the number of ads in the sample, it is unlikely that shifting the sample around at the margins would make much difference. And as we shall see, the data compare well with other estimates gleaned from content analyses of advertising, suggesting that I have a pretty good estimate of the key variables.

A third concern might be that I limited my attention to spots authorized by the candidates' campaigns. This would include ads directly paid for by the campaign, paid for by the party, or by other groups sponsored by the candidate. So, in 1972, ads paid for by Democrats for Nixon are included in this sample. What are missing from this sample are ads from interest groups either attacking or supporting particular candidates. But recall that my focus is on the link between candidates and the public, which means that ads sponsored by interest groups fall outside of the bounds of this project. Candidates do not have an official say in what goes into these ads and hence do not speak to this link between politicians and voters. Given this rule, perhaps the most famous negative ad of recent times—the Willie Horton spot—is not part of the analysis (although see chapter 6 for a discussion of this controversial commercial). Including such spots would involve a wholly different project. In the particular case of Bush's ads, the themes of the Willie Horton ad appeared in other spots authorized by the vice president's campaign (i.e., the Revolving Door spot, see Mendelberg 2001), making this omission of little empirical consequence. Moreover, according to Goldstein and Freedman (2002), independent groups aired less than 10% of the total amount of ads in the 2000 presidential election. In 2004, the rise of "527" ads may yield a different conclusion. The amount of money spent on 527 ads was still not all that large in comparison to what the candidates' spent,[26] but the news media talked a lot about these commercials, whether it was the Swift Boat ads or the MoveOn.org spots. I will talk about the news media's role in the process and how it affects the actual amount of negativity that is aired in all these commercials. But since I am interested in investigating the link between candidates and the public, these ads are not part of my story.

In addition, I did not code ads that were near duplicates of earlier spots. In some elections, there have been a number of very similar ads. With technological advances, it is easier to make one or two small changes in a spot. For instance, Dukakis's campaign ran a series of ads called the Packaging of the President. In one spot, a reference is made that the Japanese might someday buy the White House—a negative comment about the amount of foreign investment in the country. Two days later a new version of the ad was produced by the Dukakis campaign and the only change was that rather than saying "Japanese" the actor referred to "foreign interests." This difference, while an interesting story, did not affect my coding of the ad. Hence, I analyzed only one ad, so as to avoid double counting of themes.[27]

Besides near duplicate ads, some thirty-second or twenty-second spots are simply shortened versions of longer sixty-second spots. Reagan's campaigns in 1980 and 1984, for instance, cut a sizable number of their sixty-second spots into thirty-second editions. In these cases, I coded only the sixty-second spot. As with the near duplicates mentioned above, there is little reason to double count the topics in these spots.

A fifth criterion was that I excluded any spot directed at a specific state for the general election. For example, if an ad had a local politician, such as a governor, endorsing a candidate for specific reasons tied to the state, that spot was dropped. These reasons were not part of the general strategy set forth by the candidates to convince voters to support them. These ads were usually efforts to make use of the popularity of a local political figure. Of course, some ads may have been aired in just a handful of states. That would not disqualify a spot from inclusion in the sample. Other commercials that had a regional appeal, such as ads focusing on offshore oil drilling, were included in the analysis. The reason is that these spots can cover a huge area of the country, like the entire West Coast. As a result, only in cases where I knew for sure that the ad was aimed at a single state audience did I bump it from the analysis. There were not a lot of these ads (less than 4%), but they did occasionally arise and were nearly all endorsement spots with narrowly tailored messages.

Finally, I did not code ads in Spanish. The reason is practical—I do not know the language, nor did any of my coders. But this decision, dictated by ignorance, turns out not to be a serious problem. Many ads aimed at Latino audiences are often Spanish language versions of existing spots (Subervi-Velez, Herrera, and Begay 1987).[28] This claim may be less and less true as the Spanish-speaking population grows and as the two parties vie over its support. In 2000, there were just a handful of presidential ads aired in Spanish. For the most part, they dealt with issues mentioned in the other spots, such as education, environment, and health care.[29] These ads do not appear to be offering a vastly different set of appeals, but it will be important to remain sensitive to this matter—especially as the importance of the Latino vote continues to grow.

Table 2.1 shows the number of sixty-second (or shorter) spots that I coded each year. This table provides an account of the distribution of ads across the eleven presidential elections. My overall sample is reasonably close to what Benoit accumulated,[30] while Kaid and Johnston (2000, 40) use substantially more ads from the Kanter Archive, examining 1134

Table 2.1. Number of Advertisements Coded by Year and
Campaign, 1960–2000

1960			1984	
Kennedy	44		Mondale	38
Nixon	31		Reagan	27
1964			1988	
Johnson	17		Dukakis	75
Goldwater	26		Bush	26
1968			1992	
Humphrey	27		Clinton	29
Nixon	15		Bush	18
1972			1996	
McGovern	31		Clinton	49
Nixon	18		Dole	37
1976			2000	
Carter	33		Gore	42
Ford	39		Bush	33
1980				
Carter	60			
Reagan	80			

Notes: Nearly all advertisements from 1960 to 1996 came
from the Julian P. Kanter Political Commercial Archieve at the
University of Oklahoma. In 2000, the data come from the
CD-ROM *In Their Own Words: Sourcebook for the 2000
Presidential Election*, Stanford University.

spots. They wanted to provide a through mapping of presidential ads, so
they did not eliminate ads, as I did, from their dataset.

THE CONTENT ANALYSIS

The actual content analysis of these 795 ads[31] involved a code sheet of
nearly fifteen pages, covering topics from the traits of the candidates to the
slogan at the end of the commercial (see the appendix for details). I sought
to gather as much information as possible about the ads. To assess the contribution of political commercials to the information environment, it is
essential that one take a close look at the content.

Of course, I measured the tone of the appeal. Recalling the definition
presented above, any mention of a theme or reason to vote for one candidate was treated as "positive"; any criticism or reason to vote against the
opposition was treated as "negative." In addition, I captured three different types of appeals: policy, traits, and values. Most previous content analyses draw the main distinction between issues and traits (e.g., Benoit 1999;

Kaid and Johnston 2000). I thought it was important to differentiate between appeals to broad themes, such as hope and the future, and references to policy matters, such as inflation or crime. If, for instance, you lump values with issues, the share of attention paid to policy would appear to be greater than actually the case. The bottom line is that a reference to the future is not the same thing as discussion of education policy.

My coding scheme is flexible enough, however, that scholars can combine the two if they see fit for future research. For this book, I focus attention on the role policy issues played in the attacks candidates make in their advertising. This approach makes that goal more attainable.

I created a set of codes that identified general themes and values in the ads. If the "spirit of America" was mentioned, that comment was coded. If prosperity was discussed, that too was coded separately. I included "hard work," "hope," "change," and the "future," as explicit terms in the code sheet. Overall, there were ninety-eight different references to values or general themes in the ads.

A separate section was also created for coding the personal traits of the candidates. In these ads, nearly two hundred different traits (both positive and negative) were coded. Some of the codes included "good leader," "untrustworthy," "inexperienced," and "cares about people like you." Reference to character is especially important, since scholars and observers often worry about the harsh, personal tone political campaigns are perceived to possess. My data will address head on such concerns.

A core part of the analysis represented an attempt to capture thoroughly the substantive issues raised by the presidential contenders.[32] I wanted to know in detail the nature and tone of appeals candidates made to the public in these ads. Using previous work on issues driving presidential elections (e.g., Kelley 1983; Sundquist 1983), I developed nearly one thousand different themes, both positive and negative, that candidates could mention. The topics ranged from concerns about unemployment to worries over states' rights. In each case, the specific appeal was captured. If taxes were mentioned, was it an appeal to lower taxes, to raise the taxes of the wealthy, or that the opponent would raise taxes on the middle class? For education, did the candidate talk about a general concern for the issue? Or did the nominee warn about the cuts in federal funding proposed by the opposition? In this way, I can look at the different positive and negative issue appeals that candidates made to the public.

While I started out with roughly 1000 different codes for issues, I approached the data collection with a willingness to create new codes as new issues were discussed. There was no way to anticipate all the possible issues discussed by these nominees. If a candidate introduced a new issue not previously included in the scheme, I sought to accommodate it. In this way, my coding was flexible and reactive. I did not try to force new themes into existing codes (this is also true for both "values" and "traits"). The end result was over 1800 codes by the end of the data collection. The data, as a result, are very rich, providing an opportunity to map in detail the negative and positive appeals presidential candidates have made over the last forty years.[33]

One obvious question with any content analysis concerns reliability of the coding. Before I went to Oklahoma, I obtained a set of ads from the Kanter Archive for the 1968 and 1988 presidential elections. I coded these ads ahead of time to help develop the coding sheet and to test for reliability. While I did not check the reliability of all the ads I coded from 1968 and 1988, a research assistant coded a random sample of 30 from the nearly 140 ads from 1968 and 1988. In this sample, we agreed 91% of the time, providing me with sufficient confidence to proceed with the analysis.[34] I also tested for whether as time unfolded, my coding changed. It was possible that I might be "learning" how to code, which would interfere with the comparability of the results. During my initial stay in Oklahoma, I recoded a random sample of 15 ads that I had examined three days earlier. The agreement was over 93%. As a final test, I compared my coding of ads prior to my visit at the Kanter Archive and after my departure. Even then, the reliability was 91%.

Two Examples

To provide some context for how I coded these ads, I will describe the procedure for a Clinton spot from 1996. It is a good example, since it has a wide array of appeals to code:

> It's sad. All Bob Dole offers are **negative attacks**. President Clinton appointed a *four-star general drug czar*, expanded *school antidrug programs*. Dole tried to **slash anti-drug programs** *50 percent*. Voted **against creating a drug czar**. President Clinton is protecting *our children*. Breaking up *violent gangs*, *drug test teens before getting a driver's license*. *Curfews* and *school uniforms* to instill discipline. All Bob Dole offers are **negative attacks**. President Clinton is protecting *our children, our values*.

According to my scheme, there were four negative appeals leveled against Bob Dole in this spot (see the boldface passages). Two of them involve references to "negative attacks." Another was Dole's slashing of "antidrug programs." The final negative appeal was Dole's opposition to a "drug czar."

By contrast, Clinton racked up six positive issue appeals (appointed "drug czar," expanded "antidrug programs," broke up violent "gangs," and supported "drug tests" for teens before getting a driver's license, curfews, and school uniforms). The first two issues have their own separate coding category in my scheme, as does the fourth on drug tests. The references to stopping gang violence were placed under "lower crime." Furthermore, there are three "values" within this spot. Two of them would be treated as references to Clinton's support of children. The final would be a general reference to Clinton's support of our values. All in all, there would be thirteen appeals gleaned from this spot under my coding scheme.

Now consider this Ford ad attacking (mostly) Carter's personal traits:

> All the things we've read about Jimmy Carter I think are true, that **he is fuzzy on a lot of the issues.** He **changes his mind on the stand every other day or so.** He **contradicts himself from one day to another.** Well, **he's changed his opinions from one day to the next.** It's much too **wishy-washy.** He's very, very **wishy-washy.** He seems to be a little **wishy-washy.** I—if he would **stand up and say what he's for** he'd be a little bit easier to, uh, to **understand and maybe to believe.** I *like President Ford*, the man *who will tell you just exactly where he does stand.*[35]

For this spot, there would be a total of eleven appeals. The first seven are attacks on Carter's "wishy-washiness" or changing his mind. There are explicit codes for such charges in my scheme. The last two negative trait appeals would count as "not standing up" and saying what he believes. Ford would get two positive trait codes. The first is a simple "I like President Ford," the other would be you know where he "stands." In sum, this spot is about the general topic of integrity and trust, which is well represented by my coding scheme.

POTENTIAL CONCERNS

Before I present my actual measure of negativity derived from this content analysis, I will address three potential weaknesses of the data. These concerns are all reasonable, but do not undermine the value of the data for answering the questions driving this book. Because no data are perfect, it is best to tackle these worries now. In the end, the findings are sensible enough (as one can see below) that one should develop a high level of comfort with this body of evidence.

First, this content analysis focused primarily on the spoken and written word. Originally, I attempted to code the visual aspects of the ads, but I could not attain an acceptable level of reliability.[36] The visual aspects of the commercials apparently resonate differently with different people, as perhaps their producers intended. Only when the visual provided the context and there were no written or spoken words did I code those appeals. The best example of this would be the famous Daisy spot from the 1964 Johnson campaign. The nuclear explosion in the ad was coded as a reference to nuclear war. Recall, that following the mushroom cloud, Johnson said "these are the stakes," which is a statement referencing that visual. There are only a handful of ads in the entire data set where this happened.[37]

Some may find this focus on the spoken and written word to be a problem. Clearly, the visuals communicate many important messages in the ads. But without coding reliability, there was little point in procceding. More importantly, it is my experience that the visuals and the verbal (and the written) usually go hand in hand. That is, if a candidate is talking about education, the ad is likely to have pictures of children in schools or teachers in a classroom. The spot is not likely to have pictures of military people filling the screen. This interconnection between the audio and visual messages makes sense and has drawn comment from one of the most famous advertisers of recent times, Tony Schwartz. Schwartz (1974) argues that the audio component of TV advertising is underappreciated and it is an important way spots influence voters. Alex Castellanos echoed Schwartz's view, contending that the audio is more important to the candidate's message than the visuals. In fact, Castellanos made reference to the often used phrase "a picture is worth a thousand words." As he did, he noted the irony that it is a phrase comprising a string of words that conveyed the importance of the visual side of the equation.[38] Castellanos left no doubt that the text of the ad was its central contribution to the information environment.

As a test of this thesis, I examined a random sample of twenty-five ads.[39] In twenty-four of them the visuals reinforced the written and/or the spoken word.[40]

A second problem is that my data measure only the *explicit* appeals candidates make in their spots. The work of Tali Mendelberg (2001) shows quite convincingly the import of *implicit* appeals in political campaigns. The end result is that my data surely underestimate the importance of racial issues in presidential campaigns, since racial appeals have gone "underground" (see Mendelberg 2001). In the 1960s, racial issues did constitute, according to my data, a nontrivial part of the candidates' agendas.[41] However, by the 1980s and 1990s, this proportion dropped to near zero, which corresponds to the shift in thinking on how to play the so-called race card. My data, therefore, square with Mendelberg's argument that racial appeals have become much more subtle and indirect, which should provide additional faith in the coding of the data. Having said that, I do not think my data speak effectively to the role of race in presidential campaigns. Fortunately, this book is not about racial issues. Even so, it is sensible to acknowledge this weakness of the data.

The final worry confronting these data is that I do not know how often and where the ads were aired, requiring me to weight each ad equally. Ken Goldstein and colleagues have made use of a new technology that helps to lessen this problem for the 1996, 2000, and future presidential elections (e.g., Goldstein and Freedman 2002). The Campaign Media Analysis Group (CMAG) tracks when and where ads are aired in the nation's largest media markets. This innovation is important and will continue to provide valuable insights, but those insights are limited only to elections since 1996.

This issue of weighting is, in general, a tricky one. Jamieson, Waldman, and Sheer (2000) weighted their measures of negativity by campaign spending and it did little to change their basic findings. In one of the most comprehensive studies of the issue, Markus Prior (2001) assessed the various weighting strategies. He compares an unweighted procedure to frequency of airing to advertising rates (another plausible weighting scheme). In Prior's study of Columbus, Ohio in 1996, he finds that there was little difference for Clinton's spots across the three strategies, while he finds differences in the Dole case. It is not clear how to interpret the mixed results of this case study. Moreover, since my focus is on the content of appeals within the ads and not the impact of specific ads on voters, my approach is well suited to meet my needs. In 1992, Clinton, to no surprise, talked heavily about the economy in his spots. That theme appears in ad after ad. Some ads were surely aired more than others, but when aggregating across these ads, I capture the key point: it was the economy, stupid. In my conversation with Alex Castellanos, he confirms this idea. Because candidates usually have a large number of ads covering key themes, he thought that it is "safe to assume" that each spot will be shown at similar rates to the public.

Even so, this general issue remains open for debate. Prior (2001), for example, points out problems with the CMAG approach, noting that cable television systems do not overlap well with the major media markets, as defined by CMAG, which introduces yet another problem. Even if we solve all these issues, a new "far more daunting" one looms on the horizon: "analyzing ad exposure on the internet" (Prior 2001, 343).

The debate over weighting is far from over—new questions and new technologies will arise that will make this a fertile area for future inquiry. In the meantime, I shall stick with the equal weighting assumption. To study the last forty years of presidential elections, one has little choice.[42]

NEGATIVITY IN PRESIDENTIAL CAMPAIGNS

My data capture the *appeals* candidates make to the public within each spot. There are on average 12.1 appeals across each of the 795 spots. Of the 9590 total appeals from 1960 to 2000, 32% are attacks on the opposition. In other words, about one-third are negative. By organizing the data this way, I employ a much more fine-grained measure of negativity than simply identifying ads as either negative, positive, or contrast. Consider that of 795 spots I have examined, 28% are negative, 24% contrast ads, and 48% positive ads. Those proportions are useful to know, but there remains some uncertainty about the *overall* amount of negativity in presidential campaigns. What should we do with contrast ads; divide them in half, putting 50% of them in the positive camp and the other 50% in the negative camp? If so, then we could say that 40% of the campaign advertising was negative.[43] But this allocation is misleading, because it overrepresents the amount of negativity for two reasons. First, among contrast ads about 60% of all appeals in these commercials are positive. Second, some negative ads often throw in one or two positive appeals to lessen the blow. Such spots are not contrast ads, at least by how Jamieson, Waldman, and Sheer (2000) define them. But they do suggest some slippage between these categories. These data underscore the advantage of a more precise measure for assessing the overall content of political advertising.

Figure 2.1 presents my measure of the negativity in presidential campaigns from 1960 to 2004.[44] As one can see, there is a clear upward trend in negativity. On average, there has been a 2.7 percentage point increase in negativity across each of the twelve campaigns.[45] There is, of course, some interesting variation, such as the steep rise between 1960 and 1964 in negativity and the slight drop in 2000. It is worth noting that even in the most negative campaign, 2004, there was about a fifty-fifty split between positive and negative appeals. One would get the impression from the media that voters are drowning in a sea of negativity. These data do not provide much support for such dire claims. Even so, this graph serves as the centerpiece of this book. Negativity is indeed on the rise, just as many observers have feared. This finding underscores further the need to undertake a thorough evaluation of the quality of information contained in these attacks.

I want to comment a bit about the estimate of negativity for the 2004 presidential campaign. I have *not* undertaken a detailed content analysis of the spots, but I did count the number of negative, positive, and contrast ads aired by Bush and Kerry to forge a preliminary "guess." Assuming that the ads from 2004 contained the same rate of negative and

Figure 2.1. Amount of Negativity in Presidential Campaigns, 1960–2004

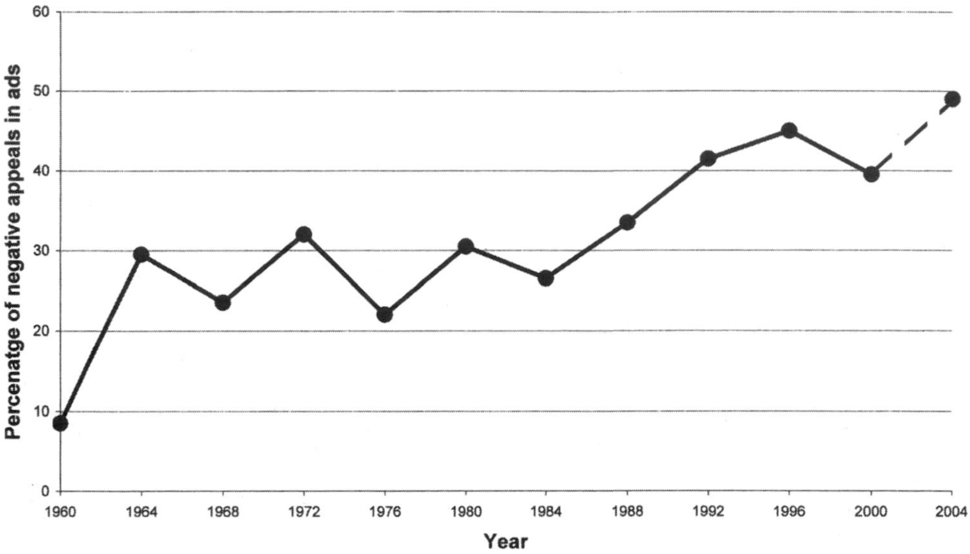

positive appeals as their recent counterparts, I generated as estimate for the share of negativity in 2004.[46] The Bush-Kerry contest appears to be the most negative in the last forty-four years—49% of the appeals constituted attacks. Bush relied more on negative ads than did Kerry—53% to 31%. Kerry aired far more contrast ads (43%) than Bush (13%). This estimate is very preliminary, but it seems reasonable to believe that the 2004 campaign was the most negative in recent memory and this proportion confirms that impression. I will not make extensive use of this estimate. But I thought it important to show that negativity continues to be on the rise.

Before we accept the measure of negativity reported in figure 2.1 as sound, it is important to compare my results to other measures of negativity over the same time period. In searching the literature, I have found four other efforts to measure negativity in presidential campaigns—Lynda Kaid and Anne Johnston, Kathleen Jamieson, Darrell West, and William Benoit.[47] Figure 2.2 compares the five measures. As one can see, they are pretty much all telling the same story—negativity is increasing in presidential elections. The agreement is impressive, especially since we measure negativity differently and employ a different set of ads.

My measure, for example, correlates 0.78 with Jamieson's, an impressive 0.93 with Kaid and Johnston's, and a staggering 0.97 with Benoit's. The correlation with West's measure drops to 0.59. West's measure, as we will see, is capturing something different than the other four.[48]

Figure 2.2. Comparing Measures of Negativity, 1960–96

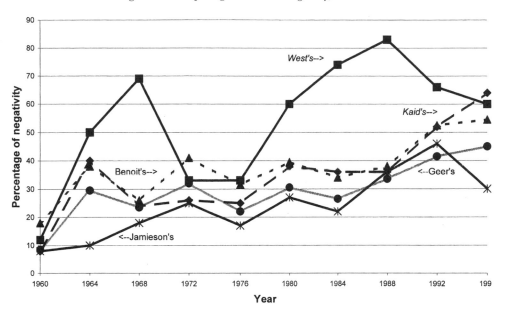

While these correlations are impressive, they only tap over-time variance. It is worth, therefore, discussing a few simple summary statistics for these competing measures of negativity. Jamieson reports the lowest amount of negativity (24% overall), while Kaid and Johnston and Benoit are higher (40% and 37%, respectively), with West topping the charts at 54%. My average rating stands at around 30%.[49] If one looks closely at figure 2.2, Kaid and Johnston consistently report more negativity than Jamieson and I. One reason for this gap probably lies in the fact that they treat ads as either positive or negative (Jamieson, Waldman, and Sheer 2000). By not including comparative or contrast ads in their analytical scheme, they are introducing measurement error. According to my argument earlier, they end up overestimating the amount of negativity in campaigns through their coding scheme. They are able to capture *change* in the rate of negativity quite well, but estimates about the frequency of attacks in a particular election should be judged with some caution.

In the case of Benoit (1999), the answer probably can be found in the differences in the coding schemes we employ.[50] Benoit (1999) employs a "functional analysis" to motivate his coding scheme. That approach yields one clear difference from mine: I gather much more information from the ads than does Benoit. He reports in the 1960 to 1996 time period 4245 pieces of information from his 761 spots. I coded 8478 appeals from my 720 ads. In short, I have about twice as many appeals as does Benoit. Given the strong correlation between our measures, I am confident that our data are tracking what we want quite well—we just have different objectives behind our data collection.

I will now address the modest differences between Jamieson and me, especially since Jamieson's work is so prominent in the field. One explanation springs to mind. A key difference between my sample and hers involves the fact that she includes ads longer than one minute. Longer ads are much more likely to be positive than shorter ones. For example, 18% of the appeals in the sixty-second spots in my sample are negative. For thirty-second spots, the proportion swells to 42%. There are only a handful sixty-second negative ads (5% of the total). The public apparently is not likely to react favorably to extended criticism. If true, five-minute ads, which Jamieson examines, are likely to be more positive on average than the typical thirty-second ad. Hence, Jamieson's sample should (and does) yield a lower estimate of negativity than mine.

There is one problem facing Jamieson's data involving the 1964 election that merits comment. By nearly all accounts, it was a negative campaign. Some of the most famous attack ads of all time come from that contest. Yet, Jamieson's data suggest the race was nearly as positive as 1960. This finding seems implausible. The explanation for this low estimate is unclear.[51] If we drop the 1964 case from the comparison, our two measures become more closely related. The simple correlation between the two indicators rises to 0.87 and the difference in the means drops to less than four percentage points (29.2% to 25.4%).

There are, as hinted earlier, substantial differences between my findings and West's. It is important to discuss them, since these differences underscore a key lesson. Much of the explanation for these differences lies in the competing samples employed. West examines "prominent" ads. The objective is to study the important spots, the ones that were most discussed in the campaigns. These prominent ads come from two sources. The first is an analysis of those spots reported in Jamieson's second edition of *Packaging the President*. This covers the time period from 1952 to 1988. From 1992 to 2000, prominent ads constitute those spots that appear in stories in the *CBS Evening News*. All in all, West has 422 ads in this data set.

The idea of looking only at prominent ads can offer useful insights. One could, of course, quarrel with West's definition of "prominent." Namely, do the ads discussed by Jamieson and by *CBS News* qualify as prominent? Surely the sample taps those ads that caught journalists' and pundits' attention, but whether they were prominent for voters is far from clear.

Questions aside, West's data suggest that presidential campaigns have been far more negative than I report above. From 1960 to 2000, West reports a 55% average rate of negativity. For my data from that same period, the proportion is nearly 30%. Actually, that 55% underreports the amount of negativity in his *general* election ads, since he does have primary ads mixed in with this sample. For example, West finds that 91% of Bush's general election ads were negative (2001, 69). My data show that only 27% of Bush's ads were negative, with another 24% qualifying as contrast spots (see also Goldstein and Freedman 2002). West's data speak to the fact that political observers often find negativity more interesting than positive rhetoric (see also Jamieson, Waldman, and Sheer 2000). As a result, the differences between West's data and my data are not a problem. These data sets offer insights on different questions. That is, West's data do not speak effectively to the link between voters and politicians, but more about the link between journalists (and pundits) and the public. The interest of political observers in negative ads is important and it is the theme that I shall address in chapter 6.

I have spent some time here trying to discuss the differences between these four data sets. Given that each of us is employing somewhat different samples and coding schemes designed to answer different questions, it is hardly a surprise that there is not complete agreement. However, figure 2.2 provides strong evidence that we have captured the same basic development—negativity is on the rise. This kind of confirmation should increase the confidence scholars place in *all* of these data sets.

A FURTHER LOOK AT TRENDS IN NEGATIVITY

We know that the frequency of attack in presidential ads has been on the rise over the last forty years. In what follows, I push the analysis a bit further. My objective is twofold. First, I want to present a few trends, building upon figure 2.1. By doing so, I can present some descriptive information that will advance our understanding of negativity in the race for the White House. Second, this undertaking allows me to build additional confidence in the data. The patterns below offer few surprises, which should facilitate greater faith in the merits of these data. This faith becomes more important in later chapters when findings do not reveal what conventional wisdom predicts.

I started by looking at the trends in negativity among Democratic and Republican nominees. There is little reason to think that there should be much of a partisan difference in the amount of negativity. There is no social science theory I know of that that would hypothesize that Democrats or Republicans will be more likely to attack members of the other party. Data confirm that intuition. The nominees of both parties show an increased rate of negativity, as we would expect, but there are not clear and consistent partisan differences. Over the last eleven elections, the Democrats do hold a slight edge—33% of their appeals were negative to 31% for the Republicans. Democrats attacked more in six of the eleven races, the Republicans more in three contests, with two essentially even. This gap is not significant in either a statistical or substantive sense. Even so, one could posit that the fact that Democrats have lost six out of these eleven contests might account for this small difference. Conventional wisdom suggests that the losing candidate is more likely to attack (e.g., Riker 1996). I addressed this follow-up hypothesis by examining the amount of negativity by winning and losing candidates. The differences are minimal. Among winners, 31% of their appeals were negative. For losers, the proportion is just 33%. The major outlier is 1964, where Johnson made extensive use of the attack ad even though he was substantially ahead in the polls and ended up winning in a landslide.

I suspect these nonfindings may be tied to the general *competitiveness* of presidential elections. There is work that shows congressional elections become more negative as they become more competitive (e.g., Kahn and Kenney 1999; 2004). Yet for my data, there is no relationship in these data between closeness of the presidential election and negativity.[52] The reason for these different findings may be that presidential elections are always "competitive" by the standards employed by congressional scholars (e.g., Jacobson 2003). There is, in short, not as much variance as we see in races for the House of Representatives or the Senate. Even in the most lopsided presidential contests, there is still a degree of competition that is absent in most congressional races.

Perhaps a better comparison would be the negativity of the in-versus the out-party. The normal story is that party out of power is more negative than the incumbent. The out-party has to criticize the incumbent party to make its case to the public. The differences again are small, but are in the hypothesized direction. On average, incumbents have a 30% rate of negativity, while challengers have 34%. The out-party nominee is more negative in seven of eleven contests, with the incumbent attacking more just three times. A noticeable outlier, again, is 1964, where Johnson is nearly twice as negative as Goldwater. This modest difference surely reflects in part the fact that some incumbents, like Bush in 1992, were trailing in the polls, leading them to be more negative than usual. With the higher rate of negativity by President Bush in 2004, this gap is likely narrow even further.

Finally, I examine the trend in intracampaign negativity. The hypothesis here is that as election day approaches, the contest should get more heated and the ads more negative. In addition, nominees no longer need to air as many biographical commercials and instead try to establish the key differences between the candidates (Geer 1998). I can test this

Figure 2.3. Amount of Negativity by Date of Advertisement

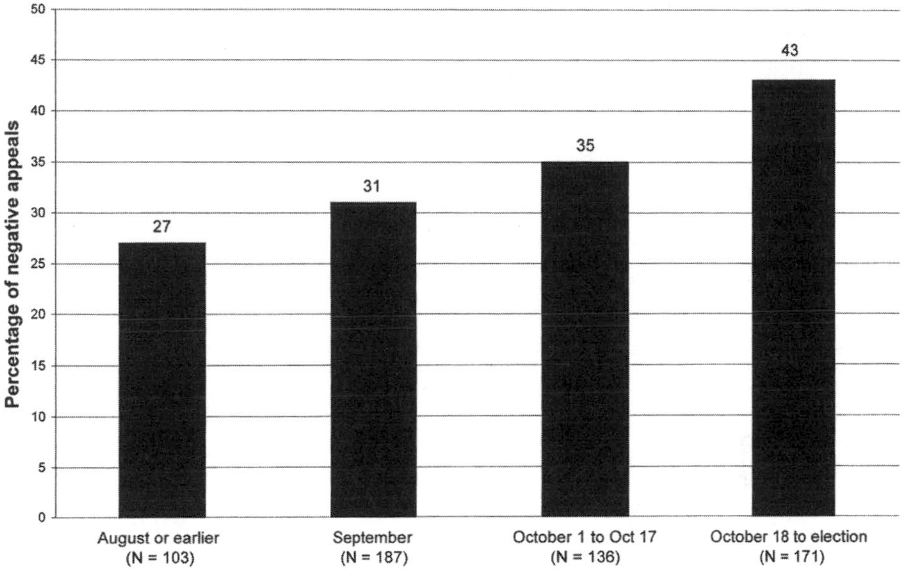

hypothesis, since from 1972 to 2000 I know the date the ad was created for nearly all the spots I coded.[53] Figure 2.3 presents the breakdown of negativity in four general periods: August or earlier, September, the first part of October, and the last part of October up to the day of the election.[54] The pattern is as expected—ads become more negative as the race comes to a close. There is a 60% increase in negativity for the ads created at the end of the campaign compared to those from August (or earlier). That is a substantial change. However, it is worth pointing out that even in the early stages of the fall campaign, candidates still attack each other— about a quarter of the time. Negativity is not something candidates save until the end of the campaign. They begin raising doubts about their opponents from the outset.

CONCLUSION

We are now ready to begin our evaluation of negativity in presidential campaigns. The data are not only sound, but they provide a detailed reading of the messages candidates have sent to the public over the last forty years. We have learned that negativity is on the rise. The pundits are, therefore, correct: presidential candidates are more willing to attack their opponents than just a few decades ago. But the question remains: does this development undermine the electoral process? Is negativity something to worry about? It is to these general questions that this book will now turn.

CHAPTER THREE

The Information Environment
and Negativity

The critics of negativity agree that attacks weaken the information available to voters. John McCain, one of the most popular politicians in the country, contends that negativity does "little to further beneficial debate and healthy political dialogue."[1] J. H. Clinger (1987, 746) believes that negative advertising has created an "increasing intellectual and ethical bankruptcy of modern political debate," which is undermining the "very future of democratic self-government." Stephen Carter (1998, 119) joins in, arguing that with negative ads, "public dialogue is debased, so we voters, who supposedly are sovereign, have more and more trouble figuring out who stands for what." These, as well as many other critics, believe that when candidates attack each other during a campaign, citizens do not learn anything useful. According to this view, negative exchanges are much like children fighting where one witnesses little more than name-calling and perhaps some shoving back and forth. The underlying assumption is that positive appeals are more *substantive* than negative appeals.[2]

This chapter not only challenges the conventional wisdom about negative campaigning, but turns it on its head. Negative appeals, I will argue, *enrich* the information environment *more* than positive appeals. To support this claim, I will develop an argument that explains why negative appeals improve the quality of information available to the public more than positive appeals. This argument provides the theoretical cornerstone for much of my analysis in this and later chapters.

Before we embark on that path, there are two tasks that demand attention. First, I will provide a brief accounting of the evidence that now exists concerning the ability of ads to inform the public. While this book, as mentioned earlier, is not about the impact of ads on voters, an underlying assumption of this project is that the content of ads influences the public's knowledge about the respective qualifications of candidates. My goal here is simply to demonstrate that this starting point is reasonable. Second, I will establish a set of criteria that serve as the basis to judge whether negativity has an informative function. This is very much a normative undertaking, and I want to be clear about my standards.

DO ADS INFORM THE PUBLIC?

Thomas Patterson and Robert McClure (1976, 111) argued thirty years ago that "spot commercials . . . educate the public." This view, at the time, flew in the face of the general assumption that short sound bites could not possibly inform the public. Most scholars believed that ads did not educate voters, they just manipulated them. Robert Spero (1980) made such an argument, as did McGinniss (1969) in his famous book on the 1968 Nixon campaign. David Ogilvy, a pioneer in the advertising field, claimed that political ads were "the most deceptive, misleading, unfair, and untruthful of all advertising" (quoted in Zhao and Chaffee 1995, 42).

Whatever one thinks of this debate, it is clear that ads at least possess the *potential* to inform the public. Even spots that are sixty seconds or shorter contain a wealth of information. There are, as mentioned in the last chapter, an average of twelve separate appeals per ad. Each appeal can be thought of as a piece of information. There is, as one might guess, a good deal of variation by candidate. Goldwater's spots were typical, netting 12.7 appeals per spot. Reagan's 1980 campaign was near the low end of the distribution at about 9.0 appeals per advertisement. Clinton, by contrast, topped the charts at 20.6 appeals per spot. This high rate is consistent with Clinton's interest in the details of public policy and his obvious desire to communicate his accomplishments.[3]

Over the last forty years, there has been a movement toward shorter ads. From 1960 to 1968, for example, slightly over 50% of the spots in my sample were sixty seconds long. In the presidential elections from 1992 to 2000, the proportion shrank to 5%. Might the rise of shorter spots lessen the amount of information candidates send to the public? It is certainly reasonable to hypothesize that the shift to the shorter format decreases the amount of information presented to the voters. My data, however, suggest that nearly the opposite is true. Sixty-second spots possess, on average, 13.5 appeals. For thirty-second ads, the average number of appeals is 11.8. If one considers appeals per second, spots lasting just half a minute contain much more information (0.39 appeals per second) than their longer counterparts (0.23 appeals per second). This evidence suggests that the shift to the shorter format led to ads that were more efficient in the amount of information they provided.

Regardless of these results, some commentators may still want candidates to engage in lengthy, detailed exchanges on the pressing issues of the day as voters listen intently to every word. Perhaps that is ideal, but it is a situation that flies in the face of what we know about voters and candidates. The public is not interested in spending hours learning the details about politics (e.g., Converse 1964; Popkin 1991; Keeter and Zukin 1996; Zaller 2004), nor is it even sensible for them to do so (Downs 1957). Even though voters do not come close to meeting these ideals, the truth is that citizens can learn quite a bit in thirty-seconds. During that half a minute, candidates can indicate their views on a variety of issues and/or raise doubts about their opponents. While we tend to dismiss spots as being too short, it is worth noting that the thirty-second time frame is about *four* times longer than the sound bites provided by the national, network news these days. Farnsworth and Lichter (2003, 81) report that direct statements by the candidates shrank to 7.8 seconds during the 2000 presidential election (see also Adatto 1990).

Candidate advertising on television possesses more than just the potential to inform. Convincing evidence now exists showing that ads do inform the public. Patterson and McClure (1976) made that point long ago. But their findings were largely based on recall measures, which confronted methodological problems (see Vavreck 2003). More recent work, which has taken advantage of methodological improvements, confirms that ads do inform the public (e.g., Ansolabehere and Iyengar 1995; Just et al. 1996; Freedman, Franz, and Goldstein 2004; Kahn and Kenney 1999). Ansolabehere and Iyengar (1995, 59), for example, contend that ads "enlighten voters and enable them to take account of issues and policies when choosing between the candidates" (see also Valentino et al. 2002; Zhao and Chafee 1993; Just et al. 1990). Among the reasons they offer for this effect is the "brevity of the advertising message" (1995, 60). These scholars note that the "great majority of voters bypass or ignore information that entails more than minimal acquisition costs, preferring to use messages that are simple to digest and easily obtained. Of course, campaign advertising meets the demand for both simplicity and access" (1995, 60).

Perhaps the most impressive work to date is by Freedman, Franz, and Goldstein (2004). They have marshaled a convincing body of evidence that shows citizens do learn from advertising. They employ a combination of survey data with state of the art measures of exposure to political ads to demonstrate that ads educate the public about the candidates.

They also find that less informed voters are especially likely to profit from these sound bites, which further underscores the importance of ads in the political process. Recall that I argued earlier that ads provide an important link between citizens and politicians. This link appears to be real. These impressive results lead Freedman and colleagues (2004, 725) to conclude that "ads represent the multivitamins of American politics." That observation captures nicely the point that these small bits of information are far more useful to voters than many observers claim.

THE INFORMATIONAL NEEDS OF VOTERS

What type of information helps voters make good choices? This is a normative question that requires a set of judgments about what are the best standards by which to judge what constitutes "good." Over forty years ago, Stanley Kelley (1960, 5) wrote what remains today the single best scholarly effort to develop "standards for evaluating campaign discussion." Kelley (1960, 6) understood, however, that regardless of the merits of his particular argument, the standards he offered were "not the only ones that could be adopted." People's values and goals differ, leading to potential disagreement. Pendleton Herring (1940), for example, put much more emphasis on the importance of the personality of candidates than did Kelley in judging the type of information voters need. Herring believed you needed someone in office you could trust and who had sound judgment. Is Herring wrong? No. Such disagreement just reminds us that it is "difficult to define and measure campaign substance" (Simon 2002, 2).

With all due respect to Herring, most conceptions of an "informative" campaign revolve around issues or policy in some way. The belief is that discussion of issues prior to an election is an important indicator of a good campaign—one where voters would have the chance to learn about the candidates' plans for government. The more issues play a role, the more informative a campaign should be. Most political scientists certainly subscribe to this view concerning the importance of policy; just consider the amount of attention scholars have paid to studying the subject of *issue voting*.[4] That interest is fueled in part by the belief that such voting is superior to citizens casting ballots on the basis of personality. Edward Carmines and James Stimson (1989, 79) observe that "the common—indeed universal—view has been that voting choices based on policy concerns are superior to decisions based on party loyalty or candidate image."

As a result, one part of my investigation will be to assess the varying importance of issues in presidential campaigns. The general point is that the more informative a campaign is, the more it focuses on policy debates. This claim, while simplistic, provides a good starting point. It does not, however, mean that traits are unimportant for voters as they choose between candidates. As I noted earlier, Herring (1940) makes a strong case for the importance of voters knowing the personal characteristics of candidates when casting ballots. In fact, chapter 4 will assess the role of personal characteristics in presidential campaigns, in general, and whether the information contained in negative appeals, in particular, is useful for voters.

A second criterion follows the axiom "the more evidence, the better." The notion here is a simple one. Claims backed by evidence are superior to stand-alone assertions. Kelley (1960, 16) contends that the question of reason and evidence is a key test of whether the campaign advances the prospect of voters making rational decisions: "Do campaigners offer evidence for their assertions and give reasons for favoring (or for having favored) particular policies?" Dennis Thompson (1970, 104) concurs, noting that "one piece of rational propaganda will be said to be *more cognitive* than another to the extent it uses evidence which is more factual than intuitive." This standard has worked its way into more practical efforts to improve campaigns. The Project for Campaign Conduct, for example, argues that advertisements should "support their claims with evidence."[5] So, even if a candidate runs a heavily issue-oriented campaign, but little evidence is offered to support those claims, it would not be viewed as informative. The fear would be that the claims, lacking evidence, might be false and misrepresentative.

A third standard, which is related to the one noted above, is whether the information in campaigns "expose the grounds on which candidates disagree" (Kelley 1960, 14). Kelley argues that such discussion during campaigns helps to promote a more informed electorate and, hence, more rational voters. Thompson (1970, 104) again supports Kelley's contention, arguing that the informative propaganda "reveals the differences among opposing views." The reasoning is that when candidates spell out their differences more clearly, voters will be able to make decisions that are consistent with their own preferences on policy. When a candidate, for example, favors "economic growth," that appeal is hardly going to help voters understand what contenders plan to do once in office, nor will it help sort out the differences between the nominees. On the other hand, specific information about the candidate's tax policy or willingness to increase the minimum wage would be useful and help voters make "rational" choices.

The fourth standard offers one last, important twist. It is quite possible that a campaign that talks a lot about issues, offers evidence for its positions, and does so in a way that lays out differences between candidates clearly could still be suboptimal. The topics discussed also need to be *relevant* to governing.[6] The general idea here is that candidates should be talking about important issues, not matters that are of limited value or of little consequence to the country. If a candidate spent a great deal of time talking about how best to handle foreign aid and price supports for grain producers, I doubt the public would become very well-informed about the issues salient to them. While a handful of citizens might find such matters important, most would not. This point also applies to discussion of personal traits. Candidates should be talking about traits that speak to a candidate's qualifications for office, such as competence or honesty. Any effort to engage in unwarranted name-calling would not be useful information for voters' decisions.

For purposes of clarification, let me list the four standards I will employ to judge the quality of negative and positive appeals made by candidates in campaigns:

1. The more issues are discussed, the better.
2. The more evidence is presented, the better.
3. The clearer the differences between candidates, the better.
4. The more relevant the appeal is to governing, the better.

These criteria will be applied by *comparing* the qualities of positive to those of negative campaign appeals. The question, then, becomes: do negative appeals in ads do a better or worse job in advancing the quality of information available to the public than positive appeals? This comparative perspective avoids the many land mines associated with making absolute judgments about whether the quality of information meets a particular standard. However, some readers may question this approach, since they have doubts about the informational value of any short advertisement. If so, any arguments and evidence I would present in regards to the informative nature of attack ads are not likely to be persuasive. I would, however, point out that many of the criticisms of negativity in ads rest on the assumption that positive appeals are superior and should be encouraged in campaigns. These critics believe that if we could only lessen the frequency of thirty-second attack ads, the quality of campaigns would improve. That commonly-held view is making an implicit comparison between negative and positive appeals. I am, therefore, employing the same type of comparative perspective.

SOME ALTERNATIVE CRITERIA

As noted earlier, one could easily argue for other standards. For example, Adam Simon (2002) makes the case that campaigns should be judged by whether they promote dialogue between the candidates and avoid what

James Bryce (1891) and others have decried about campaigns—the tendency for candidates to talk past each other. This is a worthy goal. In fact, debates are valuable institutions in campaigns for these very reasons (see also Kelley 1960; Thompson 1970; Bartels et al. 1998). However, political ads are not forms of propaganda that lend themselves to this kind of standard. The spot represents an effort by one candidate to send messages to voters; it is not a format designed to promote direct exchanges between candidates. In fact, part of the competitive struggle is for candidates to offer different agendas to the public and let them choose which set of issues they most want government to address.

It is also worth pointing out that issues that both candidates want to talk about may not be the kinds of issues voters need to hear about. Assume that an issue is either a strength or a weakness for the two major party nominees.[7] Assume further that candidates will tend to talk about their strengths and avoid addressing their weaknesses. With these two starting points, one can envision the four possible outcomes generated by a simple two by two table (see Geer 1998). In only one scenario— strength, strength—is there an incentive for both candidates to engage in a direct exchange (i.e., dialogue). Yet, the issues in this cell are *not* likely to be the most important issues facing the country. An important issue usually involves some problem that has yet to be solved. If true, then the party in power is not likely to want to talk about the matter, which would lessen the chance of direct dialogue.[8] My point is that campaign issues are not likely to fall randomly across the possible outcomes, meaning that, on average, issues of *less* importance to the public will end up in the joint dialogue box where both candidates will address the issue.

Actually, this tendency to talk past each other in campaigns becomes less pronounced when candidates have the option to attack—a point alluded to in the first chapter. Candidates in their positive propaganda want to talk about those issues that favor them and duck everything else; but attacks are just the opposite. The opposition wants to raise those issues that the candidate wants to duck. By going negative, the opposition can force a response from the candidate, generating dialogue and discussion of issues that might otherwise not be discussed.

Another potentially important criterion would be the *accuracy* of the information in ads. The standard of "the more evidence, the better" mentioned earlier is a close cousin. It seems reasonable to believe that ads with more documentation should be more accurate. Nevertheless, there are important differences.

As discussed in the introduction, I will not assess explicitly whether information from an ad is accurate or not. Obviously, campaigns that convey accurate information are superior to those that lie and mislead. In fact, a key complaint against negativity is that it promotes distortions and lies about the competing candidates. The problem is that it is very hard to establish the *truth*.[9] Moreover, ads, like all propaganda, *stretch* the truth. Campaigns put forth the most positive account possible of their candidate and paint the least flattering picture of the opposition.[10] However, exaggeration is not the same thing as lying and/or being dishonest. Reasonable people can disagree about how best to present the "facts." Republicans, for example, will offer different interpretations of the facts than Democrats. Where one falls politically will almost inevitably influence whether particular information is judged to be "accurate" or "inaccurate."

As a result, there is no clear set of guidelines that can clearly establish what is true or false. Efforts to establish whether information in campaigns is misleading strike me as a very slippery slope. It is for these reasons that I chose to establish the standard of evidence. In a way, this standard addresses some of these important concerns. Additionally, it is possible to determine whether evidence exists or not in a reasonably objective fashion (as we shall see below).

NEGATIVITY AND THE QUALITY OF INFORMATION

The old saying—"if you do not have anything nice to say, don't say anything at all"—appears to pervade many people's thinking about negativity in campaigns. There is an assumption that we should try to be upbeat and positive about things. That if we are critical, we only create more unhappiness and more criticism, forging a downward spiral of increasing negativity. There is a further belief among many reformers that to solve problems we need to offer a "positive agenda." By being critical, we are not able to make progress. Instead, we just bicker while the nation's problems go unsolved.

There is appeal to such a view. We are often uncomfortable when others fight. If someone walks into a restaurant and hears two customers fighting, he or she is likely to choose another place to eat. We usually want people to get along. The view that people like to avoid conflict has been central to some recent scholarship. Hibbing and Theiss-Morse (1995, 2002) contend that the public is disturbed by open conflict within the halls of Congress and that these fights undermine the public's assessment of that institution. In fact, a key reason why Congress is viewed less favorably than the other institutions appears to be tied to this perception of what we might call bickering. The public wants to avoid disagreement, according to these scholars.

Yet open debate and disagreement are hallmarks of democratic government. We want to be able to discuss what are the best policies for the country and that requires criticism and open (and often frank) discussion. The problem is, at what point does disagreement become bickering? Reasonable disagreements hold much more legitimacy than artificial or exaggerated ones. In the end, the decision of whether it is legitimate or exaggerated is often fueled by the evaluators' partisan perspective—a theme I raised earlier.

While having aversions to conflict is understandable, it does not mean that people cannot learn from disagreement. Children usually do not like spinach, but it is still good for them. Many adults do not like to exercise, but it is beneficial for them. If we evaluated things only by whether we liked them or not, we would not do a lot of things that are good for us. An informed decision—on nearly any subject—requires that we know the good *and* bad points of the various options. Imagine for a second buying a car without knowing about its problems. That would be a significant risk. In American elections, we usually have to choose between two candidates. Each candidate will happily provide voters with their good points, but they are unlikely to supply their bad points. That, as noted earlier, comes from the opposition often in the form of attack advertising.

My starting assumption is that we need to know the "negative" to make an informed decision. Perhaps learning such things is not pleasant, but it is essential to an informed decision. But there is more. I will also argue that negativity is *more* informative than positive information. Negative information is more about issues than positive information; it relies more on evidence to back up claims than positive information, is more specific in discussion of issues than positive information, and is more likely to tackle concerns of interest to the public than positive information. In effect, attacks provide a better source of information for voters to make decisions than positive information. Nevertheless, I do not believe we should only have negative information. Rather, the rise of negativity we saw in the previous chapter is not a development we should view with fear and concern; it is a trend that has far more benefits than most observers think, especially given the standards developed above. Let me now develop my reasoning.

Negative versus Positive Campaign Appeals: An Important Asymmetry

There has been a sizable amount of work that has discussed various "negativity effects." For example, the public appears to give more weight to negative information than positive information (e.g., Lau 1982; 1985). Kernell (1977) talked about "negative" voting, where citizens punish incumbents for "negative" outcomes more than they reward them for good outcomes (see also Erikson 1988). Campbell, Converse, Miller, and Stokes, the authors of *The American Voter* (1960, 554), developed a similar argument, noting that "changes in the party balance are induced primarily by negative rather than positive attitudes towards the party controlling the executive branch." The basic point is that scholars have theorized about various types of *asymmetries* concerning negativity (broadly defined).

Here, I will advocate a different idea, one that builds on the notion that there are differences between negative and positive information. Specifically, I posit that there is an *asymmetry* between how candidates present positive and negative information in their propaganda. Politicians, when attacking the opposition, face a different set of constraints than when promoting themselves during a campaign. It comes under the general rubric of "innocent, until proven guilty."

Assume your firm has hired two new temporary employees, James and Megan. They both know they are competing for the one permanent job open in the company, making it a zero sum game. You have hired them and, thus, have some information about each person. But you do not know either very well. In one scenario, James tells you that he has repaired some equipment that you knew had broken down. You would assume that positive information about James to be true. You would not be likely to ask for proof of the claim. However, imagine instead that James, rather than fixing the equipment, claimed that Megan had sabotaged the equipment. For that negative information about Megan to be accepted as true, you would want proof of it. Once proof was provided, you would accept the claim. Without it, you would be unwilling to view such a serious charge as true and you would in fact have doubts about James's qualifications for the job. In short, you would not only assume innocence until proven otherwise, but penalize anyone for making unsubstantiated charges.

Some examples from the 1988 presidential campaign provide more relevant examples that underscore this differential need for evidence among positive and negative commercials. Vice President Bush ran the following ad:

> I want a kinder and gentler nation. . . . I am a quiet man. But I hear the quiet people others don't—the ones who raise the family, pay the taxes, meet the mortgage. And I hear them. And I am moved.

Notice that no evidence is presented to document the claims, just an effort by Bush to make these statements with feeling, with conviction. How would Dukakis challenge these claims? Could he simply counter by saying that Bush is not a "quiet man," that he is not "moved" by the needs of others? Such a response would not have been very effective. Instead, Dukakis needed to provide reasons for *why* Bush did not "hear" the needs of "quiet people." Essentially, Dukakis could talk about Bush's positions on issues that might question this compassion. Consider the following ad aired by the then governor:

> [Bush] sat by while the administration tried to cut $200 billion out of Social Security. In fact in 1985 Bush personally cast the tie-breaking Senate vote to cut $20 billion in benefits. And now suddenly George Bush tells you he's on your side. He didn't vote for you. Why should you vote for him?

The comparison of these two ads illustrates my basic point. In the first spot, we learn that Bush cares, without much evidence. In the second, we learn two pieces of information about Bush not caring: he tried to cut $200 billion from Social Security and then cast a tie breaking vote to cut $20 billion in benefits.

Additionally, let us consider Bush's attack on Dukakis for being "soft on crime." That theme was a staple of the Bush campaign in 1988. However, Bush could not simply say Dukakis was not tough on criminals. If Bush had made only that claim about Dukakis, the response from the Democratic nominee would be simple: "I am tough on crime." An opinion can usually be refuted and it certainly can be more easily refuted than a fact.[11] Bush went further in his advertising, noting that Dukakis "vetoed mandatory jail sentences for drug dealers," "opposed capital punishment in all cases," and "even vetoed the death penalty for cop killers."

My argument, in sum, is that when politicians present negative messages, they need to provide evidence to make them credible. Positive appeals require less evidence to make them credible, because the public will be more receptive to something good than something bad.[12] Scholars have occasionally hinted about this imbalance. Jamieson (1992, 103), for example, observes that "the stronger the attack, the greater the amount of specific factual content." West (2001, 70) makes a similar point, noting that "political strategists need to be clear about the facts in the case of challenges from the media," given that "reporters often dissect negative ads and demand evidence to support specific claims." In these cases, scholars saw a connection between negativity and evidence. I go a step further and argue that *in general* criticism requires more evidence to succeed, because viewers are going to be skeptical without documentation.

Before one accepts this argument, I must present evidence to support it. I have sought to assess the merits of this argument in two ways. First, I have interviewed a handful of prominent consultants to secure their thoughts on negativity. Second, I have undertaken additional content analyses designed explicitly to test this idea.

Political Consultants

The asymmetry between positive and negative appeals is quite consistent with how political consultants think about attack ads.[13] For example, Alex Castellanos, George W. Bush's media advisor, stated that "negative ads require more proof than positive spots, because people have gotten to know the candidates and you cannot say critical things without good reason." At another point in the conversation, he confirmed the earlier point claiming that in a negative ad candidates need to "prove their case." Greg Stevens, the creator of the Tank ad in 1988, concurs, noting that "attack ads require evidence." In fact, Stevens told a story about the creation of the Tank ad that underscores my core point. When Stevens saw the new coverage of Governor Dukakis riding in the tank, he knew he had a great spot. So he quickly put one together that highlighted many of Dukakis's positions on defense policy and sent the spot to the Bush campaign. They liked the ad, but wanted to check the accuracy of all claims before they would air it. Stevens had already checked the facts, but the Bush people did it yet again. They wanted to make sure they had "their facts straight," which delayed the airing of the ad (much to Stevens's consternation). This extra attention shows the role of evidence in attack politics.

Similar comments arose in interviews with Carter Eskew, Gore's media advisor in 2000, and local consultants in Tennessee and Virginia, Bill Fletcher and Jennifer Tierney. *The War Room*, the documentary on the Clinton campaign in 1992, provides an example of this general tendency. Carville and company, as they discussed crafting an attack ad against George Bush, stressed the need to keep the spot "factual." This belief was reinforced even further when interviewing Mike Murphy, a prominent Republican consultant who has worked on Lamar Alexander's presidential campaigns and most recently Arnold Schwarzenegger's successful bid to become Governor of California. He talked about the need for evidence when creating attack ads so the spot will "be seen as fair by viewers." Interestingly, at the start of my conversation with Murphy, I mentioned that I wanted to talk about negative and positive ads. Without any prompting he stated: "We have a joke in the business: the only difference between negative and positive ads is that negative ads have facts in them."

These interviews were all very revealing in that each of the individuals I interviewed made similar points. They all viewed negative ads as possessing more evidence than positive spots. Many of them commented about how academics and observers often lose sight of this basic point. It is also worth pointing out that campaigns dedicate part of their staff and significant resources to "opposition research." That is, candidates assign key people in their staff to investigate the past records of their opposition, looking for evidence of bad decisions, problematic votes, misstatements, and so on. However, this investigation is looking at the empirical record. It is not about making things up. It is about doing, as the phrase indicates, some *research*.[14]

Content Analysis

These interviews bolster my argument. But before accepting this asymmetry as correct, I sought to assess systematically the empirical validity of the core point: negative appeals will be more likely to have evidence supporting their claims than positive appeals. Since this asymmetry lies at the heart of my argument about how negative appeals can enrich the information environment, it is critical that I marshal compelling evidence.

In my original content analysis, I did not code for the amount of evidence used to document a particular claim. While my coding scheme does permit tests of some important hypotheses that follow from this asymmetry (as we will see), I had to collect new data to test for this asymmetry.

I started by reexamining a set of ads from 2000 available on the CD-ROM *In Their Own Words*. The results were quite striking. Among the nineteen positive ads from Bush and Gore in 2000, only one spot sought to document its claims with any type of evidence. The nominees offered their plans on health care and the economy, but they apparently did not feel compelled to provide any documentation to support these positions. The opposite was true for negative ads. Of the fourteen spots I looked at from the 2000 campaign, thirteen of them took the effort to provide the documentation for at least one of the negative appeals. For example, when Gore attacked Bush for appointing "a chemical company lobbyist to enforce environmental laws" in Texas, the claim was backed up by identifying the source—the *Washington Post,* October 15, 1999. When Bush questioned Gore's ability to improve education by noting that "our students rank last in the world in math and physics," that claim was documented by showing the statement came from the "U.S. Dept. of Education, 1998."

Perhaps the differences in 2000 reflect the impact of ad watches and the news media's intense scrutiny of political ads. Hence, my more general point about the need for evidence is not correct. It is simply a product of the current political environment, as West (2001) suggested earlier. As a result, I had to gather more evidence over a longer span of time.

I reexamined a sizable sample of ads from 1964, 1968, 1984, 1998, 1996, and 2000, measuring explicitly for any documentation of its claims.[15] For these data (as for the examples noted above), I defined "evidence" as specific statistics (e.g., "for the last three and a half years every

American has been staggered by the economic record of the Carter Administration. Food prices up over 35%. Auto prices up over 31%. Home prices up over 46%. Clothing up over 20%. Transportation up over 50%"). I also counted as evidence claims with specific references (e.g., *Washington Post*, July 29, 1987), or used a direct quote (e.g., "sometimes I think we would be better off if we sawed off the eastern seaboard and let it float out to sea," *Saturday Evening Post*, August 31, 1963). Under this framework, I did *not* undertake any formal verification of the evidence. I am only comparing the tendency of negative and positive ads to contain some sort of documentation for their claims.

The differences reported in figure 3.1 between positive and negative ads are substantial and highly supportive of my central contention. In each year under study, negative ads were much more likely to provide clear evidence to support their point than positive ads. This pattern is *not* tied to the development of ad watches in the 1990s. It is plausible that the slight increase we see among the verification of negative ads in 1996 and 2000 could be attributable to the threat of ad watches. But the basic pattern was in place prior to the idea that journalists would be good watchdogs of advertising.

Figure 3.1 only presents the frequency of evidence in positive and negative ads. Contrast ads, which mix negative and positive appeals within the same spot, are not part of this analysis. Such ads offer an additional test of this proposition. Are candidates in their contrast ads more likely to offer verification of their negative claims than their positive ones? This is a powerful test because I can see *within the same ad* whether evidence and documentation is more likely in certain types of appeals. I began by comparing the rate of verifiability within Clinton's 1996 contrast ads. The president ran a large number of comparative ads in the election—the most of any campaign in my dataset. Specifically, I examined thirty-seven contrast ads from the Clinton campaign.[16] Among these spots, 90% contain verification of negative appeals. This proportion drops to 50% for positive appeals. I also looked at the Bush and Gore contrast ads in 2000. While I examined only eleven contrast ads from that contest, 91% of negative appeals had verification compared to 36% of the positive appeals. The pattern holds— negative appeals are more likely to be documented than positive appeals.

I extended my empirical investigation into the congressional arena. If my claim is indeed a general one, it should work for elections other than presidential. Fortunately, Lynn Vavreck (2001) has collected data on ads aired in the 1998 congressional elections that speak to this very issue. Vavreck coded for whether the appeal in an ad was "sourced" (i.e., documented). Among appeals concerning taxes, 37% of negative statements were sourced while only 12% of positive statements. For social security, 73% of negative appeals were documented compared to just 11% of

Figure 3.1. Share of Documented Negative and Positive Ads

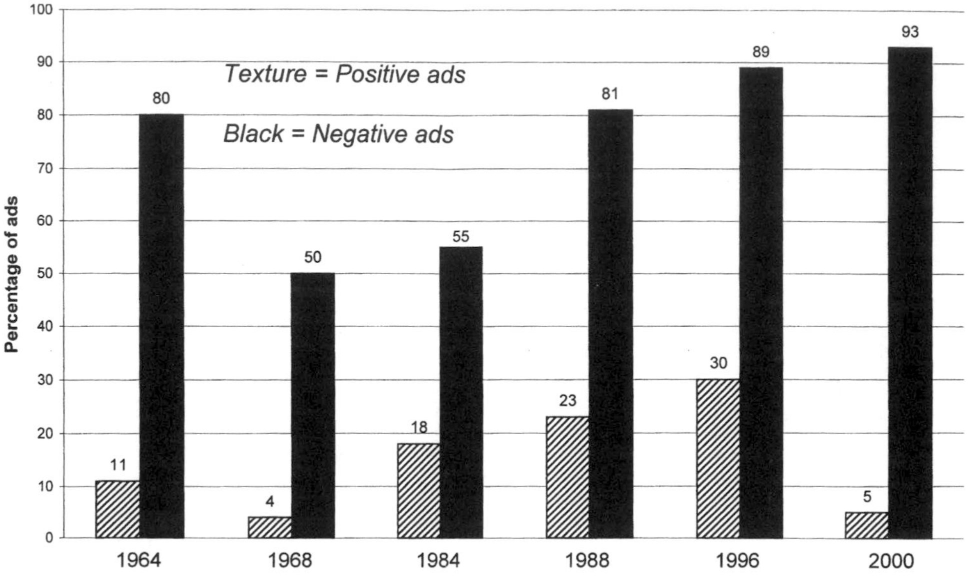

positive appeals. These data further confirm the presence of an asymmetry in the use of evidence for negative and positive appeals.[17]

A Closer Look at 1964

The presidential election of 1964 is particularly illustrative of my general claim. This contest took place more than twenty years prior to any discussion of ad watches and the election was an early example of a negative campaign on television.[18] The Johnson campaign attacked Goldwater heavily on a number of grounds, ranging from concerns about nuclear war to social security. In fact, nearly 40% of all of Johnson's appeals were criticisms of Goldwater. The senator returned the favor only 20% of the time. When examining closely these criticisms, it is clear that Johnson's strategists sought to document their attacks. For example, a number of ads made use of statements by Goldwater, using specific quotes from speeches, interviews, and press conferences. One ad said: "In a *Saturday Evening Post* article dated August 31, 1963, Barry Goldwater said, 'You know, I think we ought to sell TVA.' This is a promise. President Johnson will not sell TVA. Vote for him on November 3rd. The stakes are too high for you to stay home." Or consider the following segment from a Johnson attack ad:

On at least seven different occasions Barry Goldwater has said he would drastically change the social security system. In the Chattanooga, *Tennessee Times*, a *Face the Nation* interview, in the *New York Times Magazine*, in a continental classroom TV interview, in the *New York Journal American*, in a speech he made only last January in Concord, New Hampshire, and in the *Congressional Record*. Even his running mate, William Miller, admits that Barry Goldwater's voluntary plan would wreck your Social Security.

These are classic examples of documentation of attacks. By doing so, the Johnson campaign left little doubt about where Goldwater stood on key issues, underscoring quite nicely this asymmetrical pattern between negative and positive appeals.

The most famous negative ad of that campaign (and perhaps of all time) was, of course, the Daisy spot. However, that ad did *not* contain any evidence according to my scheme. There were no quotes, statistics, or other documentation supporting the claims made in that controversial ad. Instead, it depicted a little girl picking a daisy, with an ominous voice counting down until the world was engulfed in a nuclear explosion. It was an ad that hit many emotions, but it did not contain any evidence to document its points. The ad also did not make a single reference to Goldwater. The ad talked about the "stakes" and the need to "love each other," but no explicit attack was leveled against the senator from Arizona. It was, instead, implied. The only way to make the connection to Goldwater was to know that he had made some statements that suggested tactical use of nuclear weapons was a viable military option. Hence, it was the viewer who had to make the connection. In other words, the audience's prior information about Goldwater provided the evidence.[19]

Two other examples from 1964 are worthy of mention; both of which involve ads Johnson's team did *not* run. In one spot they sought to tie Goldwater to the Ku Klux Klan. It made reference to the KKK's endorsement of the Republican nominee while showing men marching in white, hooded robes. The spot was very hard-hitting given what the KKK symbolized to the American public. The problem with the ad was that Goldwater had twice repudiated the Klan's support. In the end, it was never aired. As one Johnson aide explained: "It strained the available evidence, it was going too far." In another ad a voice talked about "the need for nuclear restraint as a pregnant woman and daughter are seen strolling idyllically through a lush park" (Jamieson 1996, 197, 202). The problem was that no scientific evidence existed to show that nuclear fallout harmed fetuses. Johnson's advisors rejected the ad because of this lack of evidence. These cases underscore nicely my point that attacks require evidence and documentation.

This asymmetry has the effect of making attacks more substantive in the sense that negative appeals are more likely than positive claims to be backed up with evidence. Such a pattern is important in its own right.

Recall that one of the criteria for assessing the information environment was use of evidence. By this standard, negative appeals have an important edge over positive appeals. I will now turn to additional implications for the quality of the information environment that follow from this rhetorical asymmetry in the tone of campaign appeals.

ISSUES AND NEGATIVITY

As I argued earlier, the bigger the role issues play in a campaign, the better. What does this asymmetry argument predict? We know that evidence and documentation are more likely to be part of negative appeals than positive appeals. But that does not speak directly to the relative importance of issues and traits in a campaign. We can, however, develop some hypotheses.

If politicians need evidence to support attacks, candidates should go "where the ducks are" when criticizing the opposition.[20] In other words, candidates cannot just make up grounds for attack, they will need to stick to the record and evaluate the record of the opposition. This argument suggests that the kinds of attacks will depend, to a great extent, on the electoral context. In presidential campaigns, we should expect *issues* to be the subject of attacks more than personal traits. Presidential candidates usually have a long record that serves as the grist for the opposition's mills. The record, which may include previous votes in Congress, bills signed (and vetoed) as governor, and speeches delivered, provides the kind of evidence that can be used by the opposition. Politicians, of course, have personal reputations as well. Any candidate, however, who wins the presidential nomination, will be at least a credible candidate. A standard-bearer is likely to have sufficient credentials that will curtail the kind of harsh personal criticism you might see when a total novice runs for Congress. Moreover, the lengthy and demanding presidential nomination process is a good test of a candidates' mettle. Any one who survives this marathon is likely to be a strong candidate—someone without the kind of personal flaws that we often see in candidates running for local office.

We should, therefore, expect traits to play a bigger role in attacks in state and local elections. There are three reasons. First, many candidates running are not very qualified for the office—they have not jumped through the hoops of a Bob Dole, Al Gore, or Walter Mondale. That means some local and state candidates will be attacked simply for not being qualified for the office. Richard Fenno (1978) makes a similar point when talking about the hurdles nonincumbents face in seeking election to the House. He explains that these candidates must demonstrate that they are qualified enough to hold the office.

Second, local candidates are often relatively new to the political process and do not have a long track record of giving speeches, voting in a legislature, or signing bills into law. If attacks follow the evidence, then personal traits will be a frequent subject of attack for such candidates. How much experience does the candidate possess? Were they successful at previous jobs? Are they respected in the community? What have they accomplished in their personal and professional lives? All of these questions would be posed by an incumbent when facing a politically inexperienced challenger.

Third, in congressional or state legislative races, there are a large number of candidates running. As the number grows, we can expect that some of these candidates are not going to be very good. This is simply the law of large numbers. Therefore, the variance in the quality of candidates will produce some nasty attacks. In 2002, for example, there was a great deal of controversy over an ad in Montana that painted a challenger for the senate seat in a highly uncomplimentary fashion. Some observers interpreted the ad as suggesting the candidate was gay.[21] It was a pretty hard-hitting spot that listed various problems tied to the failed business of this individual. Were these attacks unfair? Scurrilous? It is hard to be sure. But the key point would be that this candidate probably did not meet Fenno's standards of being minimally qualified and was attacked for that very fact.

This line of argument has two explicit theoretical payoffs. First, it hypothesizes that issues should be more likely the subject of attack than personal traits at the presidential level. The second payoff is that it suggests there are conditions in which we can expect attacks to be more heavily based on traits: the lower level offices, such as Congress or a state legislature. Hence, it is possible that the conventional wisdom—that attacks are personal in nature—has merit, but that wisdom is context dependent. Keep in mind that such attacks need not be bad or unwarranted. Recall that the quality of the candidates will vary greatly in local elections and that variance (i.e., the presence of weak candidates) may help explain harsh personal attacks. In other words, it is reasonable for "bad" candidates to be attacked personally. This interpretation is consistent with my argument that negative appeals will stick closer to the evidence than positive appeals.

I will start by noting the distribution of appeals in presidential ads across the three categories of appeals (i.e., issues, traits, and values) talked about in the previous chapter. Issues constitute 56% of all appeals in these ads—a finding that might surprise some observers who view ads as devoid of policy content.[22] About a quarter of all appeals concern the personal characteristics of candidates (26%). The remaining 18% are references to what I term values—topics such as freedom, neighborhood, and family.

Figure 3.2 sorts the distribution of the three types of appeals made in political spots by tone, which allows me to test the hypothesis that attacks are more issue oriented than positive messages. As one can see, negative appeals are far more issue oriented than positive appeals. The differences are quite dramatic. Nearly three quarters of all attacks at the presidential level are about issues. For positive appeals, that proportion drops to just below 50%. Upon closer inspection of the figure, the difference seems to be in the value category. That is, attacks rarely mention values explicitly. Among the many references to values, just slightly less than 3% were negative references. This tiny proportion makes sense. Positive spots might have children running through fields with narrators talking about the future and the need to build community, or they can speak about the greatness of America. Attack ads, by comparison, are hard hitting and are not going to have what might be called fluff in such spots.

The findings in figure 3.2 offer strong confirmation of my claim that negative appeals have a substantive edge over positive appeals in that the former is much more about policy than the latter.

Figure 3.3 separates the previous findings by year to see if this relationship has changed over time. If my hypothesis is correct that negative propaganda requires more evidence than positive rhetoric, we should not see any changes in the pattern over the years. One might argue that the news media's increasing interest in attacks have led candidates to focus more on issues so as to avoid boomerang effects. It is possible, in an era of ad watches, that politicians view attacks on issues as safer bets. But the data lend little support to such a hypothesis. In each year, the candidates' negativity is more issue oriented than their positive appeals. The fact that the solid line (which shows the proportion of attacks that deal with issues) is always higher than the dotted line (which reports the share of positive appeals about issues) illustrates this point.[23]

It is important to take one more cut at these data before moving to the next hypothesis. Jamieson et al. (2000, 1998) have argued that it is important to sort out attack ads from contrast ads. Perhaps it is not attack ads that are issue oriented as much as it is contrast ads, where candidates compare the record. If this counterhypothesis is valid, then such a finding would place an important caveat on my general empirical claim, since the format of the attack would be part of the explanation. Figure 3.4 looks at all thirty-second negative, contrast, and positive spots.[24] As the figure illustrates, the rival explanation fails. Attack and contrast ads pay the same

Figure 3.2. Share of Issues, Traits, and Values by Tone of Appeal, 1960–2000

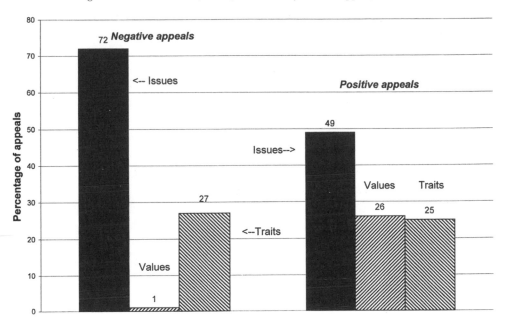

Figure 3.3. Attention Paid to Issues by Tone of Appeal, 1960–2000

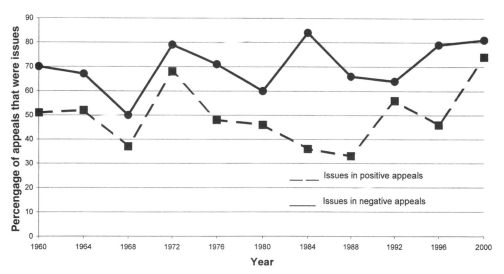

amount of attention to issues—67% of all appeals in these two formats concern policy. However, when one looks more closely at contrast ads, an interesting pattern does arise. Among only the negative appeals in comparative spots, 77% concerned issues. Among the positive appeals in those same spots, the proportion drops to 59%. So, attacks are more issue based

Figure 3.4. Share of Issues, Traits, and Values by Type of Ad

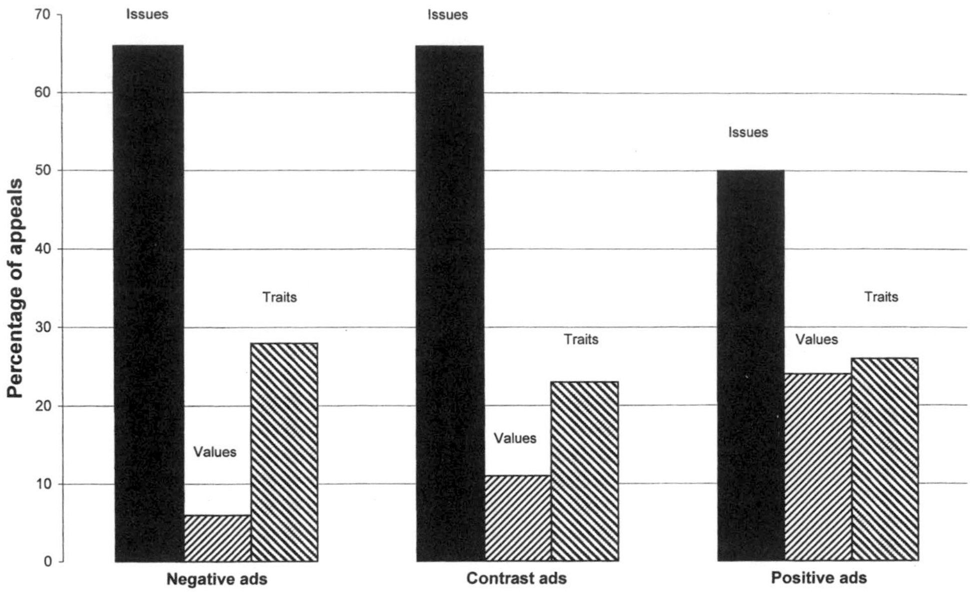

than positive appeals even within the contrast format. That pattern does not directly support the counter hypothesis, since comparative ads per se are not more issue oriented than attack ads. But it does show that within the same ad, attacks remain more about issues than positive appeals.

Under my argument that negative appeals need more evidence than positive appeals, there should also be some differences in the attention paid to issues between challengers and incumbents. Specifically, challengers should attack incumbents more on issues while incumbents will aim more fire on their challengers' traits. This hypothesis follows from the notion that incumbents have usually been in office for nearly four years, providing numerous policies to target. Presidents will have signed bills, delivered speeches, and been at the helm during some bad times. Moreover, simply being president means it would be harder to question the chief executive as inexperienced. I am not suggesting that challengers will only attack on policy grounds—just more frequently than for incumbents' policy attacks on them. At the same time, challengers will be less experienced than incumbents and therefore more likely to be questioned on that ground. The data support the hypothesis. Over three quarters of the attacks leveled by challengers against incumbents were about issues. The proportion, although still sizable, drops thirteen percentage points for the attacks incumbents made against challengers.[25] A nice example of this general pattern involves the two Reagan elections. In 1980, Carter, the experienced incumbent, attacked Reagan heavily on personal grounds. In fact, 65% of all Carter's attacks dealt with the character traits of Reagan. Just four years later, Mondale rarely attacked President Reagan personally—just 9% of his negative appeals concerned traits.

CONCLUSION

This chapter has accomplished two important goals. First, I have shown that there are two aspects of negative appeals that enrich the information environment available for voters. One, negative information is more issue oriented than positive appeals. Two, that attacks are more likely to be supported by evidence than self-promotional claims. These findings show some of the benefits of negativity for the information environment.

The second accomplishment is that I have provided a theoretical understanding of negativity that accounts for these empirical patterns. The asymmetry between negative and positive appeals will be important in upcoming chapters as well. The fact that attacks need more documentation than positive appeals has important implications. For example, we should see attack ads sticking closely to the actual record of the opposition. We should not see things just made up about the other party's nominee. If this is true, we can expect negative information to be more *useful* than positive appeals in informing the public about the pressing concerns of the day. In the next two chapters, I will develop the logic behind this general claim and present evidence to support it, starting with an assessment of personal traits in presidential advertising.

CHAPTER FOUR

Evaluating Character Attacks

There is one singular new development in American politics that violates fair play, and that is negative advertising, the paid commercial, usually on TV or radio, that is a sneak attack on a decent person. Not only is the negative ad the sleaziest new element in politics it may also be the most dangerous. The first victim is the person under attack. But the greater victim is the integrity and credibility of the political system itself.

HOWARD BAKER, FORMER SENATOR FROM TENNESSEE[1]

Senator Baker is not alone in this concern. Perhaps the single biggest worry about negativity is that the attacks tend to be personal, nasty, and scurrilous (Jamieson 1992; Swint 1998). There is a belief that voters do not learn anything useful from such attacks and that the criticisms alienate voters (Patterson 2002; Buchanan 2004). For example, a Gallup poll from July 2000 reports that 70% of the public thinks it is "unfair" to discuss an opponent's extramarital relationship. Nearly 60% of the electorate does not think candidates should mention their opponent's use of illegal drugs, providing this use was prior to running for public office. Attacks on an opponent's family appear totally off-limits—just 3% of the public view such attacks as acceptable (Stevens et al. 2003, 30). This dislike of personal attacks is strong among the public. In fact, citizens often equate "negativity" with character attack (Freedman, Wood, and Lawton 1999; Stevens et al. 2003).

By contrast, the public does not express as much concern over criticism about a candidate's views on issues and matters of policy. Only 5% of the public thinks it "unfair" for a candidate to discuss their opponent's views on issues like education or military spending (see Brooks 2000a). In general, the electorate thinks it is fair game to question a candidate's past legislative or executive record (Freedman, Wood, and Lawton 1999; Stevens et al. 2003).

Journalists and other political observers share the public's dislike of personal attacks. David Broder (2002), for example, complains about negative ads because of the "trivialization and avoidance of serious issues and the proliferation of personal attacks." During the 2000 presidential contest, the Bush campaign was criticized for airing "a commercial that mocks Vice President Gore's credibility, showing footage of Gore's infamous Buddhist temple visit and his boast that he helped create the Internet."[2] Gore was hardly above such tactics, questioning in "a tough new advertisement that bluntly questions whether Mr. Bush is 'ready to lead America.'"[3]

While any hint of personal attack draws commentary from the news media and from the candidates involved, such criticism is hardly new. In fact, Senator Baker was simply wrong to have suggested that negative ads have introduced personal attacks into politics. George Washington faced harsh personal criticism, as did John Adams and Thomas Jefferson. In fact, the famous duel between Aaron Burr and Alexander Hamilton was a product of character attack during a political campaign. Hamilton did not personally like or trust Burr and often criticized him on these very grounds. When Burr was seeking the governorship of New York, Hamilton issued some very hard-hitting personal attacks on Burr, which Burr strongly resented. That resentment led Burr to challenge Hamilton to a duel to settle their differences.[4] While a duel is an unusual way to settle such disputes, it is clear that personal attacks have drawn strong reactions from combatants and observers. One can thumb through the pages of American history and see the many attacks leveled against the personal traits of well known political figures.

The goals of this chapter are not only to offer some systematic evidence about the role of personal attacks in presidential campaigns, but to provide some assessment of them. Even though it is difficult to establish unambiguous standards for evaluation, all indications are that the negative trait appeals contained in paid advertising are not undermining the information environment and perhaps even enriching it. The overall goal of this chapter is to ease concerns about any possible adverse consequences of harsh personal attacks in presidential campaigns.

A FEW EXAMPLES OF PERSONAL ATTACKS

With so many elections in the United States, it is easy to find instances of outrageous, personal attacks. A prime example involves a congressional race in 1996 in California. James Fay, a challenger for a House seat, talked about incumbent "Pete Stark's whore" in some of his campaign literature.[5] This was a nasty, backhanded reference to Fay's claim that Stark was a "whore for the insurance industry." Fay lost badly in this race. Such outrageous claims surely reflect both the candidate's own desperation and that fact that he was not a quality challenger.[6] However, in looking for such examples at the presidential level, there are not many instances of nasty personal attacks. I searched explicitly for such attacks over the last forty years. While my search was not exhaustive, I did examine over 400 presidential ads with this criterion in mind.[7] Below are two of the most hard-hitting, negative trait ads from this search[8]:

1992 Bush Attack Ad

He said he was never drafted. Then he admitted he was drafted. Then he said he forgot being drafted. He said he was never deferred from the draft. Then he said he was. He said he never received special treatment. But he did receive special treatment. The question then was avoiding the draft. Now for Bill Clinton it is a question of avoiding the truth.

In the background is a cover from *Time* magazine from April 22, 1992 that has an ominous picture of Clinton (actually the "negative" from a photograph), with the headline "Why Voters Don't Trust Clinton."

1964 Johnson Attack Ad

In a *Saturday Evening Post* article dated August 31st, 1963, Barry Goldwater said "sometimes I think this country would be better off if we could just saw off the eastern seaboard and let it float out to sea." Can a man who makes statements like this be expected to serve all the people justly and fairly?

The central visual is a map of the United States, with a saw cutting off the eastern seaboard. You hear the sound of sawing and then eventually the east coast drops into the Atlantic Ocean, making a splashing sound.

While impressions will surely vary, these ads do not seem scurrilous, vulgar, coarse, or abusive. These ads, while quite pointed, contain credible information—a result consistent with the argument developed in the previous chapter about the greater need for accuracy when attacking. Clinton, for example, did change his answers to questions about his draft status. In fact, he faced sufficient questioning about his responses that *Time* magazine had a cover story in April about Clinton's trustworthiness. With such concerns in the media and among the public, it seems fair game for President Bush to raise them in his spots. In the case of Johnson's attack on Goldwater, the Senator from Arizona is quoted from an ill-advised statement he made prior to the campaign. The comment was not something that reflected well on a presidential candidate, and the Democrats made extensive use of it.[9]

Perhaps I am looking at the glass half full. It is quite possible for reasonable observers to find these ads offensive. These different judgments would in the end be a matter of taste. However, compare these appeals to examples from the 1800s. In 1864, for example, Lincoln was referred to as "a liar, thief, buffoon, ignoramus, swindler, and butcher." Thomas Jefferson was accused of supporting "murder, robbery, rape, adultery, and incest." In 1884, the Democrats offered the following battle cry "Blaine, Blaine, James G. Blaine, the continental liar from the state of Maine."[10] Perhaps the best known mudslinging of that era came in 1828, which I discussed earlier. Those attacks extended beyond Jackson (he was labeled a murderer among other things) and included his wife and his mother, both who were tarred as prostitutes.[11]

I am not sure how much importance should be placed upon the partisan attacks of that era. The press was controlled by political parties and the atmosphere was highly charged. Examining more recent elections, such as the Truman-Dewey contest, offers a better perspective. This campaign, which was the last one prior to the start of televised advertising, witnessed some of the harshest attacks of any presidential election. Truman was the sponsor of these attacks, as he sought to criticize the Republicans as the party of extremism. In a speech on October 25, 1948, Truman addressed a large crowd in Chicago with opening comments about Franklin Roosevelt and how FDR saw the threat posed by the Nazis. Truman, then claimed that the current

> danger to our democracy does not come . . . from those extremes. It comes mainly from the powerful reactionary forces which are silently undermining our democratic institutions. . . . If the antidemocratic forces in this country continue to work unchecked, this nation could awake a few years from now to find that the Bill of Rights has become a scrap of paper.

These "forces," Truman argued, worked "through the Republican Party." These "forces" also wanted to consolidate economic power. As Truman then argued,

> when a few men get control of the economy of a nation, they find a front man to run the country for them. Before Hitler came to power, control over the German economy had passed into the hands of a small group of rich manufacturers, bankers, and landowners. These men decided that Germany had to have a tough ruthless dictator who would play their game and crush the strong German labor unions. So they put money and influence behind Adolf Hitler. We know the rest of the story. (Karabell 2000, 247–48)

Truman continued with the scathing analogy, attacking the Republicans and Dewey. It should be noted that Truman did not mention Dewey's name explicitly, but the point was clear. While I cannot claim to be an expert on Dewey, comparing the Republicans and their nominee to the Nazis and Hitler seems to fit the definition of "scurrilous." This incident helps to put the two examples from 1964 and 1992 in clearer perspective. The attack by Truman was not unique, but part of a larger pattern of negativity in that contest. Karabell in assessing the 1948 election, observed that "Truman had broken all the unwritten protocols of personal attacks" (2000, 249).

PERSONAL ATTACKS: SYSTEMATIC EVIDENCE

Even though there is great concern about personal attacks in paid advertising, table 4.1 makes one clear point. Over the last eleven presidential elections, there have been only a handful of ads attacking solely on traits. Just 4% of all ads aired from 1960 to 2000 qualified as "negative-trait" spots. By comparison, "negative-issue" ads comprise 16% of the total sample. If we look instead at the distribution of all appeals, not ads, a similar pattern arises. Among all 9590 appeals between 1960 and 2000, just 8% were personal attacks. Again, this proportion is small when compared to the share of appeals that involved attacks on issues (23%). If we limit our focus to only negative appeals, just 27% involved personal criticism of the candidates and 72% focused on matters of policy. Finally, among only traits appeals, attacks constituted just 33% of them.

Overall, it seems hard to argue that personal attacks are excessive in presidential elections. While there would surely be disagreement over what constitutes excessive, this rate of attack falls short of the kind of expectations that are generated by the news media's coverage of presidential elections. Some observers might like to lower these proportions, but personality is an important criterion when considering candidates for office (see Herring 1940). Therefore, some discussion of a presidential candidate's character flaws seems quite appropriate.

To provide additional context for these initial findings, I undertook a deeper historical look at this question. I had a research assistant code

Table 4.1. Tone of Ad by Substantive Content, 1960–2000*

Tone of ad	Substantive content of ad		
	Traits only	Issues only	Both
Positive (%)	8	25	8
Contrast (%)	2	15	7
Negative (%)	4	16	8

*Notes: Total number of ads for this analysis is 723. There are 72 ads that did not fit into this scheme, so they were dropped from these results. Examples include ads that were so general that they did not discuss traits or issues, focusing instead on values.

presidential advertisements printed in the *New York Times* from fourteen campaigns between 1916 and 1956.[12] This sample is, of course, not representative, but it moves beyond the kind of anecdotes that I reference above. These more systematic data indicate that the amount of trait negativity appears much the same as in the 1960 to 2000 period. Of all appeals on traits between 1916 and 1956, 33% were attacks on the opposition—exactly the same amount as in the era of TV. If one examines the share of trait attacks among *all* appeals, the proportion is 10%, which is two percentage points higher than my ad data. Finally, when considering all attacks in these print ads, 30% dealt with character, compared to 27% for TV ads.[13] There is, in short, little difference between these two data sets.[14] While these data are not ideal, the findings lend additional weight to my argument that personal attacks over the last forty years are not excessive in presidential elections (or, at the very least, that the rise of TV advertising has not fueled an increase in character attack).

The findings so far are simple means aggregated across the last forty years, which could be covering up potentially important trends. As discussed in chapter 2, negativity in presidential campaigns is on the rise. Are negative trait appeals also on the rise, as commentary from political observers would lead us to believe? The answer depends on how one views the question. If one examines the rate of negativity among only references to personal characteristics, the story is a bit mixed. The election of 1960 stands out as a contest where neither candidate was very negative about the other's personality. Of all of Nixon's references to personal characteristics in 1960, only 7% were personal attacks against Kennedy. Among Kennedy's references to traits, just 16% were critical of Nixon.[15] From 1964 to 1988 there was no clear trend, with the average rate of attack between the two major party nominees ranging from 20% to 36%. In 1968, for example, 26% of Humphrey's references to character were attacks on Nixon. Eight years later, 21% of both Carter and Ford trait appeals were negative. Of Ronald Reagan's discussion of personal characteristics, 34% were attacks on Carter. Starting in 1992, this measure of negativity starts to move upward. The Bush reelection campaign stands out in this regard. In 1992, 75% of all of the elder Bush's references to traits were attacks on Clinton's character. This is by far the all time high under the period of study. The next closest was George W. Bush's attacks on Al Gore's character, which stood at 57% of all trait appeals.

These data, however, represent only one approach to the problem. If we want to assess more fully the overall trends in negativity of presidential campaigns, we need to consider the importance of trait attacks in light of other appeals. Figure 4.1 does just that, examining the importance of trait attacks as a proportion of *all* attacks. These data help to answer

Figure 4.1. Share of Personal Attacks among Negative Appeals, 1960–2000

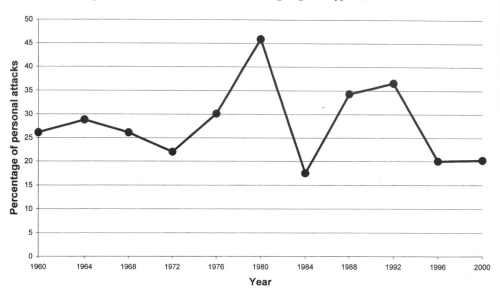

whether personal attacks are serving as an increasing share of negativity in presidential campaigns. The graph shows clearly that there is no increase in the importance of traits as subjects of attack. The 1980 campaign hit an all time high, with Carter heavily questioning Reagan's competence. In that campaign, nearly two-thirds of Carter's negative appeals dealt with Reagan's personal traits. George Bush's attacks on Clinton in 1992 constituted nearly half of all his negative appeals (48%). On the other hand, 1996 and 2000 represented the two *lowest* rates of personal attacks—a finding that undermines the thesis that the number of personal attacks are on the rise.

Another way to look at this question is to examine the share of trait attacks as a product of *all* appeals. The idea is simply to see if presidential advertising in general is increasingly using personal attacks as a way to appeal to voters (see figure 5.1 in the next chapter). It is pretty clear that the increase in negativity is *not* a product of more personal attacks. The pattern looks more random than anything else, with elections like 1964, 1980, and 1992 turning more heavily to personal criticism than contests like 1960 or 1984. This pattern is important, since it implicitly means that attacks on issues underlie the rise of negativity. That point will be demonstrated in the next chapter. It also means that evaluating the content of issue attacks becomes even more pressing, a subject that will be taken up in chapters 5 and 7.

EVALUATING THE TYPES OF TRAIT ATTACKS

My objective in the previous section was to provide a set of findings that ease concerns about personal attacks being "excessive" or "scurrilous" in recent presidential campaigns. But even so presidential candidates do question each other's personal qualifications for office. It is just not at an alarming or an increasing rate (at least by some standards). While ads attacking solely on character traits are rare, table 4.1 does show that about 20% of all ads contained some type of personal criticism.[16] Moreover, as we already know about one-third of all attacks in presidential campaigns focus on personal traits. Therefore, even though the rate of attack does not square with popular concern, the general topic warrants closer investigation since we need to know whether this information holds value for the electorate.

Below I will move toward such an assessment by sorting out the different themes underlying trait appeals. My data provide a unique opportunity to understand the specific personal criticisms raised by the candidates and to assess their merits. Since these data include nearly 200 different codes for references to personal characteristics in presidential ads, I can take a closer look than previously possible for scholars.

With so many different codes, it is essential that I adopt an analytical scheme for organizing these many themes. In developing a set of helpful categories, I wanted to be guided by what kinds of information voters *should* want about the personal traits of their potential presidents. In other words, what kinds of personal information would assist citizens to make good choices? Fortunately, previous scholars have addressed this question, helping to pave the way for this analysis (e.g., Kinder et al. 1980; Kinder 1986; Miller et al. 1986; Funk 1999).

Donald Kinder and colleagues (1980) report on the findings from a 1979 Center for Political Studies national survey that asked respondents about the attributes of an "ideal" president. They observe that a "successful would-be president is not only technically adept (e.g., 'knowledgeable,' 'appoints good advisors'), but also capable of facing hard choices and tackling formidable problems" (1980, 320). These scholars go on to argue (1980, 320) that "trust *is* important, if not essential, for an ideal president." In sorting through all these data, the "most important qualities," according to them, "seem to be competence and trust" (1980, 320).[17]

A few years later Kinder (1986) followed up this research with an even more sophisticated effort to understand the public's perceptions of presidential character. In that work, he identifies four key characteristics of voters thinking about personality: competence, leadership, integrity, and empathy. Carolyn Funk (1999) recently built upon Kinder's analysis and reaffirmed the validity of these categories, although she combines "competence" with "leadership" for her own analyses.

Kinder's categories should not be controversial; they are consistent with an array of thinking on the subject. Pendleton Herring (1940, 289), for example, felt that honesty and sincerity were essential traits for a successful president and something that campaigns should discuss. Some fifty years earlier, James Bryce echoed a similar theme, arguing that "both the integrity and ability of the rival candidates deserve to be carefully weighed by the electors and ought to affect the result."[18] From a very different perspective, Anthony Downs (1957, 107) weighs in on this matter, noting that parties must be reliable if they are to get the "votes of rational citizens." James Fearon (1999, 68) also identifies a "good type" of candidate as one who is "honest and principled (hard to buy off) and who is skilled."

Building upon Kinder's scheme, I have coded the trait data along five dimensions: competence, integrity, leadership, compassion, and other. Competence includes references (favorable or unfavorable) to experience, intelligence, and general abilities to get the job done. Integrity includes comments about trustworthiness, a willingness to stand up for principles, or a tendency to "flip-flop." Leadership includes references to respect, whether the candidate is behind or ahead of his time, and whether the contender possesses "vision." Compassion includes explicit references to caring, concern about people, or lack of sensitivity to the needs of others. The "other" category captures a range of traits, including a sense of humor and comments about the candidate's religious ties.[19] It is just a collection of largely idiosyncratic traits.

As figure 4.2 shows, I have used this five-part analytical scheme to compare the content of negative and positive traits. It is clear that the themes raised in attacks are quite different in composition than those raised in self-promotion.[20] The single biggest difference occurs in the "integrity" category. Nearly 50% of all trait attacks question candidates' honesty and integrity. Among positive appeals, the proportion drops to just 7%. In fact, three-fourths of all the personal criticisms by presidential candidates concern either "(in)competence" or "(lack of) integrity." The proportion among positive appeals drops to under 50% for these two themes. Scholars ranging from Bryce to Kinder argue that it is these two traits that are the most important in evaluating presidential candidates and negative appeals focus far more heavily on them—honesty in particular.

It is worth commenting briefly upon this finding. The attention to integrity when going on the attack makes strategic sense. If a candidate is able to question the opposition's honesty, that appeal may also cause voters to wonder about whether that individual's positions on issues can be trusted. In many ways, attacks on integrity kill two birds with one

Figure 4.2. Distribution of Negative and Positive Traits, 1960–2000

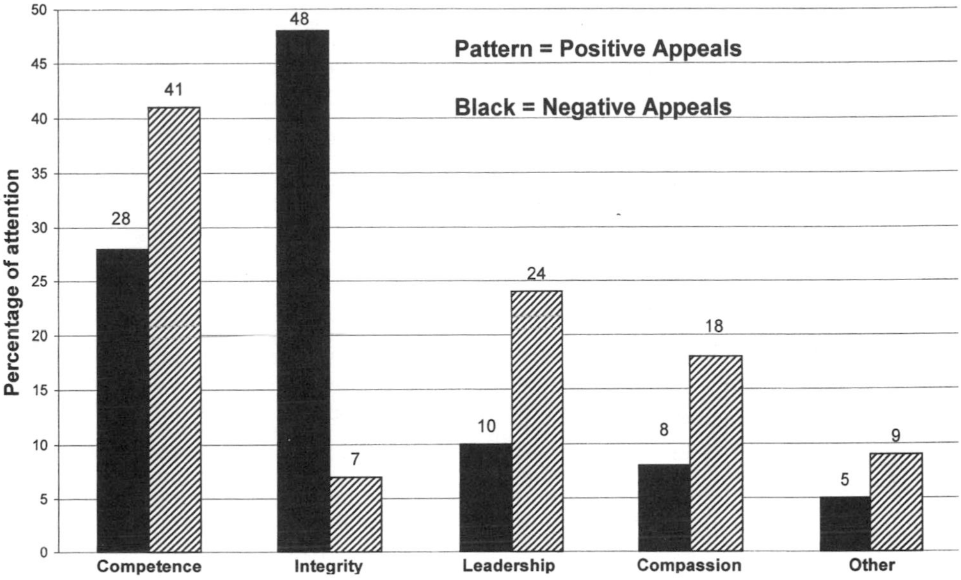

stone. The candidate raises doubts about the personal qualifications of the opposition as well as their ability to deliver on what they have promised in their program for government. Downs (1957) makes this very point when he discusses the importance of parties being reliable in both the positions they take on issues and delivering on the promises they make. In addition, the heavy emphasis on matters surrounding honesty and integrity speaks to my argument developed in the previous chapter about the asymmetrical need for evidence when going on the attack. If a politician has lied to the public or changed their mind on a matter of policy, there is usually a record of it. That information can be used to *document* such a personal attack. By comparison, it would be far harder to verify that a candidate is a bad leader. What kind of evidence might be available to document such a claim? Along the same lines, it would also be difficult to offer evidence that shows that someone does not care. In both cases, candidates do not attack very frequently on such grounds. I will say more about attacking on integrity later in the chapter.

The fact that attacks focus more on competence and integrity is potentially a good sign when trying to evaluate how negativity contributes to the quality of information available to voters. It is premature, however, to reach any conclusions that such appeals enrich the information environment, since we do not have any evidence that establishes whether these attacks are defensible or at least credible. In the following two sections, I will seek to evaluate the quality of information available in the positive- and negative-trait appeals of presidential candidates. While the standards I propose are reasonable, they are by no means the final word. As Kelley (1960, 87) reminds us, "what is legitimate or illegitimate in personal attack is . . . subject to no absolute definition." With that caveat in mind, let me now turn to these assessments.

EVALUATING EXPERIENCE

Candidates have records that speak clearly to their experience. What offices have they held? How long have they held them? Have they done good jobs? We should expect attacks to focus heavily on such concerns: not only is it an obvious basis for evaluating the respective merits of candidates, but there is a body of evidence that can be used to document such claims. As figure 4.2 shows, 28% of all trait attacks concern the general subject of competence. Nominees discuss their own ability to do a good job even more often, netting 41% of all positive trait appeals.

The frequent references to "competence" provides an opportunity to assess whether the rate of such appeals correspond with the actual record of candidates. In other words, are these appeals consistent with the amount of previous political experience? While competence obviously involves more than just previous office holding, there should be a connection between the appeals in the campaign and the actual résumé of the candidate. Of course, given my general argument, there should be a differential correspondence between actual experience and the tone of these references to competence.

My first test involves a simple hypothesis: challengers are more likely to be attacked for inexperience than incumbents. The reason is obvious: the incumbent is president and has, by definition, experience. Now one should not expect a perfect relationship, since being in office might demonstrate that the incumbent is incompetent and not right for the job. But even so, there should be a connection. Figure 4.3 confirms this hypothesis. Challengers were attacked two and one half times more often than incumbents on this dimension. In particular, when attacking on traits, incumbents questioned the challenger's experience 41% of the time. Challengers just raised this theme 16% of the time among their personal attacks.

To provide a further test of this hypothesized relationship, I created an index to capture the previous political experience of the twenty-two major party nominees. I developed a ten-point scale.[21] I then correlated this measure of experience with the attention paid to experience in the candidate's positive and negative rhetoric. For example, as a candidate's

Figure 4.3. Comparison of Incumbents' and Challengers' Character Attacks, 1960–2000

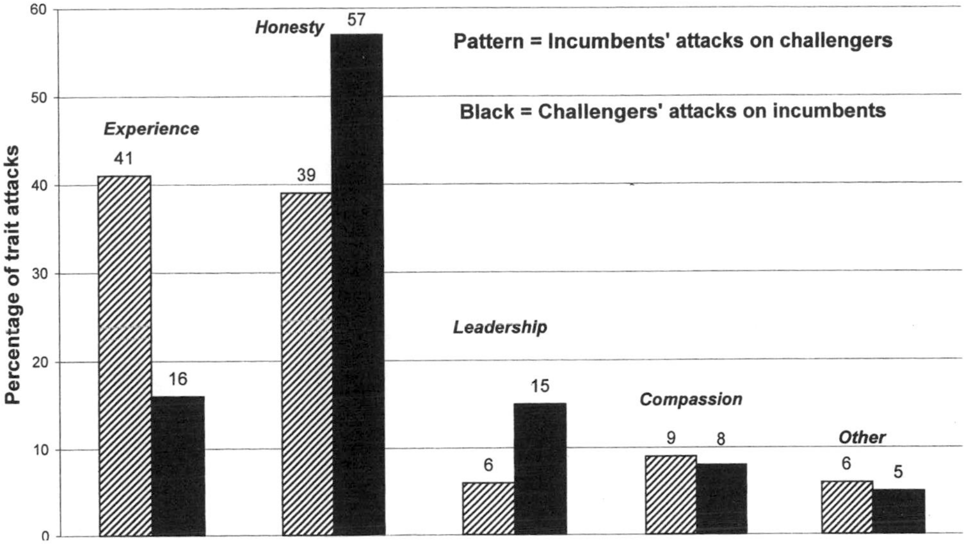

experience increases, there should be a corresponding increase in references to competence in the ads.[22] This hypothesis draws modest support. The correlation across the twenty-two cases is 0.39.[23] It is not overwhelming, but there is a relationship.[24] This connection is slightly stronger for negative appeals, as hypothesized earlier. As a candidate's experience decreases, there should be an increase in attacks by the opposition. The correlation in this case is –0.46.[25] I do not think it is reasonable (or wise) to make a big deal over this small of a difference. The point is that attacks, like self-promotional appeals, appear to have some basis in reality and are consistent with objective evidence.

Correlations, while useful, provide little substantive feel for these empirical relationships. Therefore, I ran some simple regressions to generate explicit estimates of the relationship between these variables. Specifically:

Share of Personal Attacks about Competence = $a_1 + b_1$ *(Actual Experience)* + e

If one compares an inexperienced candidate to a sitting president, the frequency of attack on that basis is five times higher for a relative novice than for an incumbent.[26] If one compares an inexperienced candidate to an incumbent president, you can expect the latter to mention favorably their experience three times more often than the former.[27] A challenger, when attacking an incumbent president, can be expected to dedicate only 3% of all his attacks on the theme of (in)competence.[28]

INVOKING PUBLIC OPINION AS A STANDARD

While experience is a trait that can be assessed somewhat objectively, the other traits offer a far greater hurdle. Integrity is obviously very important, especially given the frequency of attacks on that dimension. But how do we decide whether such attacks advance or hinder the political debate? How can one measure objectively the honesty of a candidate? President Clinton certainly had many detractors who claimed he was not honest. The Monica Lewinsky scandal fueled such claims, but that perception existed prior to that incident. Even so, his defenders would take issue with such claims and point out the many examples of Clinton delivering on his promises. The point is not to get into a debate about Clinton's integrity, but to show how any effort to assess the presence of that trait in a candidate is the social science equivalent of quicksand.

The same problem faces assessing a candidate's ability to lead as well as their compassion. Leadership is exceptionally hard to define (e.g., Neustadt 1990; Bass 1981; Geer 1996). As James MacGregor Burns (1978, 2) once observed that "leadership is one of the . . . least understood phenomena on earth." It is easy to identify leadership after the fact. If we see an outcome we like, we often conclude that the person in charge was a good leader. Ronald Reagan, for example, ran the nation during a time of economic prosperity (at least after 1982) and is often hailed as someone who possessed great leadership skills (Gergen 2000). However prior to being president, there were great concerns within the public about his ability to lead the nation. Similar difficulties would confront a sound assessment of compassion. Clinton was famous for "feeling the pain" of others. Bob Dole, by comparison, came across to many observers as not caring. Nonetheless, it strikes me as problematic to conclude that Dole was not compassionate or even that he cared less about helping people than did Clinton.

How do we move past these kinds of seat of the pants assessments? My answer is to use public opinion as a guide. That is, investigate whether the appeals candidates make in their ads about traits compare favorably with the public's assessment of them. The notion is that if the public is uneasy about a candidate's integrity or competence, an attack on that ground is more defensible. If, on the other hand, candidates' attacks on topics are not consistent with public sentiment, that finding would show that attacks are less grounded in actual perceptions and are, instead, simply aimed at undermining candidates in any way possible.

To develop such a test, I made use of data from the National Election Studies (NES). Specifically, I employed the public's likes and dislikes of presidential candidates from 1960 to 2000. These data have many advantages. First, NES data is high quality, publicly available, and widely used by scholars. Second, these questions have the same wording in each of these eleven elections, permitting comparisons over forty years. Third, these questions employ an open-ended format, which provides a flexible way to match my ad data with the survey data.[29] Fourth, the open-ended format taps the salient attitudes of the public toward the presidential nominees (see RePass 1971; Kelley 1983; Geer 1991). Finally, these questions ask explicitly what respondents *like* and *dislike* about the contenders, providing an opportunity to measure the tone of their attitudes.

For each of the twenty-two presidential candidates, I created a measure of the importance of each of these traits in the public's personal evaluation of them. Each respondent has the opportunity to offer five likes and five dislikes about each of the Democratic and Republican nominees. Citizens rarely offer twenty responses, but they offer enough comments to provide a rich set of evidence about the public's attitudes toward these candidates. I limited my attention only to the responses that dealt with character and personality. I excluded all references to policy. Even with these restrictions, I have around 40,000 unique comments about these candidates' personality between 1960 and 2000, which averages to nearly two comments per respondent.

Using this extensive array of data of likes and dislikes, I created a measure of the attitudes toward each of these candidates on the five dimensions used above—competence, integrity, leadership, compassion, and other. Consequently, for each candidate I have ten measures of personality. These measures are simply the average number of comments in each of the categories. The values range from 0.01 to 0.76.[30] For example, the public rarely "dislikes" Democratic nominees for not being compassionate. In 1964, for example, the average number of comments about Johnson not "caring" was nearly nonexistent, equaling only 0.01. By comparison, the public often commented favorably about Johnson's competence (0.76).

It is also worth noting that these data work very much like one would predict. In 1992, the public had concerns about Clinton's integrity—0.25 average comments on that dimension. That share grew in 1996 to 0.42. In 1972, the public gave Nixon high marks for competence (0.55), while expressing some worry about McGovern's ability to lead (0.28). In 2000, Gore was viewed as more competent than Bush, but also far less trustworthy.[31]

There is, however, one concern with these data—the all-too-common problem of endogenity. The questions are asked in the preelection section of the NES survey, with the actual date of the interview ranging from around September 1 to the day before the formal casting of ballots. The information gleaned from these data, as a result, could reflect the goings-on of the campaign, in general, and the content of advertising, in particular. Therefore, if a candidate focuses on his opponent's lack of integrity, that appeal could work its way into the public conscience. As a result, any relationship I find could be misleading. Given the general view that campaigns do not have massive effects on public opinion (e.g., Finkel 1993; Holbrook 1996; Campbell 2000), it is not likely that ads have powerful influences. But the concern is a real one and cannot be ignored.

To address this concern, I made use of the date of interview to purge the effects of the fall campaign from these data.[32] I regressed the date of the interview on the respondents' comments about the candidate's personality. By assigning the first day of interviews in the campaign a zero and arranging all other dates from that starting point, I generated estimates that purged the effect of the campaign. Specifically, the constant from that regression (i.e., setting the date of the interview to zero) reflects the estimated value for the public's attitudes at the start of the campaign.[33]

The purged results do not change greatly from the original NES data. In fact, the two measures correlate at 0.94.[34] The few big changes that do make sense. For example, Humphrey's favorable competence score was 0.45. But when purged, it declined to 0.31. That shift reflects that the public increasingly viewed Humphrey as more competent as the campaign unfolded—a finding consistent with his comeback in the polls. As mentioned earlier, Gore was not thought of as trustworthy (0.30). The purged value was 0.19, suggesting that the campaign led the public over time to judge Gore less favorably on this dimension. However, the magnitude of these changes was the exception, not the rule.

In the results that follow, I only use the purged values. I did run all analyses with both the corrected and uncorrected measures. Given the strong correlation, the results did not change much. However, the strength of the findings was slightly weaker with the purged data, so I present them below.

Results

With public opinion as the standard, the question now becomes whether positive or negative trait appeals fall more in line with citizens' judgments of the candidates. Remember, the goal here is to determine if attacks enrich the information environment by presenting information that is consistent with preexisting perceptions of the public. As a simple, yet revealing test, of this question, I regressed the likes for each of the five-trait categories as a predictor of self-promotional appeals. The parallel regression used the dislikes to explain the trait attacks in presidential campaigns. The results are presented graphically in figure 4.4.[35] As one can see, the dislikes have a stronger

Figure 4.4. Impact of Public Opinion on Trait Appeals, 1960–2000

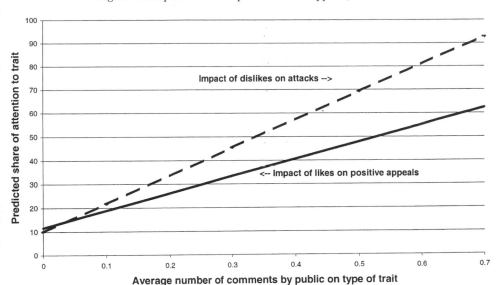

relationship to the ad data than the likes.[36] For example, if the public gives a candidate a 0.15 score on competence, we can expect that nominee to discuss it 22% of the time in his positive trait appeals. On the other hand, if the public rates the candidates much more favorably on this dimension (0.75), that proportion climbs to 66%. By comparison, if the public gives a candidate a 0.15 score on (in)competence, we can expect the opposition to raise that subject 27% of the time among their trait attacks. If the public's dislike rating soars to 0.75, we can expect an almost single-minded attack on this dimension (98%).

These findings clearly show that the positive and negative appeals of presidential candidates reflect public opinion. It would be hard to argue that the negative appeals are simply made up by candidates trying to attack the opposition on any and all possible grounds. Moreover, the findings suggest that, on average, attacks mirror public opinion more closely than positive appeals. The differences are not stark and I would not want to overstate the importance of this finding. But to put the matter differently, it would be very difficult to contend in light of these data that character attacks are more misleading than the positive appeals presidential candidates make about their personal qualifications for the White House.

The findings above are aggregated across the different types of trait appeals. Table 4.2 disaggregates the results by type of appeal.[37] The first part of the table presents the actual coefficients when running these

Table 4.2. Regression Estimates for Relationship between Trait Appeals
and Public Opinion

	Negative appeals			Positive appeals		
	Intercept	Slope	R^2	Intercept	Slope	R^2
Competence	6.9	97.1**	0.26	16.7*	66.3**	0.28
Integrity	27.4***	168.3***	0.27	−0.5	63.7***	0.41
Leadership	9.4	15.9	0.01	11.6	126.4*	0.15
Caring	−1.2	405.5**	0.23	18.6	22.4	0.00

	Predicted values from regression					
	Negative appeals			Positive appeals		
	Lowest[1]	Mean[2]	Highest[3]	Lowest	Mean	Highest
Competence (%)	7	23	54	17	40	73
Integrity (%)	27	51	96	0	8	17
Leadership (%)	9	11	14	12	24	38
Caring (%)	0	7	19	19	20	21

Notes: Sample size for each regression is 22:2 nominees for the 11 presidential campaigns.

[1]Reports the intercept, the predicted value when the independent variable is set to 0.

[2]Uses the mean value for that variable to generate this predicted value.

[3]Uses the highest value recorded in the 11 campaigns covered by the NES.

* significant at 0.10

** significant at 0.05

*** significant at 0.01

subregressions. As would be expected, most of the slopes are statistically significant and positive, which is consistent with the above information. The actual size of the coefficients is not easily compared, since some categories draw more comment in the public than others, so we need to know the variance of the independent variable to make sense of the estimates. Hence, the second half of the table lays out a series of predicted values for campaign appeals in light of credible values for public opinion on that trait dimension. In most cases, the appeals candidates make in their ads correspond to public opinion; negative leadership and positive caring are the two exceptions. As with earlier analyses, much of the action takes place around the themes of competence and integrity. If the public views a candidate as experienced, the campaign should stress that topic heavily. The same process is true for when the public has doubts about a candidate's competence or integrity.

I want to draw particular attention to the intercept, which usually is not viewed as important. For this analysis, it is valuable. Specifically, it tells us the predicted amount of attention paid to that type of appeal when the public makes *no* mention of the topic in the likes or dislikes. That estimate, therefore, provides insight into whether candidates talk about a theme even when the public does not.

The finding that warrants the most attention involves attacks on integrity. The results suggest that even if the public has no worries about a candidate's honesty and trustworthiness, candidates still attack on that dimension and do so heavily—to the order of 27%. Additionally, as the public expresses concern about a candidate's integrity, the opposition seizes on it disproportionately. To some extent this pattern is true for "lack of caring," but there are just a handful of attacks on this trait. That is not true, however, for integrity. Candidates spend a considerable amount of time raising doubts about their opponent's honesty and credibility.

This result is cause for concern and raises the possibility that candidates when attacked on integrity are going overboard and therefore not enriching the information environment. In what follows, I will take a closer look at this specific appeal in order to understand better whether or not this is a cause for concern.

A Closer Look at Integrity

As mentioned earlier, scholars have long stressed the importance of integrity in assessing the qualifications of a candidate. It is clear that this theme is discussed during campaigns largely within the context of attacks. Candidates do not talk much about their own honesty (recall figure 4.2), but it appears fair game for criticism. However, by the standards of public opinion, the amount of attention is excessive. Of course, one could counter that the public needs to know about this trait and so extra attention is not a problem. It is an important criterion for all the reasons scholars like Kinder, Fearon, and Kelley argue. Even so, it seems pretty clear that candidates focus more heavily on it than appears warranted (as defined by my standards).

It is worth recalling that the amount of attention paid to this theme supports the argument I made in the last chapter about the need for evidence. Candidates, when attacking, cannot make things up, if they want their criticisms to work. The need for evidence shows itself in the trait appeals by the extensive attention paid to integrity. It is a topic about which one can locate evidence. Have candidates changed their mind on an issue? Have they made statements in the campaign that are inconsistent with previous positions and votes? Have they been accused of being misleading or perhaps not entirely forthcoming on some matter? Any candidate who manages to win the nomination is very likely to have a long enough resume to find many inconsistencies. In 2004, for example, the Bush campaign closely examined John Kerry's "thirty-two years of votes and public pronouncements," according to Bush media advisor Mark McKinnon, looking for inconsistencies once the senator became the likely Democratic nominee.[38] The end result was lots of attacks on this front, including one of the more memorable attack ads from 2004, which used footage of Senator Kerry on a windsurfer to illustrate the point that he could not be trusted, that he tacked too much. The opposition has every incentive to raise such doubts, since such information is not only important to voters, it is something that can be documented and thus viewed as credible.[39]

If my argument is correct that integrity is an effective target for attack because it is easier to document those kinds of claims than whether the opposition is an ineffective leader or uncaring, then we should not see much change over time in the rate of attack. On the other hand, one could imagine that with declining levels of trust (see Hetherington 2004), attacks on such grounds have been increasing. If so, then my interpretation seems less plausible.

To test these competing hypotheses, I looked at the question from a number of angles. If one examines the share of all personal attacks that dealt with integrity, there is no increase over time. In both 1968 and 1972, candidates made integrity a centerpiece of their personal criticisms.[40] Nixon was an obvious target for such attacks, as was Humphrey and McGovern. The Minnesotan used a weather vane to represent Nixon's willingness to change his mind, depending on which way the wind blew. Nixon turned the tables on McGovern in 1972, using the same weathervane imagery against the senator. These proportions from 1968 and 1972 are very comparable to the last three presidential elections. It is worth noting that while Clinton was attacked heavily over concerns about trust, Dole was not. That makes sense, since Dole was viewed as someone of great integrity—a "war hero." In general, these data have face validity. Those candidates who were viewed as honest did not get attacked as much on this point as those like Nixon and Clinton.

Figure 4.5 offers another cut at this issue by looking at the role of integrity attacks among all negative appeals (which includes references to both issues and traits). There is a big spike in 1992, where both Clinton and Bush attacked each other on this. Other than that notable increase, there is very little change over time, suggesting attacks about

Figure 4.5. Share of All Attacks About Integrity, 1960–2000

integrity are not on the rise—not just a product of the current political environment. It is probably safe to conclude that questions about candidates' integrity are something that has been around as long as campaigns have been.

Integrity matters to the public and candidates clearly focus on the topic when attacking. Even so, I would be hard-pressed to argue that this line of attack is not overused and surely exaggerated. The finding that even if the public expressed *no* doubts about a candidate's honesty, the opposition would still attack on it underscores this point. It is of some comfort that this pattern is not on the rise. My belief is that this result speaks more to the problems underlying political life (see Kelley 1998). Politicians often face tough choices. Do they stick to their past positions? Or do they try to adapt to any changes in public opinion? If they fail to respond to public opinion, they are not likely to hold office very long. If they respond too much to public opinion, politicians will be attacked for being untrustworthy. It is a tough balancing act that ends up providing a lot of fuel for the opposition's attacks. In the end, I do not believe these findings sketch an optimistic picture for this aspect of the information environment provided by advertising. Candidates do appear to be going overboard, but at least they are doing so with some evidence to support their claims. Moreover, given the central role of integrity in judging a candidate's qualifications for office, perhaps this bit of excess is at least tolerable.

CONCLUSION

The findings in this chapter offer a number of lessons about the role of personal attacks in presidential campaigns. First, personal attacks in presidential campaigns do not appear to be excessively harsh, nor are they particularly frequent. The concerns among political observers about personal attacks seem unwarranted in light of these data. Second, the rise of negativity over the last forty years is *not* tied to increasing personal attacks. This means by implication that issues must be the driving force behind the increase I report in figure 2.1. Third, personal attacks have at least as much, if not more, credibility than positive trait appeals. We saw, for instance, that previous political experience of nominees compares reasonably well with how often competence and experience are mentioned in political ads. Moreover, the trait appeals raised in ads square with public opinion in general. There is a notable exception when it comes to attacks on integrity, but even those attacks appear to be part of the general dynamic behind negativity—the need for evidence.

With concerns about personal attacks in presidential campaigns eased a bit, the stakes have been raised for the next chapter. Are the many attacks on issues informative for the public? With the heavy and increasing emphasis on issues, this form of negativity becomes central to my task of evaluating the merits of attack advertising. It is to that topic I will now turn.

CHAPTER FIVE

Evaluating the Content of Negative and Positive Issue Appeals

At this point, we have learned three important lessons about attack advertising. First, attacks are more likely than positive appeals to be about issues. Second, attacks are more likely than positive appeals to be backed with verifiable evidence. Third, personal attacks are not excessive (despite conventional wisdom), clearly not on the rise, and actually have the potential (in most cases) to enrich the information environment available to voters. These are all good things and should give us reason to lessen our concerns about the pernicious effects of negative advertising. However, work still remains before anyone should accept my general claim that attack advertising advances democratic politics.

In particular, I have yet to assess the specific issues candidates raise when they attack the opposition. Are negative appeals about important issues—topics that are relevant to the citizens? We have seen that trait attacks are often on salient concerns. Do issue attacks work in similar ways? How do attacks compare to the positive issues raised by candidates? Do nominees tend to attack on issues more peripheral to the lives of voters than self-promotional issues? Since campaign appeals tend to be vague (Stokes 1963), are attacks more or less vague than positive appeals? Which type of appeal is more likely to allow voters to sort out the differences between candidates? These are the types of questions I raised when discussing standards to assess the quality of campaigns (recall chapter 3).

There is a widespread belief that attacks are designed to mislead voters and misrepresent the positions of the opposition, which suggests that negativity is not likely to be informative for voters. I argue that in fact we should expect just the opposite, using the logic of the asymmetry argument developed in chapter 3. I will provide evidence consistent with this claim.

This chapter serves in many ways as the centerpiece of my argument. The reasons are threefold. First, attacks in presidential campaigns, as previously mentioned, tend to be more issue oriented than self-promotional appeals. So, if it turns out that the issues raised in these assaults are not of value to the decisions of voters, it poses a serious problem for my defense. Second, most normative conceptions of a "good" campaign hinge on the kinds of issues that are raised during the struggle for votes (Kelley 1960; Buchanan 2004). If the policy attacks made during a campaign were found to be lacking, it would pose a serious problem for my general argument. Third, the rise in negativity documented in chapter 2 and discussed by so many political observers is mostly tied to an increased willingness to attack on issues. Figure 5.1 makes this point very clearly. Just as with the rise of negativity in general, attacks on issues are on the rise as well. In fact, there is a 0.93 correlation between "overall" negativity and "issue" negativity.[1] This pattern stands in contrast to the changing rate in personal attacks over the last forty years. There is a very slight increase, but as one can see from figure 5.1 most of the action lies with "issues." These differential trends provide even greater urgency to assess the kinds of issues raised in presidential campaigns.

My goal in this chapter, therefore, is to provide compelling evidence

Figure 5.1. Trends in Negativity, 1960–2000

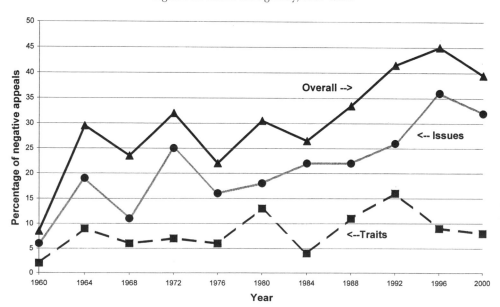

that attacks are *more likely* to be specific (i.e., less vague), *more likely* to be about issues the public considers important, and *more likely* to concern real problems facing government.[2] Such appeals, therefore, have a greater potential to inform the public in meaningful ways than the rhetoric that appears in positive political ads. This general conclusion underscores how negativity in campaigns enriches the information environment and thereby, advances the prospects for democratic government.

THE ISSUE AGENDAS OF PRESIDENTIAL CANDIDATES

My data afford the opportunity to understand with some precision the kinds of appeals candidates make to the public through their advertising. There have been previous efforts to understand the agendas of presidential candidates (e.g., Petrocik 1996; Budge, Robertson, and Heard 1987; Monroe 1983; Page 1976). But these efforts usually rely on speeches and party platforms as their base of evidence, which does not shed direct light on the appeals candidates make to the *public* during the course of the *campaign*—the democratic link I am investigating. Perhaps more importantly, this previous work has usually not differentiated between attacks and self-promotional themes. Part of the reason for this is that platforms tend to be highly positive documents where the party lays out its vision for the future. There are only a handful of attacks in these documents.[3] Speeches contain some criticism, but tend to be more positive than political ads. Jamieson (1992) argues that the reason is that a candidate cannot be viewed as excessively negative when personally delivering the message. So attacks are often left to advertisements and other sources of propaganda. As a result, these previous efforts have not been able to examine an important piece of the electoral puzzle.

The Coding

With over 1800 codes for issues alone, a central task was to decide how best to organize them. I experimented with a number of schemes to assess the utility of various approaches. Table 5.1 presents one way to organize the issues candidates raised in their ads. This organizational scheme is broad, representing bundles of issues, such as social or economic issues. The purpose here is to be both descriptive and to provide some face validity to the data. Petrocik (1996) and others, for example, have written about "issue ownership"—the idea that parties have a reputation for being able to handle that issue successfully. Such ownership is stable and reflects the "party constituencies in modern party systems" (Petrocik 1996, 827). For example, Democrats should talk much more about "New

Table 5.1. Broad Issues Raised in Presidential Advertising, 1960–2000

	All spots[1]	Democratic ads	Republican ads
Economic (%)[2]	27	24	32
Government management (%)[3]	10	6	12
New Deal (%)[4]	26	31	18
Social (%)[5]	9	11	7
Foreign policy/defense (%)[6]	16	12	21
Other (%)[7]	11	15	7
Number of ads	795	445	350
Number of appeals	5404	3043	2361

[1]I calculated the proportions in this table by looking at all ads during this forty-year time period. I did not sort it out by presidential campaign.

[2]Includes all references to the economy, including comments about taxes, inflation, jobs, and economic times.

[3]Includes all references to government spending (general), deficits, national debt, management of bureaucracy.

[4]Includes references to issues such as education, social security, welfare, Medicare. See Kelley (1983, 1988) for complete definition.

[5]Includes references to crime, abortion, gun control, and policy toward drug use.

[6]Includes all references to handing of war, dealing with other nations, defense spending, weapons programs, and so on.

[7]Includes such issues as the environment, transportation, urban affairs, and other domestic issues outside of those noted above that drew periodic attention in presidential campaigns.

Deal" issues than Republicans. The Democrats built their reputation in a large degree on handling such issues as Social Security, Medicare, and other social-welfare programs (Kelley 1988). That reputation remains a defining feature of party competition even though the New Deal era has long since passed. The data support that claim—over 30% of all issue appeals by Democrats were about such concerns. Republicans, by contrast, paid more attention to foreign policy and defense matters, downplaying "New Deal" concerns.

While this scheme sheds some light on how candidates compete for votes, the categories are too broad. First, candidates tend to raise more specific issues than just "social" or "New Deal" issues. They instead talk about crime, gun control, social security, or health care. Second, by lumping issues under these broad labels, we may miss the opportunity to learn more about the specific kinds of appeals candidates make. For example, table 5.1 suggests the Democrats talk more about social issues than the Republicans, which is not what we would expect (see Petrocik 1996).

That finding, in part, is a product of lumping discussion of such issues as crime, gun control, and drug policy all under one heading. As we will see, the Republicans do talk more about crime than the Democrats, which is consistent with conventional wisdom.

In devising a more detailed scheme for organizing these issues, I sought to identify the main bases of competition between the candidates (e.g., Kelley 1983, 1988; Sundquist 1983; Petrocik 1996). Democrats and Republicans have battled over health care, inflation, education, and the deficit—to name a few. My arrangement captures most of the major issues that have been discussed in presidential campaigns over the last forty years. In any particular year, a new issue could become quite salient and then fade into the background. I did not try to account for those temporary blips on the radar screen. For example, in 1968 Hubert Humphrey made urban decay a reasonably important issue in his political ads, dedicating 7% of his appeals on issues to that topic.[4] No other candidate before or after him paid much attention to that issue, but given the problems confronting cities in 1968, it is no surprise that Humphrey did so. In 1972, Nixon gave airtime to the issue of busing (5%). In 1988, Dukakis paid a great deal of attention to the issue of illegal use of drugs and their entry into the country (20%).[5] I limited my attention to more durable issues which divide the parties.

It is also worth mentioning an issue that has been important in presidential politics, but draws almost no attention in political ads—abortion. Over the entire forty-year time span covered by my data set, abortion was mentioned in only three ads—each aired by a Democrat (Mondale and Clinton). There is not a single reference to abortion in any Republican ads in my data set, and even within the Mondale and Clinton (1996) campaigns, the issue was not prominent.[6] This finding underscores the fact that abortion is more of an elite game for the parties and not a theme that presidential nominees want to address in their appeals to the mass public.

While these stories hold interest, I want to look for more general patterns. Table 5.2 presents the key issues raised by Democratic and Republican nominees, sorting out negative appeals from positive appeals by party. Again, using the idea of issue ownership as standard to judge the quality of these data, we should find that the Democrats, for example, should talk more about Social Security and health care. Republicans, by contrast, should stress issues like crime and government spending far more than the Democrats. The results confirm these expectations. Democrats talk more about health care and social security than the Republicans, while nominees from the GOP stress crime and government spending more.

Table 5.2. Specific Issues Raised in Presidential Advertising, 1960–2000

	Republicans*			Democrats*		
	Positive	Negative	Total	Positive	Negative	Total
Government Activism (%)	3.5	4.3	4.1	0.6	1.2	0.8
Jobs (%)	5.6	2.5	4.5	5.6	5.8	4.6
Inflation (%)	4.7	9.4	5.6	1.0	2.6	1.7
Taxes (%)	6.3	15.7	9.1	8.9	7.7	8.1
Government spending (%)	2.8	6.2	3.1	0.7	0.5	0.6
Deficit (%)	2.1	4.1	2.9	2.2	2.2	2.1
Health (%)	3.0	3.5	3.2	7.5	7.7	7.3
Social Security (%)	6.6	0.6	4.4	4.8	7.8	6.5
Education (%)	5.8	2.5	4.8	8.6	5.2	7.2
Poverty/welfare (%)	1.6	2.2	2.1	6.3	2.5	4.4
Race (%)	0.9	0	0.8	1.6	0.7	1.3
Crime (%)	4.2	7.9	5.8	3.1	3.0	2.9
Foreign Policy (%)	21.8	11.4	20.0	9.4	9.7	9.5
Defense (%)	6.8	5.3	6.4	8.2	6.6	7.2
Environment (%)	0.4	2.0	1.2	3.0	5.1	3.7

*These proportions are the average attention paid to that issue across the eleven presidential campaigns in each party from 1960 to 2000.

Of course, within these general patterns, there are specific stories that illustrate the unique features of each campaign and the payoffs to sorting negative from positive issue appeals. Table 5.3 presents each candidate's favorite issue. George Bush talked a lot about crime in 1988—something that has drawn scholarly attention (see Mendelberg 2002). In fact, over one quarter of his attacks against Dukakis on issues dealt with the subject of crime. In 1964, Johnson stressed Social Security, attacking Goldwater on that issue alone one-third of the time. In 2000, George W. Bush tried, like his father, to be the education candidate. Nearly one-half of his positive issue appeals (46%) dealt with the issue of education. Richard Nixon made foreign policy the centerpiece of his campaign against Kennedy in 1960. There is also the famous 1992 Clinton "war room" slogan: "It's the economy, stupid." Over 50% of his positive appeals and 85% of his attacks on Bush dealt with the economy.

There are also systematic differences between the negative and positive agendas of the candidates. For example, the Republicans focused heavily on taxes, but the vast majority of that discussion involved attacks on the Democrats. The Democrats turned the table on the GOP when it came to Social Security, attacking them on this issue more frequently than raising

Table 5.3. Presidential Candidates' Favorite Issues, 1960–2000

	Positive		Negative	
	Issue	Attention (%)[1]	Issue	Attention (%)
1960				
Kennedy	Education	25	Education	25
Nixon	Foreign policy	61	Budget/deficit	15
1964				
Johnson	Poverty/welfare	29	Social Security	34
Goldwater	Foreign policy	48	Crime	14
1968				
Humphrey	Education	12	Defense policy	17
Nixon	Crime	28	Crime	41
1972				
McGovern	Taxes	17	Inflation	14
Nixon	Foreign policy	42	Foreign policy	32
1976				
Carter	Taxes	14	Unemployment	15
Ford	Foreign policy	17	Taxes	29
1980				
Carter	Foreign policy	27	Foreign policy	25
Reagan	Unemployment	11	Inflation	34
1984				
Mondale	Defense policy	40	Defense policy	25
Reagan	Unemployment	19	Taxes	28
1988				
Dukakis	Environment	12	Environment	16
Bush	Foreign policy	15	Crime	27
1992				
Clinton	Taxes	17	Economic times	32
Bush	Foreign policy	16	Taxes	34
1996				
Clinton	Taxes	12	Health care	19
Dole	Taxes	26	Taxes	22
2000				
Gore	Health care	29	Health care	21
Bush	Education	46	Education	26

[1]Attention is calculated by dividing the number of positive (or negative) appeals on the issue by all positive (or negative) appeals.

it in their own favor. In fact, by distinguishing between negative and positive appeals, a new wrinkle in the concept of issue ownership develops. Issue ownership predicts that nominees will talk more about the issues they "own" than the opposition. This is a sensible prediction that is supported by the data. For example, there is 0.72 correlation between the *relative* attention paid[7] to these fifteen issues and whether the party "owns" the issue or not.[8] That correlation is hardly a surprise and bolsters the general analysis.

The more interesting story lies in differences between the positive and negative appeals within the fifteen issues. If one examines relative attention paid to these issues when candidates go on the attack, the correlation with owning the issue increases to 0.80. Among the positive appeals, the correlation drops to 0.51. The point here is that a key test of issue ownership is whether the party will *attack* the opposition. This makes theoretical sense. The GOP might well spend time talking about why they will protect Social Security, but would they attack the Democrats on such grounds? The answer is not very often—less than 1% of the time across the eleven campaigns. Therefore, if a party owns an issue, it is reasonable to believe they have enough credibility on that issue with the public that they can effectively raise doubts about the opposition's views on that matter.

It appears that the agendas of candidates vary when they go negative or positive, suggesting that they are indeed sending different messages to the public. For example, if I compare what the Republicans say about themselves (i.e., positive) to what they say about the Democrats (i.e., negative), the correlation is 0.38. For the Democrats, the comparable statistic is 0.54. I do not want to read a great deal into the meaning of these correlations, but they do show that the positive and negative agendas of the candidates are different. An even more interesting story arises when one compares interparty agendas. For example, the Democrats and Republicans attack each other on very different grounds. There is almost no relationship between the two "negative" agendas (0.05). The positive agendas of parties also have a limited relationship to each other (0.15). If you compare what the Democratic nominees say about themselves to what the Republicans' attack them on, the correlation is just 0.21. The same relationship exists when you correlate the Republican positive agenda to the Democratic negative agenda. These statistics show quite clearly that the Democrats and Republicans do talk past each other, as James Bryce observed long ago, and that tendency becomes even clearer when looking at the party agendas by tone.

WHAT CONSTITUTES AN "IMPORTANT" ISSUE?

When perusing the data presented in tables 5.1 and 5.2, it appears that the topics raised in candidates' negative appeals are reasonable. Clinton attacking Bush on the economy in 1992 is certainly defensible. The economy had been in a slump and Clinton was reminding voters of this fact. One could not question the importance of education as an issue and the attention that Governor Bush gave it in 2000. The public often expresses concern about education. With the cold war still raging in 1984, Mondale's frequent attacks on Reagan's defense policy have credibility, especially with the ongoing debate over the so called star wars plan. Of course, the same can be said for candidate's positive appeals. Goldwater's interest in foreign policy has merit. He felt it was important to talk about his plans for how he would handle Russia and other nations. President Carter's emphasis on that issue in 1980 made sense, given his success with the Camp David Peace Accords. Nevertheless, it is essential that we move beyond such impressionistic readings of "important" issues and instead develop systematic tests that assess the quality of candidates' negative and positive issue appeals.

The key to this undertaking is to find ways to measure objectively what constitutes an "important" issue. One might argue that any issue candidates raise during the course of the campaign is important in the sense that it matters to the candidates. That is hardly convincing as a standard. Not only because it is tautological, but that standard confuses good campaign tactics with what is a good (or important) issue. In what follows, I offer two ways to define an important issue. First, do candidates attack on issues that are salient to the public? So, as an issue becomes more pressing to the electorate, do we see presidential contenders discussing it more or less? If it is the former, that is good news for our assessment of attack politics. If it is the latter, that would be a source of concern. Moreover, how do these patterns of responsiveness compare across negative and positive appeals? It is this question that speaks directly to the informational payoffs of attack advertising.

Second, do candidates attack on issues that reflect changes in actual conditions facing the country? For example, if unemployment increases under the incumbent administration, do we see challengers attack on that basis in the election? If crime rates soar, does the incumbent come under increasing attack for this surge? This strategy moves us past questions about what might be affecting public opinion and focuses instead on objective indicators of the state of the country. By employing two sets of standards, there is an even greater opportunity to assess the substantive nature of attacks in presidential campaigns.

HYPOTHESES

In chapter 3, I contended that negative appeals will prove more informative for voters than positive appeals because the former stick closer to the evidence. Under this framework, I expect negative appeals to track the kind of problems that confront the country, whether those problems are defined by public opinion or more objective indicators of the economy. Since negative appeals are more likely to be backed by evidence than positive appeals, it should affect the specific issues on which candidates attack. They cannot just make up themes, they need to follow the trail of evidence—or at least follow it more closely than for positive appeals. If this is the case, then negative appeals are more informative than positive appeals.

Consider the 2004 presidential campaign. In late October 2003, as Democratic hopefuls were scrambling for their party's nomination, they were attacking President Bush largely on his handling of the economy and postwar Iraq. There were good reasons to do so. After Bush had declared an end to the hostilities in Iraq on May 1, soldiers continued to die in various ambushes and suicide bombings. As the death toll continued to rise, so did the Democrats' complaints about Bush's policy in Iraq. They had the evidence to make the claim work: men and women were dying with little end in sight. If the killing stopped and Iraq became peaceful, the Democrats would no longer have the grounds to continue the attack. They would need a new issue, focusing on where the evidence could be found.

The state of the economy tells a similar story. During the first three years of the Bush administration, the nation lost millions of jobs and piled up a huge deficit. The economy was struggling, despite the Bush tax cuts. Bush kept stressing the importance of these tax cuts and that patience was needed. On October 30, 2003 an important piece of data was released: GDP had jumped 7.2% in the third quarter—the strongest level of economic growth since 1984. The terms of the debate changed with that evidence. Bush was quick to claim credit for the growth, citing the surge as evidence "the tax relief we passed is working."[9]

Bush's quick reaction is hardly a surprise. But, for the Democrats, this evidence posed a problem. An article in the *New York Times* commented two days after the GDP figure was released:

> The rapid change in outlook—underscored by figures released on Thursday showing the fastest quarterly economic growth since 1984—is already forcing the Democratic presidential candidates to calibrate their attacks on Mr. Bush's economic record in ways they did not have to just a week ago.

Democrats turned attention to the weak job market and to the huge deficit. Even then, fears existed that this growth in GDP would lead to more job creation and a shrinking of the projected deficit. Changes in Bush's favor on these fronts would have posed even greater challenges to any Democrat's quest to win the presidency.

The point of this brief discussion is to demonstrate that political attacks cannot just be made up. There needs to be some basis for the attack for voters, journalists, and other elites to pay attention. This constraint offers reasons to believe that negativity does have the potential to be informative. On the positive side, candidates can talk about their plans and aspirations for the country. They can claim with little constraint to favor a "robust economy," "new jobs," "a clean environment," and "a world class education for our children." Few would question these goals or candidates' desire to achieve such goals.

This argument, it should be noted, focuses on the role of the out-party. It is the party out of power that drives the attacks on the incumbents' record. In their effort to gain power, they will use the record of the incumbent as a springboard to the White House. This claim is consistent with scholars who have advocated a responsible party model for government (Schattschneider 1942; Epstein 1986; Aldrich 1995). To have accountable parties and, therefore, democratic government, the out-party must be a critic of the in-party. This point is not new, but it seems to have been forgotten. The famous American Political Science Review published in 1950 argued strongly for an effective opposition party:

> *The fundamental requirement (for) accountability is a two-party system in which the opposition acts as the critic of the party in power, developing, defining and presenting the policy alternatives which are necessary for a true choice in reaching public decisions.* (18; italics in original)

The incumbent party's attacks on the out-party are more complicated. Their criticism will be tied to the particular record of the out-party nominee. But that record will not necessarily reflect larger trends in the country. So, if the nominee comes from a state with poor education scores or bad environmental ratings, we could expect such things to be raised, as Al Gore did in 2000 against then Governor Bush. Because Senator Dole supported legislation that led to a government shutdown, he could expect that as a candidate it would be used against him, which Clinton did in 1996. The point here is that these attacks will be driven by evidence as well, but it will be more idiosyncratic in nature and tied to the record of the particular challenger. By contrast, the incumbent president presides over the nation and thereby can be held accountable for national shifts in the state of the economy or other indicators of society's well-being.

In short, there are two related hypotheses that emerge from the discussion above.

H1: Attacks should track more on the problems of the country than should positive appeals.
H2: This relationship between negativity and the problems of the country should be stronger for the out-party, which has the incentive to raise

reasonable doubts about the accomplishments of the incumbent administration.

THE MOST IMPORTANT PROBLEM

The Gallup organization has been asking the public on a periodic basis,
"What do you think is the most important problem facing this country
today?" It is an open-ended question that allows respondents to offer
their opinions and not be constrained by a limited set of fixed responses.
This format provides a good measure of an issue's salience to the public
(see RePass 1971; Kelley 1983; Geer 1988, 1991). Gallup then combines these responses into a sizable number of issue categories.[10] Those
publicly available results provide the basis for the analysis presented
below.[11]

With the Gallup poll data in hand, I then recoded the data from the
content analysis to match the "most important" problem issues.[12] By
making use of both sources of data, I identified a set of eleven to twelve
issues for each campaign that I was able to examine over the four
decades.[13]

The task now is to see how well the public's assessment of the country's pressing issues affects the respective agendas of presidential candidates. I have four dependent variables:

1. Share of challenger's attacks on an issue[14]
2. Share of challenger's positive appeals on an issue
3. Share of incumbent's attacks on an issue[15]
4. Share of incumbent's positive appeals on an issue.

How can we assess the responsiveness of nominees' agendas to public
opinion? That relationship, in its ideal form, can be specified in a simple
linear model:

$$\textit{Frequency issue is raised} = a_1 + b_1 \textit{ (importance of issue)} + e.$$

This specification yields an important estimate: b_1, or what can be called
responsiveness.[16] For every unit increase in the share of interest in the
issue by the public, how much attention is given to the topic in political
advertising? A fully responsive campaign should yield an estimate of 1. In
other words, if there is a ten-point increase in importance for the issue
among the public, we will also see a similar ten-point increase in the attention paid to the issue in a candidates' advertising.

This approach, as a result, provides a standard to judge whether politicians respond to public opinion in their campaigns: the higher the slope,

the greater the responsiveness. As a starting point for this analysis, I will simply see if there is a significant, positive relationship between public opinion and the issue agenda of presidential campaigns. Then, we can compare the estimates across candidates' negative and positive agendas. Which is the most responsive? Which is the least? My hypothesis is that the challenger's negative appeals will be the most responsive to public opinion. Challengers, in other words, are mostly likely to attack where the public gives them the opportunity to attack.

Of course, the coefficients need not be positive. One troubling outcome would be where there is *no* relationship between the appeals of the campaign and the public's thinking. Even more troubling would be a *negative* relationship. If it turned out that as an issue grew in importance, candidates' negative appeals were less likely to tackle it, that finding would raise serious doubts about the democratic nature of attack advertising. Indeed, such a result would confirm the very worst fears of critics who complain about the negativity of political campaigns. On the other hand by this standard, any positive and statistically sound relationship would be favorable evidence for the way presidential campaigns work.

To get an estimate of the impact of these problems on the appeals candidates make, I ran a regression adding a series of controls that took account of fixed effects[17] and the potential influence of issue ownership on the appeals candidates make. I showed earlier that candidates talk about issues that their respective parties own, so by controlling for it, we can secure a more precise estimate of the effect of an issues' importance on the positive and negative agendas of the candidates.

Table 5.4 presents the coefficients. The first thing to note is that in all four cases as the public cares more about an issue, challengers and incumbents are more likely to address that issue in their negative and positive agendas. Such a relationship in and of itself speaks favorably of campaigns. Responsiveness to public opinion underscores the general properties of political campaigns, showing that they can indeed operate as democratic undertakings. Figure 5.2 provides a visual display of these relationships.

Of specific interest for my argument are the differences between the negative and positive appeals. The challenger's negative appeals are the most responsive to public opinion. As a problem grows in importance to citizens, it is the challenger's criticism that most closely responds to changes in the perception of those problems. The challenger's positive appeals are also quite responsive. These results confirm my hypothesis: if the country identifies a problem, it is most likely to find its way into the attacks that challengers' level against incumbents.

Table 5.4. Relationship between the Most Important Problem Question
and Issue Appeals in Presidential Ads, 1960–2000

	Incumbent's positive appeals		Challenger's positive appeals	
	slope	S.E.	slope	S.E.
Public that cares about the issue (%)	0.336*	0.078	0.520*	0.105
Incumbent party owns issue	3.666*	1.131	−0.103	1.519
	Incumbent party's negative appeals		Challenger's negative appeals	
	slope	S.E.	slope	S.E.
Public that cares about the issue (%)	0.316*	0.112	0.646*	0.098
Incumbent party owns issue	6.136*	1.613	2.519**	1.415

The sample size for each of these regressions is 129. There are between 11 and 12
issues for each of the 11 presidential campaigns.

* p < 0.01

** p < 0.10

Figure 5.2. Negativity and Public Opinion

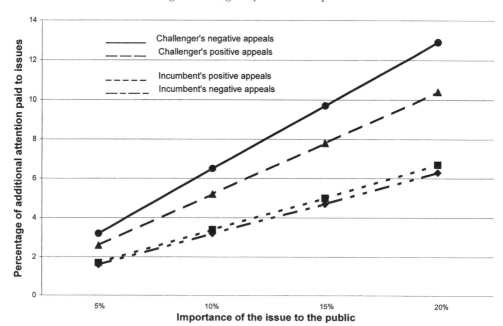

The substantive impact of these relationships is quite impressive. Consider that if an issue becomes fifteen percentage points more salient to the public, we can expect challengers to attack on that issue nearly ten percentage points more frequently. That is a decent amount of responsiveness. By contrast, a fifteen-point surge in an issue's salience to the public generates only a five-percentage point boost in the incumbent's positive appeals on that issue. It is also true that issue ownership matters more for the in-party than for the out-party. The reason for that probably speaks to the fact that incumbent parties are not as likely to discuss "problems" facing the country as are their challengers; hence, they turn to the issue their parties own as themes for their campaign.

OBJECTIVE INDICATORS AND NEGATIVITY

The analysis above certainly paints a favorable picture of attack advertising. It seems that the themes in negative appeals are not about irrelevant issues designed to distract the public. Rather, they are about issues that the public finds important. Moreover, challengers' attacks correspond more closely to these problems than the themes of the incumbents. However, this is only one standard. In what follows, I push the investigation further.

In particular, I examine the relationship between key indicators of the state of the country and the tone of challengers' and incumbents' appeals. For instance, when unemployment goes up, do challengers attack more on that issue while incumbents talk less about it? Conversely, if unemployment drops, do we see incumbents stressing the issue more, while challengers move to other topics? The answers to these questions shed further light on the informative value of advertising, because it ties the content of these appeals to actual conditions confronting the country.

There are aggregate data available that provide an opportunity to answer these kinds of questions, especially on the economic front. We have good measures over time of inflation, unemployment, and the state of the economy.[18] In addition, data on crime rates exist over this period of time that offers further opportunity to assess negativity.[19] There are good measures of defense spending and domestic spending. But it is not clear whether an increase or a decrease is a good or bad thing. By comparison, a drop in inflation or a jump in GDP has a pretty clear interpretation. Spending on key social programs, like Social Security or Medicare, is tied to key changes in the demographic profiles of the nation and will be driven by nonpolitical forces. Some issues, such as education[20] and the environment[21] do not have good time series data available to study any connection.

Even so, I have collected data for four separate issues: unemployment, inflation, the overall economy, and crime. I look at the data on an issue

Table 5.5. Relationship between Real Problems and Content
of Presidential Ads, 1960–2000

	Challenger's negative appeals	Incumbent's positive appeals
	State of the Economy (change in GDP)	
Intercept	55.32*	13.19
	(12.0)	(9.04)
Slope	−8.45*	3.13
	(3.38)	(2.55)
R^2	0.41	0.14
	Unemployment (change over four years)	
Intercept	6.61*	5.36*
	(1.69)	(1.82)
Slope	3.55*	−0.63
	(1.06)	(1.14)
R^2	0.55	0.03
	Inflation (change over four years)	
Intercept	6.17*	3.12*
	(2.45)	(1.22)
Slope	1.63*	−0.49
	(0.64)	(0.32)
R^2	0.42	0.21
	Change in crime rate	
Intercept	5.02	3.41
	(3.07)	(0.97)
Slope	1.32*	−0.21
	(0.54)	(0.16)
R^2	0.42	0.16

Numbers in parentheses are standard errors.

*$p < 0.05$

by issue basis, since combining all the issues together would be tricky given that we do not have a common measure across all issues (as in the case of the most important problem data). As a result, I will only have eleven cases for each issue—the presidential elections from 1960 to 2000. That means one must be cautious about overinterpreting any one relationship.

Table 5.5 presents the regression estimates from the eight simple regressions. In each case, I used the measure of the state of the country as a predictor for the challenger's negative appeals and the incumbent's positive appeals. I did not examine the incumbent's negative appeals, since it makes little sense that the challenger could be held accountable for the state of the country. For much the same reason, I dropped the challenger's positive appeals as well. As mentioned earlier, party government advocates would view the comparison of the challenger's negative appeals to the incumbent's positive appeals as the key issue as voters make their choices.

Despite having only eleven cases, the overall pattern is very clear. Challenger's negative appeals track much more closely to measures of real-world conditions. If there is a surge in inflation, challengers react to it. In fact, for every two-point jump in inflation, we see three percentage points more attention to the issue in the challenger's attacks. The incumbent's positive appeals work in the correct direction—as inflation decreases, they devote more attention to the issue—but the coefficient is small and not close to significance. In fact, ignoring the normal statistical tests given our small sample size, it would take a two-percentage point drop in inflation to generate just one percentage point more attention to the issue by the incumbent. For unemployment, the case is even stronger. The coefficient for the challenger's negative appeals is five times larger than that for the incumbent's positive appeals on that issue. If GDP is stagnant, one can expect the challenger's attack to be on the economic front 55% of the time. If GDP is only growing at 2%, then that proportion drops to 38%—still a sizable amount of attention, but a drop of nearly 33% in attention to the issue. If crime rates change ten percentage points from the last election, one can expect a thirteen-point surge in attention by the challenger and an overall amount of interest of 18%—nearly one-fifth of all negative appeals.

To go beyond these statistical estimates, I have provided two visual displays of these relationships for the issues of inflation and the economy (see figures 5.3 and 5.4).[22] To ease presentation, I have subtracted the share of attention the challenger paid to the issue when attacking from what the incumbent paid to it. As inflation increases, we should see this difference tilt toward the challenger (i.e., the metric becomes smaller). As the economy grows, we should see the incumbent stress it more than the challenger. The fit for these two relationships is quite impressive and reinforces the findings in table 5.5.

It is also worth noting the outliers in figure 5.3. One might fear that that these cases are driving the results; and thereby, undermining my conclusions. The two elections in question, 1980 and 1984, actually strengthen my thesis. In 1980, inflation was a serious problem—it was 13.5% in 1980 alone.[23] Given this context, Ronald Reagan made this topic an important part of his effort to unseat President Carter. In fact, 34% of his attacks on issues dealt with this single issue. Carter did not, by comparison, tout his "successes" on this front. Just four years later, inflation had dropped dramatically during the Reagan administration. What was Mondale's response during the campaign? He mentioned it just 1%

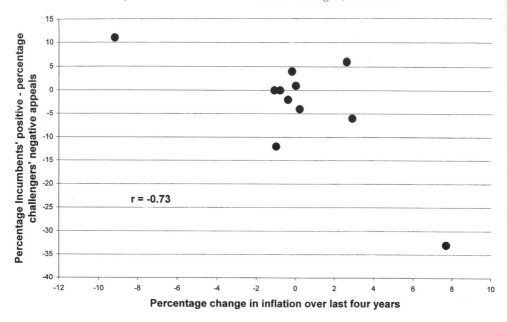

Figure 5.3. Inflation, Incumbents, and Challengers, 1960–2000

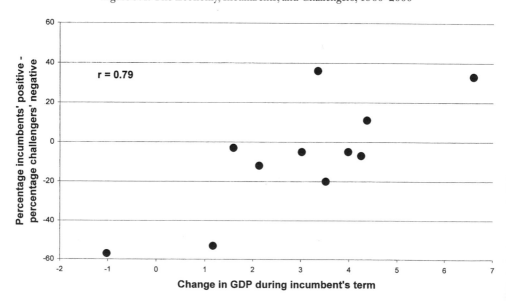

Figure 5.4. The Economy, Incumbents, and Challengers, 1960–2000

of the time, while Reagan reminded the public frequently about the lower rate of inflation.

There are additional outliers in figure 5.4 worth mentioning. In 1980, when GDP shrank about 1%, the challenger, Reagan, harped on the economy in his attacks on Carter—70% of negative appeals were aimed at the economy. Twelve years later, when the economy was growing at a little over 1%, Clinton too hammered away at this theme in comparison to the incumbent. Another example, not part of these two graphs, involves the issue of crime. One election, 1968, might be shaping the relationship. Crime rates had jumped dramatically in 1968. Nixon, as the challenger, used that fact to attack Humphrey and the Democrats. Over 40% of the Republican nominee's attacks dealt with this issue. Nixon did not invent the problem; he just took advantage of it in his quest for the White House.

These graphs and regression results confirm that attacks reflect the context of the election. They are not fabricated, but respond to actual conditions in the country. Such data show the positive aspects of negativity.

NEGATIVITY AND SORTING OUT THE DIFFERENCES

One of the standards for judging the quality of the debate during elections is whether voters can learn about the candidates' views on issues. Candidates all favor a strong economy, for example. Such information would not help voters differentiate the candidates. Instead, voters need to know specific positions of candidates on issues so as to differentiate the contenders. One way to think about this matter is to borrow Stokes's (1966, 170) now famous distinction between "valence" and "position" issues. A position issue involves advocating governmental action "from a set of alternatives over which a distribution of voters' preferences is defined" (Stokes 1966, 170). By contrast, a valence issue links the candidates or parties "with some condition that is positively or negatively valued by the electorate" (Stokes 1966, 170–71). A call for "economic growth," as mentioned above, would count as a valence appeal, while a call for a higher minimum wage would be treated as a position issue.

The judgment that position issues are superior to valence issues might be open to some debate. Candidates who call for an end to corruption or mismanagement of government, both of which are valence issues, send important and serious signals to the public. By interjecting such themes into the public debate, candidates can help citizens learn valuable information about the potential direction of government. Valence issues, therefore, are potentially useful to the electorate. However, my point is that, *on average*, campaigns become more substantive if they contain a higher share of position issues.

What differences should we see between negative and positive appeals? Consider the following example. When President Clinton traveled across the nation in search of votes, he talked about the need to grow the economy, educate our children, and lower crime rates. But when attacking, it was not credible for him to claim that Bob Dole favored an economic slowdown, did not want to educate children, and supported an increase in the number of crimes. Such claims would simply have been false. All candidates want to create jobs, educate children, and lessen crime. These are all classic valence issues, which do not offer the opportunity to distinguish between the candidates. Everyone agrees on these general goals. As a result, Clinton, when on the attack, needed to spell out why Dole's policies would yield bad outcomes for the attacks to be credible. This point is yet another manifestation of the need for evidence.

Another way to think about the point involves the relative incentives for politicians to be vague or specific in their policy statements. Downs (1957) once observed that "candidates becloud their policies in a fog of ambiguity." Page (1976, 742) seconded this claim, noting that "politicians are notoriously reluctant to take clear stands on issues of the day."[24] This view has become part of conventional wisdom. But, actually, it is incomplete. While candidates may want to be vague when discussing their views on issues, the opposite is true when they are on the attack. Rather than being ambiguous, candidates want to be *specific* when laying out the problems with the opposition's views. They want to show not only areas of disagreement between themselves and the opposition, but how ill-advised are their opponents' plans. In a sense, politicians want to underscore the risk involved in choosing the other candidate. The clearer the risk, the more likely the attack will work.[25]

If we think of this matter in simple Downsian terms, candidates have an incentive to push opponents off the median (evidence permitting) or stress issues where the opposition is already off the median. The end result will be a set of negative appeals that will better allow voters to sort out the differences between candidates—an attribute that would improve the information environment in a campaign.

Because my coding scheme is very detailed, I am able to distinguish between issue appeals that are very general in character to ones than are more specific in nature. To do so, I have operationalized Stokes's core distinction in an attempt to test whether negative appeals are more positional than positive appeals.[26] As one may recall, Stokes (1966, 170) was critical of the Downsian approach on a number of grounds, including that there was not usually "an ordered set of alternatives of governmental action that the parties may advocate and the voters prefer." For Stokes, it did not make sense to align candidates on a single spectrum of opinion.

In fact, campaigns, according to Stokes (1966, 170), "do not involve even a shriveled set of two alternatives of government action." This revised standard is a far less demanding, since now candidates only had to differentiate themselves on some issue. That is, candidates need not frame this issue along a continuum. So, for example, when Kerry advocated increasing the minimum wage, that differentiation would count as a position issue. But a call for higher wages in general would be a valence issue, since no candidate is opposed to higher wages.

Stokes's original insights hold up very well. Only 25% of appeals in presidential ads meet a loose definition of "two alternatives." The middle and right side of the figure 5.5 examine how the share of position issue varies by tone. These data support my hypothesis that negative appeals tend to be more positional in nature and less valenced. Nearly one third of attacks are positional (or specific) in presentation. By contrast, only 16% of positive appeals are specific enough for voters to sort out differences in candidates' positions. It short, negative appeals are almost twice as likely to provide voters with a choice of governmental action. I am not arguing that negativity is "positional" in an absolute sense, only that it is *more* specific than positive appeals.

I also examined this pattern across contrast, attack, and positive ads. My goal here was to see if the type of ad influences the ratio of valence to position issues. Among thirty-second spots, attack and contrast ads

Figure 5.5. Proportion of Position and Valence Appeals, 1960–2000

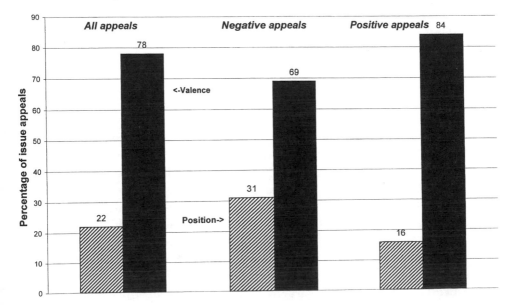

contained the same share of specific appeals (32%).[27] That proportion drops to 19% for positive ads. These findings support the earlier argument that negative appeals have a different dynamic than their counterparts. When making a positive appeal, candidates have a greater tendency to be vague, calling for a "sound Social Security system." However, when attacking the opposition, there is a greater need for evidence and reasoning. It is just not a very viable strategy for a candidate to say only that the opposition wants a weak Social Security system. Rather, an attack encourages the attacker to be specific about how that candidate poses a threat to Social Security. The data here are consistent with this position.

This argument and supporting evidence have important implications for our theoretical understanding of party competition. Scholars working within this rational choice framework have yet to differentiate theoretically between negative and positive appeals made by candidates. The general view is that candidates adopt a position and the public responds. There are at least two amendments that need to be made to such an approach. First, the perception the public has of a candidate's position on an issue is a product of two forces—what the candidates claim their position to be and what the opposition says about them. This argument suggests we may need to rethink our models that explain the public's perception of candidates' views on issues. There has been a tendency to assume that the gap between the public's view and what the candidates say about themselves is a product of misperception or ignorance of voters. It may be that we have just failed to include the opposition's statements in the equation. Second, we need to make negative campaigning, in general, part of our models of party competition. The fact that attacks are more likely to fit the ordered dimension assumption of these models is reason enough. But when you think, for example, about the idea of pushing a candidate off the median, the strategic possibilities are intriguing. It makes sense that if a candidate is off the median, it may be more rational to push the opposition out of the center than changing their own positions and moving to the center. Any time candidates shift positions, it opens them up to charges of flip-flopping. This intersection of party competition, negative campaign, and valence issues is offers some new ways to think about campaigns.

To push further empirically, I now examine how well negativity accounts for the vagueness of the appeals candidates make in their campaigns. That is, to what extent can attacks explain the variance of the specificity of the contenders' rhetoric as they pursue the Oval Office? Figure 5.6 offers one such look. There is a strong relationship between the amount of negativity in a campaign and its share of specific issue appeals. The correlation of 0.78 is impressive, as reflected in the tight fit of the data points. To forge an even more systematic reading of the quality

Figure 5.6. Issue Negativity and Position Appeals, 1960–2000

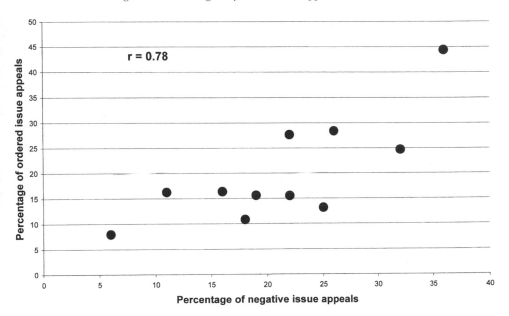

of negative appeals in political ads, I will test a multivariate account that controls for potentially confounding factors.

In the upcoming analysis, I will move from the appeal or spot as the unit of analysis to the campaign. That is, what explains why some presidential campaigns offer fewer valence appeals than others? The number of cases, therefore, is only twenty-two—eleven presidential elections for the two major parties since 1960. The dependent variable will be the share of position appeals in a nominee's ad campaign. There is a significant amount of variance. The most specific campaign was Bill Clinton's bid for reelection: 45% of all issue appeals were positional. By contrast, Richard Nixon ran an exceptionally vague campaign in 1960. He used his advertising to call for international peace and offered very few specific proposals or plans for government. Only 3% of all his issue appeals were specific in nature. The next closest was Michael Dukakis in 1988, at 6%.

The key independent variable is simply the share of negative issue appeals in the candidate's bid for the White House. A second variable is the proportion of contrast ads in the campaign. I have looked at contrast ads in some previous analyses in order to see if the ads improve the quality of the debate.[28] So far that hypothesis has not been supported, but it is worth exploring further in light of the many arguments that comparative ads are superior to pure attack ads.

Two other variables worth exploring involve the context of the

Table 5.6. Explaining the Share of Position Appeals in
Presidential Campaigns, 1960–2000

	Slope	S.E.
Constant	−6.278	17.4
Attacks (%)	0.512*	0.138
Incumbency	9.143**	4.991
Contrast (%)	0.220	0.196
Competitiveness	−0.003	0.342

N = 22

R^2 = 0.58

*p < 0.01

**p < 0.10

particular election. The first is the competitiveness of the contest. As competitiveness increases, the tendency to be vague might also increase. The reason for this hypothesis is twofold. A close campaign may encourage candidates to be risk averse and not stake out clearly defined positions. They also may not be as negative as a lopsided election where the trailing candidate is forced to go negative as a way to get back into the race. The second variable is incumbency. The incumbent will be more specific since they have a record to run on and defend. They have been adopting policy over the previous three years and they will tout their record during the campaign. Stokes (1992), over twenty-five years after he penned his original essay, noted that campaigns are often made of valence issues, whereas the running of the government forces politicians to take clear positions as they make tough policy decisions.

Table 5.6 presents the results of the regression, which shows that the model works fairly well. The share of negative issues has a sizable impact on the amount of position appeals in a campaign. For every ten percentage points of negativity, there is about a five-percentage-point jump in position appeals. The coefficient indicates that incumbents, on average, have nine percentage points more position appeals than do pure challengers.[29] Contrast ads do not meet normal standards for statistical significance, but with only twenty-two cases we need not be dogmatic about such things. The coefficient suggests that for every ten-percentage point increase in the share of contrast ads in a campaign, we will see a two-percentage point decrease in vagueness of appeals. As a result, there is some modest support for the claim that contrast ads, when controlling for the overall share of negativity, improve the quality of campaign rhetoric.[30]

Competitiveness has no apparent impact on the share of positional issues in a campaign.[31] This result, as suggested in a previous chapter, should be expected, since there is not much variation in the competitiveness of presidential elections. I would not, therefore, want to generalize these findings beyond the presidential arena.[32]

These results provide a basis to understand the relative vagueness of various presidential campaigns. Using the highest values for each of the variables under study, the predicted share of position appeals is 47%.[33] By comparison, a challenger's campaign that is very positive and relies on very few contrast spots could in fact yield a share of position issues close to zero.[34] The share of attacks alone can account for a thirty-point swing in how specific is a campaign. That is a sizable shift and one that would clearly be large enough to have an influence on the quality of the information environment in a campaign. One could point to the underlying fact that campaigns are, in general, vague, as Stokes commented many years ago. Nevertheless, that observation should not diminish the fact that negative appeals appear important in presenting information in campaigns that will allow voters to sort out the differences between candidates on the issues of the day.

CONCLUSION

The findings of this chapter paint a far more favorable picture of attack politics than conventional wisdom suggests. The information environment of the public is enriched by attacks. These attacks are on important problems facing the country and these negative appeals change in response to real-world changes in the condition of the country. It would, in light of this evidence, be far harder to argue that attacks mislead and misinform. It would be even harder to argue that positive appeals provide more useful policy information than negative appeals. In addition, attacks are more specific in their presentation of an issue than are positive appeals. Campaign appeals are in general vague, but that is especially true for self-promotional issue appeals.

The results, while satisfying for those who are concerned about the pernicious effects of negativity, also bolster the core theoretical argument of this book. Since attacks tend to be tied to evidence, that dynamic encourages negativity to be about legitimate issues. Presidential candidates are not making up issues in an effort to distract. They are in some sense playing the hand they were dealt by the context of the election.

There are two additional lessons worthy of some comment. First, the public can learn more about real-world problems from negative appeals than from positive appeals. This story is very much different from what we normally hear about the ill effects of negativity. If we think of it in terms of Gelman and King's (1993) argument that campaigns matter in that they inform the public about the condition of the country, these data add an amendment to that claim. It is the negative appeals of the challenger that help that process more than the positive appeals of the incumbents on those issues. It seems quite clear that the out-party is indeed serving its role as a critic of those in power—an outcome that speaks favorably of the campaign and the role of attacks. This is a potentially important insight, since, if true, the informative nature of campaigns draws strength from the negative side of the equation.

A second implication of these findings is that the party government theorists were correct: the opposition does play an important role in forging accountability. Attacks by the opposition seem much more likely to be of value to voters as they make their choices. Most of the discussion of negativity has ignored this theoretical issue. If the public wants to have accountability, someone has to do the accounting and that accounting is not done through positive, feel-good appeals, but through harsh political attack where voters are made aware of the problems of the incumbent. Obviously, political campaigns of challengers offer much more than just advertising in their efforts to lure voters to their side. They have many ways of sending messages to voters. Nevertheless, at least in the presidential case, these messages seem to play a critical role in allowing elections to perform their democratic functions.

We will attend more to these themes of democracy, accountability, and negativity in the final chapter. In the meantime, we are now going to take a close look at one of the most discussed negative campaigns in recent presidential history—the 1988 battle between Michael Dukakis and George Bush.

CHAPTER SIX

Dragging the Truth into the Gutter? The News Media, Negativity, and the 1988 Campaign

Observers, pundits, and scholars often view the electoral duel between George Bush and Michael Dukakis as the low point in modern presidential campaigns. Kathleen Jamieson (1988b) wrote "Our Appalling Politics" when evaluating the 1988 presidential campaign. There was a lot of be appalled about, according to critics. Some observers commented that the campaign lacked substance and meaningful debate (e.g., Buchanan 1991; Patterson 1993). But the most common complaint about 1988, as Jamieson suggested in her essay, concerned the negativity of that campaign. Wilson Carey McWilliams (1989, 178–79), for example, commented that the 1988 "campaign was more than 'negative.' It was a year when civility 'took it on the chin,' one in which . . . nastiness 'became a commodity.' " Todd Gitlin concurred, observing that "nastiness seemed to reach an all time low this year."[1] The commentary does not end there. Gary Wills viewed the 1988 campaign as "A Moral Derailing"—a theme that echoes Jamieson's. Robert Guskind and Jerry Hagstrom (1988) joined the chorus, writing a story for the *National Journal* under the banner, "In the Gutter." Bruce Buchanan (1991, 5) worried that this election may have shown that "American political practice [has drifted] too far from its ethical mooring."

Voters too shared this unfavorable view of the 1988 presidential election. In a story in the *Christian Science Monitor* at the end of the campaign, citizens expressed their disgust. One voter said simply: "I hate this campaign." A senior citizen commented "that this was the worst campaign I've seen in my life."[2] One can always find a few unhappy voters after any election. But survey data confirm these opinions were widely shared among the electorate. In an NBC News/*Wall Street Journal* poll 68% of the public agreed with the statement that the 1988 "presidential campaign has been one of the worst in recent history."[3] The fact that pollsters had not asked this question prior to 1988 speaks volumes about this campaign.[4] Much of the citizenry's unhappiness, as with the pundits cited above, surrounded the negativity of the campaign. A Harris poll at the end of October found the 75% of the public thought the television commercials in 1988 had been either "too negative" or "somewhat negative."[5] When asked about how this campaign compared to past campaigns, 62% of the public thought it had been more negative and only 7% more positive.[6]

The concerns with the negativity of the 1988 presidential election were largely tied to the tone of television advertising. This contest witnessed some of the best-known attacks ads in modern times. Phrases such as "revolving door" and "Boston Harbor"—both titles of attack ads sponsored by George Bush—have become part of the political discourse. Of course, one need only mention the name of Willie Horton and immediately we start thinking about mudslinging and racism. When I asked fellow political scientists to name the most memorable ads in presidential campaigns, they mentioned *five* different *negative* ads from this election alone—the Revolving Door, Boston Harbor, the Handler (or the Packaging of the President) ads, the Tank ad, and Willie Horton.[7] The single most mentioned ad was the 1964 Daisy spot. But no campaign came close to 1988 in the overall number of memorable spots.

What happened in 1988? Was the advertising that sleazy? Was it an instance where lies trumped the truth? Was it a campaign that ended up in the gutter? These questions are important to my assessment of negativity, because of the widespread belief that 1988 was the kind of negative campaign that undermines the ability of elections to forge healthy democratic ties between the public and elected officials. In other words, the advertising aired in the 1988 presidential election might undermine the defense of negativity I have marshaled so far. I will argue, however, that the problems of 1988 were not due directly to an unprecedented nasty advertising campaign. Instead, I will show that the news media's coverage of the election played a big role in forging this perception of a campaign in the "gutter." At least in regards to advertising, the candidates did not break any new ground in the harshness of attacks leveled. Previous elections have witnessed such negativity. What was new was the news media's interest in the subject.

By tackling the case of 1988, I will be able to integrate more fully the role of the news media in my discussion of negativity and its effects on the information environment. The fourth estate is important to this debate and has been largely absent from the pages of this book. This case also provides me the opportunity to move beyond the kind of data I have examined thus far and, instead, offer more nuanced assessments of negativity in presidential advertising. I shall start by recounting briefly what happened in the Dukakis-Bush battle so as to remind people about the context of that election.

THE SETTING

The 1988 presidential election was the first in twenty years without an incumbent running. The two challengers, George Bush and Michael Dukakis, were relative unknowns. Although Bush had been vice president for seven years, he was not a household name. In an ABC News poll in December of 1987, 21% of the public answered "don't know" to a question about whether they had a favorable or unfavorable impression of George Bush. Governor Dukakis was, of course, even less defined in the public's mind. He had been governor of Massachusetts, but did not draw national attention until he started to rack up wins in the Democratic presidential primaries and caucuses. In fact, at the start of 1988, 63% of the public did not even have an impression of Dukakis.[8] Even by June, 42% of respondents did not know much about the presumptive Democratic nominee.[9]

As the country approached the November election, the economy was doing well and the nation was at peace. Ronald Reagan had weathered the Iran-Contra scandal and remained popular with the electorate.[10] Most of the structural features that shape the outcome of elections favored the Republicans. Ray Fair (1988), for example, predicted a 52% to 48% victory for the Republican Party using data from July of 1987. The economy was even better by the summer of 1988, further pointing to a solid Republican win. Yet Bush trailed Dukakis in the polls conducted after the conclusion of the primary season. At the end of May, the governor held a thirteen percentage point lead over the vice president.[11] Bush's negatives were pretty high and it looked like an uphill battle.[12]

As the summer approached, a number of commentators predicted that Bush would have to run a nasty campaign to leap frog over Dukakis. Specifically, the vice president would need to raise Dukakis's negatives to have a chance. Both sides started to exchange fire early in the summer. On June 7 in California, Bush attacked Dukakis for not supporting the pledge of allegiance. Just ten days prior to the opening of the Democratic convention, rumors started to swirl that Dukakis faced some mental health problems. The rumors got bad enough to force Dukakis to issue a denial, which was covered by the *New York Times*. But then Reagan raised the stakes by saying that he was "not going to pick on an invalid" after a reporter ask him to comment on Dukakis's refusal release all his medical records (Germond and Witcover 1989, 360–61).

Dukakis was not above going on the attack either. He questioned the Reagan administration's record on corruption by noting that "there is an old Greek saying: A fish rots from the head first" (Germond and Witcover 1989, 359). This statement drew strong reactions, because Dukakis was attacking a personally popular president. The willingness to attack was best represented by the tone of the Democratic National Convention. Ted Kennedy and Ann Richards both delivered harsh speeches mocking the vice president. Ann Richards, for example, poked fun at Bush by noting that he had been "born with a silver foot in his mouth."

Following the Democratic convention in July, Dukakis's lead increased to seventeen percentage points in at least one poll. While that surge was tied to the bounce normally associated with national conventions (Holbrook 1996), it looked like Dukakis was in the driver's seat.

The Republicans met in mid-August in New Orleans. Bush still trailed, but Jim Baker was now in control of the campaign, which observers thought would give direction to the Bush effort. Reagan, of course, continued to cast a long shadow over Bush and the whole party. The choice of Dan Quayle did not exactly get the general election campaign off to a good start. Quayle was a surprise choice. The media wanted to know why the senator from Indiana was chosen, especially since alternatives included politicians like Bob Dole and Jack Kemp. In a press conference soon after his selection, Quayle faced some tough questions, especially about his decision to enter the National Guard rather than serve in Vietnam. He tried to explain the decision, but the questions continued. Finally, he said "I did not know in 1969 that I would be in this room today." The statement made not only Quayle look callous and calculating, but it raised doubts about Bush's judgment.[13]

Despite the controversy over Senator Quayle, Bush delivered an effective acceptance speech, and became the leader of the party. The convention had been a success, especially if we use survey data as our metric. While Bush had trailed prior to the convention, he was now ahead. In a Gallup poll immediately following the convention, Bush led Dukakis by eight points (forty-five to thirty-seven). That lead shrunk to four points a week later, but went back to eight points by early September, staying pretty much the same throughout the fall campaign.

SOMETHING HAPPENED IN 1988

It is clear that various elites became interested in negativity in general, and negative advertising in particular. Most notably, the news media's coverage of the subject soared in 1988. Figure 6.1 displays a content analysis of the number of news stories aired by the major television networks about negative advertising between 1968 and 2000 using the Vanderbilt Television News Archives.[14] As the graph clearly shows, the news media gave a great deal more attention to the negative advertising in 1988 than any previous contest under study. Interestingly, between 1968 and 1984 there was an *inverse* relationship between the amounts of attack advertising (recall figure 2.1) and the news media's attention to the subject.[15] With five cases, one must be cautious in placing too much faith in those results. Even so, two points are clear. First, the news media paid scant attention to the subject prior to 1988. Second, when they did, the coverage had little correspondence to the frequency of negativity in advertising. One can look at newspaper coverage find pretty much the same pattern. There was a fourfold increase in the number of stories on negativity in the *New York Times* and *Washington Post* from 1984 (eight) to 1988 (thirty-two). This surge in attention is nicely symbolized by the cover story in *Newsweek* in the October 31, 1988 titled "Mud in Your Eye." Never before had the subject graced the cover of a major magazine.

The rise in interest concerning negativity extends beyond journalists. Candidates joined the fray. Bush and Dukakis attacked each other, which is hardly new. But 1988 witnessed a new twist—these attacks began to be about negativity and attack advertising itself. In 1988, the nominees

Figure 6.1. Network News Attention to Negativity, 1968–2000

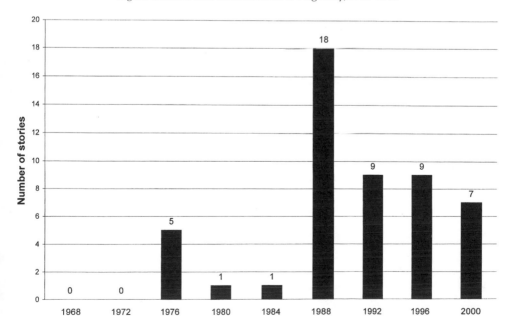

debated who was the most negative and who was responsible for the "dirty" politics. Figure 6.2 captures this development. Prior to 1988, negativity was not an issue in any presidential campaign from 1960 to 1984. That changed in 1988 quite dramatically, with seven separate ads raising the issue. Perhaps the most notable was a spot aired by Michael Dukakis that began: "I'm fed up with it. Haven't seen anything like it in twenty-five years of public life. George Bush's negative TV ads, distorting my record, full of lies and he knows it." In the same spot, Dukakis goes on to state that Bush's strategy is "about dragging the truth into the gutter."[16] This ad does not stand alone. Dukakis continued to fire back in his advertising. Another spot, which sought to counter the Revolving Door ad, began by stating "George Bush's False Advertising," and ended with the observation that "the real story about furloughs is that George Bush has taken a furlough from the truth." Candidates had complained about negative ads in the past, but airing attack ads against other attack ads was novel.

Evidence of this sudden interest in negativity can be seen elsewhere. The debate over the 1988 campaign reached such a fevered pitch that pollsters started to ask questions about negativity. Prior to the 1988 presidential campaign, there had been no questions asked about the subject during previous battles for the White House.[17] In 1988, however, eight surveys asked questions about negativity, with a Harris poll in October posing six specific questions about negative commercials on television (see figure 6.3). The most common question appears to be an effort by

Figure 6.2. Number of Presidential Ads Using Negativity as an Issue, 1960–2000

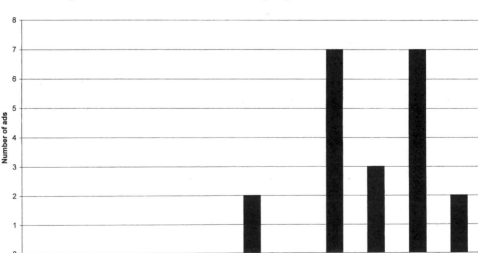

Figure 6.3. Number of Public Opinion Surveys Asking
about Negative Campaigning, 1976–2000

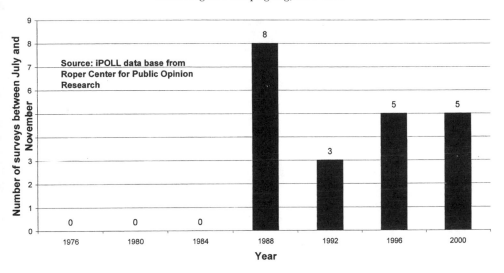

pollsters to find out whether the public blamed Bush or Dukakis for the negative campaigning in 1988. These questions are interesting because they assume, first, that the campaign was negative and, second, that one of the candidates (or perhaps both) were to blame for it.

The changing content of survey questions are good indicators of new issues that have entered the political arena. Pollsters have only limited space for new questions and add new ones only when there is a visible and important development in society. For example, I could find only one question asked about gay marriage in 2000. In 2004, pollsters asked eighty-five questions.[18] The issue of gay marriage jumped onto the political stage in 2004 and pollsters reacted. This same kind of process unfolded in 1988, as survey researchers sought to gather the public's thinking on what was suddenly a hot topic—negativity.

Scholarly interest in the subject also jumped following the 1988 campaign. Kathleen Jamieson published *Dirty Politics* in 1992. The opening paragraph of that book started with commentary about the 1988 campaign and the role of negativity in that contest. Three years later, Stephen Ansolabehere and Shanto Iyengar published *Going Negative*—an influential book that sparked an important debate about the effects of negative advertising on the public. A more systematic search in JSTOR confirms an increase in interest in the subject by scholars. In the twelve years prior to 1989, there were *no* articles in the field of political science that made reference to the phrase "negative advertising." In the twelve years following the Dukakis-Bush contest, the phrase appeared in thirty-six scholarly articles.[19]

In sum, the topic of negative advertising became part of the political landscape in 1988. Negative ads had been airing on television since 1952, but they had not become the center of attention before. What was different about this presidential struggle? Why did negativity capture the attention of political elites and the general public? The remaining segments of this chapter shall consider various explanations. In so doing, I shall reject some explanations and settle on a mix of others. This exercise will provide the springboard for some discussion about how we think about negativity and why political observers often misunderstand this subject.

WHAT EXPLAINS THE RISE IN INTEREST?

The Ads Did It

The conventional explanation for the surge in attention to the subject of negativity is that the amount of attack advertising jumped in the 1988 campaign. The news media (and other actors) were, therefore, just responding to unparalleled criticism the two presidential contenders heaped upon each other. This explanation does not, however, hold water. The 1988 campaign was *not* significantly more negative than recent presidential elections, at least according to my measures.[20] If we examine the amount of negativity in 1988 (recall figure 2.1), it was not out of line the previous six elections. Between 1964 and 1984, the average amount of negative appeals was 27%, ranging between 22% and 32%. In 1980, the amount was 31%. It is true that 1988 was three percentage points higher than 1980 (34%), but certainly not enough difference to generate the attention the subject received in 1988.

Recall that the data in figure 2.1 represent the average from the two major party nominees. Averages, as we all know, can be misleading. Perhaps Bush's "excessive" attacks were the trigger behind this surge of interest and the mean rate of attack for the two candidates covers up a more distinctive pattern. Figure 6.4 breaks out the rate of negativity for each party's nominees from 1964 to 1988. The findings do not offer much comfort to this revised hypothesis. To begin, Bush did not air more negative appeals than Dukakis. It was Dukakis who was more negative over the course of the entire campaign. This finding may surprise some observers, but the data are pretty clear on this point.[21] Moreover, Dukakis's amount of negativity was comparable to Johnson in 1964, McGovern in 1972, Reagan in 1980, and Mondale in 1984. Again, the frequency of attack seems well within the scope of recent campaigns.

Figure 6.4. The Negativity of Presidential Candidates by Party, 1960–88

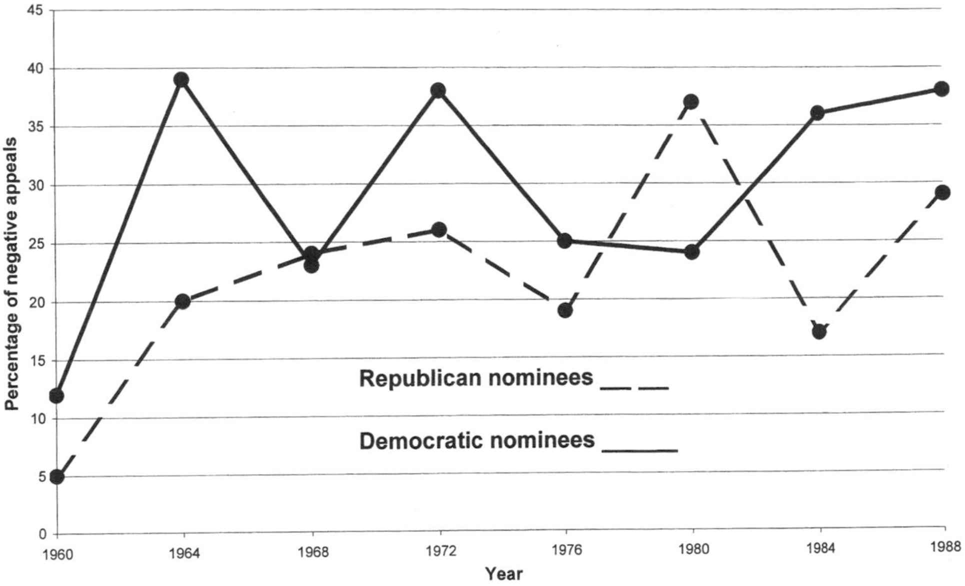

Further variations of this general theme are, however, worth exploring. For starters, what about the share of negative ads? My measure lumps all negative appeals together whether from a contrast or an attack ad. Perhaps 1988 had more pure negative ads than previous campaigns. Again, the data do not support such a hypothesis. Bush and Dukakis's ads were each about 35% negative. Thirty seven percent of Mondale's spots were negative. Reagan held the record up to that date, running 42% negative ads in 1980. In 1968, one third of Nixon's spots were negative. Another possibility is that there might have been a surge in personal attacks. Nasty exchanges about traits would be viewed as troubling by various critics, stimulating the news media's interest. But again the data do not support such a hypothesis. Of Bush's attacks, 36% were about Dukakis's traits. Among Dukakis's negative appeals, 32% deal with Bush's personal weaknesses. This is not a particularly high rate of attack. In 1976, Ford's personal attacks on Carter constituted 41% of his negative appeals. In 1980, about two-thirds of all Carter's attacks were questioning Reagan's personal qualifications for office.

Perhaps what was different about 1988 was how early the attack ads started to air. Bush did go on the attack from the start, which might account for the surge in interest. In addition, it is possible that Dukakis's higher rate of negativity may reflect the campaign's reaction to Bush's attacks, making this an important test. But, again the data do not back up this view. In 1988, the Bush campaign produced their first negative spot on September 6.[22] This is not exceptionally early. Mondale's campaign produced an attack spot on September 9, 1984. Even more to the point, the famous Daisy ad aired on September 7, 1964.

To be a bit more systematic, I sought to examine the rate of negativity in September and compare that to October for 1980, 1984, 1988. The idea here is that perhaps Bush was more negative early on and the proportion reported in figure 6.4 was misleadingly positive. Figure 6.5 compares the rate of negativity for these six presidential campaigns in September to October. This demarcation should provide at least a rough cut at the hypothesis. The data again do not lend much support to the idea. Bush was indeed more negative than Dukakis early on, but no more so than Mondale, Reagan (1980), or Carter (1980). Moreover, both Bush and Dukakis became more negative in October than they had been in September.[23] It does seem reasonable to believe that Dukakis's increase in negativity in October was partially a reaction to Bush's attacks, but these data cannot formally confirm that hypothesis. The broader point remains: the amount of negativity in these ads, however one slices it, does not appear to be the explanation for the surge of interest in the topic.

The Negative Ads Worked

Another hypothesis about the sudden surge of interest in negativity is that it worked. That is, Bush's attack ads were the key to his victory in 1988.

Figure 6.5. Negativity in September and October by Candidate, 1980–88

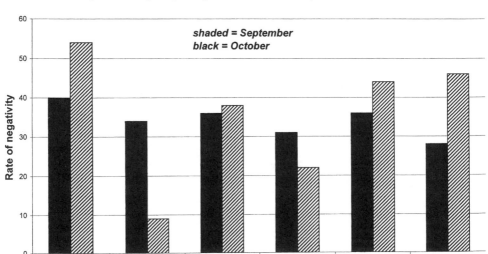

While candidates had attacked each other before, the outcome of 1988 election was shaped by them. This hypothesis is difficult to test, since we all may have different ideas about what constitutes "worked" or "shaped." A commonly held view, however, is that Bush became the front-runner and eventual winner through his attacks ads.

While there is little doubt that these ads were memorable and drew much comment from the news media then and now, we lack evidence that shows conclusively how many voters were actually influenced by these spots. There were some efforts to use survey data to assess the impact of advertising on voters in 1988 (e.g., Buchanan 1991). But these studies tend to suffer from numerous methodological problems. It is only over the last three presidential elections that scholars have started to gather the kind of data that gets at these questions effectively (e.g., Johnston, Hagen, and Jamieson 2004; Freedman and Goldstein 2002). Thus, we can do little more than guess at the actual effectiveness of these commercials. And even if we still think that these ads moved public opinion, that would hardly be new. Advertising on television had been used since 1952 and some ads, such as Ford's commercials in 1976 or Humphrey's near the end of the 1968 campaign, were credited with shifting public opinion.

We can, however, be sure of one thing. The attack ads aired by the Bush campaign did *not* catapult Bush into the lead. The reason is simple. Bush surged ahead at the end of August (Farah and Klein 1989); yet he did not start airing any negative ads until early September. As mentioned earlier, the vice president had already established a lead of eight to ten points in the polls by the time any of these spots hit the airwaves and maintained that edge pretty much the entire fall.

One might counter that these attack ads were effective in that they kept him in the lead. That is, of course, possible. But the same logic could be applied to ads from the previous years. Johnson used negative ads to maintain his comfortable lead against Goldwater. The same could be said about Nixon in 1972 or Reagan in 1984. The point is that the impact of these negative ads from 1988 could not have recast the race and, therefore, their effects were not so unique as to trigger the surge of attention in the topic. Something else must be afoot.

Racism Did It

The Willie Horton ad is one of the most famous commercials of all time, trailing only the Daisy spot from 1964 in notoriety. This spot was not sponsored by the Bush campaign and was aired in only a handful on midwestern states a handful of times.[24] With pictures of Bush and Dukakis and then images of Horton, the narrator states:

Bush and Dukakis on crime. Bush supports the death penalty for first degree murderers. Dukakis not only opposes the death penalty, he allowed first degree murderers to have weekend passes from prison. One was Willie Horton, who murdered a boy in a robbery, stabbing him nineteen times. Despite a life sentence, Horton received ten weekend passes from prison. Horton fled, kidnapped a young couple, stabbing the man and repeatedly raping his girlfriend. Weekend prison passes. Dukakis on crime.

The spot in many ways serves as a capstone to the extensive discussion about the Horton issue. In the months prior to the airing of this spot, Willie Horton drew frequent comment in the press.[25] Al Gore was the first to mention Willie Horton in his nomination battle with Dukakis. There was a *Reader's Digest* story in July 1988 that talked about the problem with the governor's furlough program. Bush advisors saw the potential of this story and started to have their candidate talk about it on the campaign trail during the summer.[26]

This journalistic attention focused on the crimes Horton committed and the furlough program run during Dukakis's tenure as governor. Race was not an explicit part of the story. Robin Toner (1988), when covering the Bush campaign for the *New York Times*, talked about how Bush mentioned Willie Horton: "a convicted murderer who escaped from the Massachusetts prison system on a weekend furlough and raped a Maryland woman." In a story in early September, the *Christian Science Monitor* had a story about Willie Horton and they used John Dilulio, an expert in criminal justice, to discuss the furlough program.[27] The theme of the story, again, was centered on crime. Mendelberg (2001, 146) confirms these impressions, showing clearly that references to race in the news media's coverage were almost nonexistent until the end of the campaign.

The "fame" of this spot has grown dramatically since the 1988 campaign. Using Lexis-Nexis, I found 998 stories in major newspapers between 1989 and 2004 when searching for "Willie Horton" in the headlines or lead paragraphs.[28] The Willie Horton ad haunts us today. Its use of crime as a theme against Dukakis was a cover for its racial tone. We now know about these subtle racial messages. But that was *not* true for most of the 1988 campaign. Mendelberg (2001) offers the most compelling and thoughtful discussion of this ad and the context surrounding the 1988 campaign, showing quite convincingly that it was not until October 21, 1988 that Willie Horton became associated with race. It was on that day that "Jesse Jackson . . . accused the Bush campaign of using Horton with racial intent" (Mendelberg 2001, 3). Prior to that point, Willie Horton ad offered only *implicit* racial appeals. Mendelberg's point is that this ad represented the effort of politicians to go underground with their racial arguments and it was only Jesse Jackson and the subsequent furor touched off by his claim that made the Willie Horton ad what it is today.

There is little doubt that Willie Horton is still with us, shaping how presidential candidates approach elections and how pundits interpret them. But the racial themes imbedded in the ad came to light too late in the campaign to have contributed significantly to the sudden interest in negativity in 1988. It might well help explain the interest since that time, but not for 1988. However, the Horton ad still may have crossed the "line" of acceptable rhetoric, given its hard-hitting attack on Dukakis's views on crime. So perhaps the spot's explicit themes did help to forge the interest in negativity. But if so, then this ad is part of a larger explanation about the content of the advertising from this campaign. It is to that subject we now turn.

The 1988 Spots Crossed the "Line"

I have shown that 1988 was not significantly more negative than other recent presidential campaigns. An obvious response is that my measures are missing something. Just consider that pollsters started to ask questions about negativity during the campaign, reflecting the sentiment that 1988 was so negative as to warrant sampling public opinion. Or consider the rise of ad watches following the 1988 campaign. The news media wanted to check misinformation in the future, and this was one solution to that problem. Lots of postelection analysis focused on this topic—just recall the commentary at the start of this chapter.

If quantitative measures of the 1988 campaign do not suggest that it was unusual, the answer may lie in the qualitative nature of these negative appeals. My data capture many things quite well, but they may not get at these more subtle indictors of attacks. Recall, I only coded the attacks, not their intensity. My data, therefore, may offer less insight into whether specific ads crossed the line. It is quite plausible to believe that the nature of the attacks were sufficiently harsh and out of bounds that the findings gleaned from this content analysis miss the mark.

To consider whether the advertising from 1988 crossed the line, I must first draw it. But herein lies the problem. Drawing such a line is a product of one's personal values and political allegiances. Consider the controversy over the Swift Boat ads in 2004. Individuals sympathetic to Kerry usually found the ads unacceptable, misleading, and unfair. People aligned with George Bush tended to view these ads as fair game. Kerry had talked about his service in Vietnam and made it a centerpiece of the Democratic convention. That tactic, Republicans argued, made attacks on his service legitimate. The senator claimed it was central to his qualifications, so his opponents sought put that service under a bright light. Democrats, of course, offer a different interpretation, claiming that these attacks were just outright lies and distortions. The bottom line is that so-called red observers are very likely to draw the line differently for Republican attack ads than blue observers. This argument is hardly surprising, but it reminds us why these assessments are very slippery and not something that readily applies itself to normal social science standards.

These disagreements over the line extend beyond partisanship. It is also a product of people's values and thinking. Establishing these distinctions is much the conceptual equivalent of a Rorschach test. Some people will see what they want to see in these inkblots. Observers who think harsh criticism is part of the political game will be more supportive, in general, of such tactics. Others who want campaigns to be more feel-good exercises will be, on average, more likely to take issue with tough negative ads. Recall, one's assessment of the contribution of negativity to political information available in a campaign is a product of the *normative* standards one brings to bear.

Consider the idea that ads should tell the "truth" and not "mislead." These are noble goals and seem like decent starting points for drawing these lines. Yet such standards are not, in fact, very useful. Campaigns are forums where candidates make the strongest case for their position. In other words, they exaggerate. All ads, positive and negative, engage in stretching the truth. It is part of politics. Thus, to say that an ad or set of ads are misleading does not do us much good. All ads are misleading, as noted in the introduction of this book. There is no such thing as an objective spot. They are all efforts to lure additional support. The problem is that commentators often assume that objective ads exist. They have in the back of their mind a fair spot that often provides the implicit basis for their assessments. As a result, this so-called line is *not* fixed, nor widely agreed upon.

Even though, I am aiming at a moving and undefined target, I shall take a close look at four of the most controversial ads from 1988—the Revolving Door, Boston Harbor, Tank, and Handler (or Packaging the President) spots. An in-depth analysis of these spots will help me move beyond my content analysis. I will, then, discuss some other ads from past elections to help put 1988 in proper perspective. I should note that this undertaking is fraught with one additional problem. My assessments are being made in 2005 (when I am writing this chapter). The context of 1988, however, was quite different. Since then we have had sixteen years of history and a lot more discussion of negativity. I wave this cautionary flag just to let readers know that the following section is just one interpretation of these ads, not *the* interpretation.

The Boston Harbor Ad

The Boston Harbor ad was the first negative commercial aired by the Bush campaign. It followed a contrast ad aired by Dukakis at the very start of September. This spot came on the heels of Bush visiting Boston Harbor in an effort to undermine Dukakis's credentials as an advocate of the environment. Dukakis had been stressing his many accomplishments as governor and Bush sought to use the polluted harbor to turn the tables. The script of the ad is as follows:

> As a candidate, Michael Dukakis called Boston Harbor "an open sewer." As governor he had the opportunity to do something about it but chose not to. The Environmental Protection Agency called his lack of action the most expensive public policy mistake in the state in the history of New England. Now Boston Harbor, the dirtiest harbor in America, will cost residents $6 billion to clean. And Michael Dukakis promises to do for America what he's done for Massachusetts.

At first glance, these claims do not appear offensive or excessively harsh. The adjectives are not over the top. Moreover, the claims are largely accurate. The harbor was polluted, and it remained so under Dukakis's tenure as governor. Incumbents take credit for all successes, whether or not they deserve it. The flip side is that incumbents get blamed for problems outside of their control. Dukakis often talked about all the jobs created on his watch. Were his policies responsible for all those gains?

Perhaps the visuals are the problem. The visuals, in general, were compelling in that they drew a graphic picture of polluted water. The soundtrack is subtle, but eerie. Again, it was not wildly out of bounds or without precedent. Near the end of the ad, a sign appears that reads: "Danger Radiation. Hazard. No Swimming." Jamieson (1988a) takes issue with the use of the sign, because it was not tied to the harbor but instead it was a warning to navy personnel not to swim in waters where nuclear subs had once resided. Yet few would quibble that Boston Harbor was heavily polluted and not fit for public use. It was, in short, a pretty effective ad in that it conveyed its message well. Hard hitting? Yes. Crossed the line? I am less convinced.

Much of the unhappiness expressed with the ad by journalists and Democrats focused on the subject matter. Republican nominees had never attacked their Democratic counterparts on the environment before. In fact, the GOP had virtually ignored the issue prior to 1988, mentioning it a total of two times out of 1386 issue appeals between 1960 and 1984 (0.1%). The Democrats raised the issue far more frequently, having mentioned it about 2% of the time over the same twenty-four years. This is not a high rate of attention compared to topics like the economy or Social Security, but the issue was widely viewed as Democratic turf (Petrocik 1996). Moreover, with the environment becoming a more important issue to the public and the Reagan administration's suspect record on the environment, the Republicans had good reason to worry. Given this context, it made good sense to raise doubts about Dukakis's record on the environment. It may be frustrating if one has Democratic stripes, but it seems fair game. It almost seems that what was "unfair" about the ad was not the content, but the strategic implications. Rather than having a real debate about environmental policy, Bush was, in effect, saying "your record on the environment also stinks."

The Revolving Door Ad

This ad is more controversial than Boston Harbor because it ties into some of the themes of the dreaded Willie Horton ad. Not only did the ad tackle the issue of crime, but some of the prisoners used in the revolving door ad were African-American and others appeared to be Hispanic, which speaks to the implicit racial themes that still dog that campaign. The ad had powerful black and white images of a scary prison with armed guards and lots of barbed wire. It is indeed hard hitting, seeking to stirs emotions of fear and anxiety. Here is what the narrator said as these black and white visuals of prisons, prison guards, and prisoners filled the screen:

> As Governor, Michael Dukakis vetoed mandatory sentences for drug dealers. He vetoed the death penalty. His revolving door prison policy gave weekend furloughs to first degree murderers not eligible for parole. While out, many committed other crimes like kidnapping and rape, and many are still at large. Now Michael Dukakis says he wants to do for America what he's done for Massachusetts. America can't afford that risk.

These claims are not false. Dukakis did veto the two bills referenced in the commercial. The seriousness of the "revolving door prison policy" is, however, open to debate. There is a statement flashed on the screen that says 268 prisoners escaped under Dukakis's furlough program. This is an exaggeration in that nearly a quarter of these "escapees" were just late in returning. Jamieson (1988a) also warns that "only one first-degree murder" was "furloughed by the Massachusetts program" and that "the typical furlough jumper was an unarmed robber, not a murderer." This spot appears guilty of common sin in propaganda: stretching the truth.

The concluding theme about American can't afford that "risk" was not unprecedented. Nixon ended his 1968 ads with the statement urging citizens to "vote like your whole world depended on it." Johnson talked about the "stakes being too high to stay at home."[29] The substance issues raised are not unique either. For example, the Democrats have been attacked on crime before—in 1968, 41% of Nixon's attacks on Humphrey dealt with crime. There was a general perception that Democrats were soft on crime and this ad played off that perception (Petrocik 1996).

Did this commercial cross the line? A case can be made for an affirmative response. But we need to make sure we do not confuse "effective" and "hard hitting" with any normative assessment that the ad went too far.

The Tank Ad

Michael Dukakis has opposed virtually every defense system we developed. He opposed new aircraft carriers. He opposed antisatellite weapons. He opposed four missile systems, including the Pershing 2 missile deployment. Dukakis opposed the stealth bomber, a ground emergency warning system against nuclear testing. He even criticized our rescue mission to Grenada and our strike on Libya. And now he wants to be our commander in chief. America can't afford that risk.

This ad drew lots of fire from the Dukakis camp, leading them to respond, as noted earlier, with an ad that used this spot as evidence that Bush was dragging the "truth" into the gutter. This ad seems clearly guilty of exaggeration (see Jamieson 1992). But Bush's advisors argued they could defend all claims made in the ad and they did check and double check the accuracy of all claims (Runkel 1989). Moreover, the overall message of the ad seems defensible: Bush was a bigger proponent of military spending than Dukakis.

As before, the actual substance of the claims made here in no way break new ground. The Democrats have often been criticized for being weak on defense. Ford attacked Carter on this front, with over 10% of all his attacks on this general subject. In one of Nixon's ads, McGovern, the audience was told, "would cut the Marines by one third, the Air Force by one third. He'd cut Navy personnel by one fourth. He would cut interceptor planes by one half, the Navy fleet by one half, and carriers from sixteen to six."[30] Such claims misrepresented the changes McGovern envisioned for the military, just as George Bush's claims did sixteen years later. McGovern planned to cut the military, but he was not going to wipe out half of our naval forces. The Democrats are hardly innocent on this front either. Mondale accused Reagan of supporting "killer weapons" (the so called star wars) in one spot. In another commercial, Mondale warned that Reagan's foreign policy had put the "whole world at stake." These spots make the Tank ad look commonplace, not unique.

The novel aspect of this ad was that the Republicans made use of footage that the Democrats had hoped would show Dukakis to be strong on defense. The appearance at the tank factory in Detroit had just the opposite effect. This adds to the frustration among Democrats and their supporters, but it is not reason to argue that the ad crossed this so-called line.

The Handler Ads

The Packaging of the President or Handler ads launched by the Dukakis campaign broke new ground as they portrayed Bush as a mere product of his advisors without views of his own. I do not know of any ad prior to 1988 that discussed the role of political advisors. For political junkies, these ads are fun and interesting. But hard hitting? Crossing the line? Probably not. The reason is that the negative messages are subtle and implicit. The themes are not harsh and do not seek to strike fear into the hearts of voters. Here is one of the transcripts:

> *First man:* We've got a disaster on our hands. After all that rehearsal I thought we had Quayle totally programmed.
> *Second man:* Not totally. Suddenly the words "President Quayle" even make me nervous.
> *First man:* Bentsen looked great. You know, what if it's too crazy.
> *Second man:* What is it?
> *First man:* Is it too late to drop him—and bring in Bob Dole?
> *Second man:* Yeah, Dole, yeah. You're right. It's too crazy.
> *Third man:* It's not that crazy. [Picks up phone] Rosemary?
> *Announcer:* They'd like to sell you a package. Wouldn't you rather choose a president?

Quayle's performance in the debate was hardly stellar and these ads clearly reference that widely shared perception. But except for mentioning that the idea of "President Quayle" might make people "nervous," there are few frontal assaults. In another commercial, the Dukakis campaign suggests that Bush has no real response to the environmental issue and so Bush's handlers plan to have him stand on "a beautiful beach" and "say he loves the environment." Again, the thrust of this spot is far different than the harsh tones and ominous imagery of the Boston Harbor ad. These spots used a stiletto; the Bush ads wielded an axe. One Democratic consultant in fact worried at the time that they might be "too subtle."[31]

These ads crossed into new territory by interjecting political advisors into the debate, but are they out of bounds? Unfair? The Republicans did not complain. Roger Ailes, for example, loved them, hoping the Democrats would pour money into them (Grove 1988). He felt this approach would not work and actually confuse voters. He was, in short, not yelling foul, as Dukakis did with some of Bush's ads. These ads drew commentary by the news media, but not on the grounds they had crossed the line.

Discussion

The negative ads just discussed do not appear to be so nasty as to forge a sudden and sizable interest in attack advertising. None of the four ads were excessively personal. Many of them are hard hitting. Did they cross the line? Most observers at the time certainly thought so. Yet that assessment seems to be an overreaction. Many will disagree with this conclusion. But let me note that this judgment rests in large part on putting the 1988 in the larger historical context. When we consider ads from elections prior to 1988, it becomes even clearer that this election was not unprecedented. I mentioned a few examples above, but even more telling is the advertising campaign of Lyndon Johnson in 1964. We have already talked about the Daisy spot from that contest. Raising the issue of nuclear war by using the innocence of a young girl seems pretty hard hitting. Of course, Goldwater's name was not mentioned in the ad. However, the Daisy spot was just one of many negative ads from that contest. Recall that Johnson's campaign was the most negative during the period from 1960 to 1988 (see figure 6.4).

The Daisy spot was not the only ad in 1964 to make use of a child. Consider the Ice Cream ad:

> Do you know what people used to do? They used to explode atomic bombs in the air. Now children should have lots of vitamin A and calcium, but they shouldn't have any strontium 90 or cesium 133. These things come from atomic bombs and they are radioactive. They can make you die. Do you know what people finally did? They got together and signed a nuclear test ban treaty. And then the radioactive poison started to go away. But now there's a man who wants to be president of the United States, and he doesn't like this treaty. He fought against it. He even voted against it. He wants to go on test-ing more bombs. His name is Barry Goldwater and if he is elected they might start testing all over again.

The visual of the ad is a young girl eating an ice cream cone. She is innocent and enjoying the cone without a care in the world. A female narrator then informs the audience that atomic bombs contain radioactive material that makes people "die." The implication is that the ice cream might well become lethal if Goldwater wins the election. Such a claim seems hard hitting by any standard. Does it cross the line? Well, Goldwater certainly thought so, but the senator did, as the ad points out, oppose the test ban treaty.

The theme of nuclear war and its implications continues to be important to the Johnson campaign. Following a nuclear explosion that engulfs the screen, an announcer states in another Johnson spot: "On October 24th, 1963, Barry Goldwater said of the nuclear bomb, 'Merely another weapon.' Merely another weapon? Vote for President Johnson. The stakes are too high for you to stay home." Like the 1988 ads, the words here are not particularly harsh. No strong claims are being made. But tough questions were being asked. The controversial part of the spot is the nuclear explosion that opens this spot. Yet Goldwater had made the statement that atomic bombs were merely another weapon. So does this spot cross the line?

A final example from 1964 involves the Confessions of a Republican spot. This spot has a person who begins by noting "I voted for Dwight Eisenhower the first time I ever voted; I voted for Nixon the last time." But with that context established, this individual offers a long series of comments about Goldwater and Johnson. Early on he states that Goldwater "scares" him. He mentions later that "so many men with strange ideas are working for Goldwater," instilling fear about Goldwater's nonmainstream views. Near the end of the spot, this person states, "when the head of the Ku Klux Klan, when all these weird groups come out in favor of the candidate of my party—either they're not Republicans or I'm not." This so-called confession contains a mix of different statements and some of them are quite hard hitting—more so than many of the Bush spots from 1988.

The point of this discussion is to argue that it is not enough to say that the ads from 1988 crossed the line. It is clear that lots of people found the ads and the whole campaign unacceptable. This general point seems sound. But this discussion has shown that the ads were not wildly inappropriate, nor entirely new. If all it took was tough negative ads to prompt a surge in attention to the topic of negativity, this surely would have happened prior to 1988. Yet as we saw earlier, it was 1988 that prompted reactions from various elites that recast the political landscape. It is not, therefore, enough to say these ads were out of bounds or unfair. Such ads were surely a *necessary* condition, but not a *sufficient* one. Something else must be part of this story. As I shall argue below, that something is the change in how journalists cover presidential elections.

The Patterson Hypothesis

The next hypothesis springs from Thomas Patterson's highly influential *Out of Order*. Patterson argues that journalists changed how they covered campaigns moving from a policy oriented focus to an interest in covering elections as a series of strategic moves, or games (1993, 82). That is, journalists have moved away from description toward interpretation. In 1960, according to his content analysis of the *New York Times*, over 90% of stories were descriptive, meaning that they talk about what happened in the campaign. Over the next thirty years, journalists started to write more and more stories that interpreted why the campaign was moving in one direction or another. These interpretive stories became increasingly more frequent. By 1976, they constituted a majority of the coverage. Patterson (1993, 74) reports a similar pattern in regards to the share of stories the focused on the "game" or "policy" implications. In the 1960s, it was about a fifty-fifty split between the two forms of coverage. By the 1980s, the game aspect of the elections dominated policy coverage by a four to one ratio.

This interest in interpreting the game of politics, whether poll standings, battleground states, where candidates visit, who won the debates are part and parcel of campaigns today. Journalists want to talk about the conflict, the disagreements, where to go to gets votes. Patterson writes:

> For reporters, controversy is the real issue of campaign politics. The press deals with charges and counter charges, rarely digging into the details of the candidates' positions. It is not simply that the press neglects issues in favor of the strategic game; issues, even when covered, are subordinated to the drama of the conflict generated between the opposing sides. (1993, 137)

This framework makes interest in negativity a natural. Attack politics symbolize the battle, the game, and the struggle for votes. A candidate goes on the attack to weaken the opposition, to lessen their support. Given the journalists are often drawn to strategy, as Patterson reminds us, attacks become a topic of obvious interest to journalists.

This potential for a surge of interest in negativity existed by 1980, given Patterson's data and argument. There were, of course, attack ads and negativity in both 1980 and 1984, yet little attention paid to it by the news media or other elites. In fact, it was positive ads that drew commentary in 1984—the famous Morning in America commercials by Reagan. These stirring ads remain the standard today, using beautiful photography and a compelling narrative to argue that "our country is prouder and stronger and better."[32] The Bush-Dukakis battle, by contrast, had memorable negative ads that sparked controversy from the key players. The attacks drew counterattacks and played to the game orientation of the news media. Both sides complained about the tactics, further fueling the interest in the subject. As Roger Ailes stated, "we got all the publicity with the negative, but we ran more positive than negative" (Runkel 1989, 155).

There had been other contests with harsh exchanges—such as 1964. Reporters paid little attention, however, to the subject. The Daisy spot drew some commentary, but it paled by comparison with what we witnessed in 1988. In searching the *New York Times* historical index, I could only locate two stories that talked about the Daisy spot and just nine stories about television advertising at all. And as Patterson would predict, most of these stories were descriptive accounts of expenditures or other aspects of the campaign. The stories did *not* evaluate the merits of the advertisements or how the spots played to the strategic aspects of the election.

My argument, in short, is that this surge in interest was the product—the interaction, if you like—of both the nature and content of the 1988 ads and the way the news media began covering presidential campaigns by the 1980s. Both ingredients needed to be present for this surge in interest to take place. The 1988 campaign was nasty. It was negative. But this was not new. What was new was the lens thorough which journalists and other political observers viewed these heated exchanges. The implications for how we think about negative advertising, in particular, and attack politics, in general, are substantial and will draw comment in the next and final section.

IMPLICATIONS AND CONCLUSION

Negative advertising on television has been part of presidential campaigns since 1952. Yet if one paid attention to the news media and other elites, negative advertising was perceived as something new as of 1988. The interest in negativity soared, far beyond what in fact was unfolding in the campaign. All this coverage left an impression that these ads were far more negative than anything we had seen before. Candidates, we were told, were rolling around in the mud, bickering, clawing, and fighting in a nasty and unproductive air war. This impression is misleading, however. The advertising in 1988, despite all the claims, did not usher in a new era of American politics. It was the news media's coverage that brought about a new era. And this change is important to our understanding of campaigns, in general, and our understanding of political advertising, in particular.

Journalists were committing the same sin they were accusing the candidates of: they were exaggerating. This form of exaggeration is potentially troubling. The public, for example, is left with the belief that presidential campaigns are dominated by negative ads; that candidates only want to attack and mislead. Yes, attacks have been on the increase, but they are still not at the rate suggested by the news media. Consider the fact that the CBS News during the 2000 campaign discussed *only* the attack ads of the two major party candidates (West 2001). Yet most of Bush and Gore's ads were positive ads—not attack ads. The positive ads received little or no air time. Such overreporting of negativity generates misperceptions about campaigns and candidates. It also creates a feeding frenzy that does not help the press report reasonably what is unfolding in the campaign.

This attention to negative ads and negativity by reporters shows little sign of waning. We saw the latest manifestation of this infatuation with the Swift Boat ads in 2004. In a Lexis-Nexis search, I found 845 articles about "swift boats" from July 1, 2004 to November 1, 2004.[33] This is an amazing amount of coverage, underscoring the news media's continuing interest in attack advertising. Consider the following passage from a story in the *Washington Post* on August 20, 2004:

> Swift Boat Veterans for Truth, which is funded in large part by Bob Perry, a Texas Republican, has knocked the Democratic nominee's campaign off stride with a small but effective advertising buy in the battleground states of Ohio, West Virginia and Wisconsin. The group spent about $500,000 on the ad, but its allegations that Kerry exaggerated his combat record to win medals have been on the Internet, the 24-hour cable channels and, most recently, the nation's major television networks and newspapers.[34]

The messages from this controversial spot reached the public not through ad buys, but through the megaphone of the news media. The following data reinforce this basic point. From August 1, 1984 to November 1, 1984, there were 9 stories in major newspapers that made reference to "negative advertising."[35] In 2004, there were 114 stories using the same criteria in a Lexis-Nexis search. This represents a more than twelvefold increase in attention to the subject by journalists. Yet 2004 was less than twice as negative as 1984. The attention paid to this subject has jumped dramatically and this shift can be tied to the 1988 election. Patterson (1993) and others warn about this excessive interest in the conflicts in politics. In light of these shifts in election coverage, Alex Castellanos's statement that "the most negative force in politics today is the news media" rings true.

It is also important to realize that the negativity of campaigns, broadly, defined involves far more than just negative advertising. Yet it is the candidates who are usually blamed for the negativity. So did the ads from 1988 drag the truth into the gutter?—the answer is no.

The 1988 campaign may have been in the gutter, but it was not attributable to the content of political ads. Many of the ads were hard hitting and Dukakis and others complained, as candidates often do. But it was the news media that interpreted these exchanges in such a way as to make us all think that we had entered a new era of nasty politics.

I want, however, to press further, because the problem extends beyond just excessive attention to negativity. Journalists and other observers need to realize the important differences between negative and positive spots that undermine their efforts to evaluate the content of political advertising. Specifically, negative commercials tend to use evidence more than positive ads (recall figure 3.1). Because attack ads use more evidence, they are, ironically, open to more criticism from the news media for being misleading than positive ads. Positive ads tend to contain more general references that are harder to take issue with. So, was it misleading for Bush in 2004 to claim he wanted to create more jobs? No, it was surely true. But when Kerry attacked Bush on the loss of jobs, he found the piece of data that made the strongest case against Bush. Is that misleading to stress the "fact" that makes Bush look the worst? Perhaps, but it depends on how you interpret that fact. Some may view it as misleading, while others will not be bothered by such claims. The end result is that negative ads will be viewed by political observers to be more misleading than positive ads *because* the former makes more use of evidence than the latter.

I have some data that highlight this problem. In 2004, FactCheck.org assessed the accuracy of the ads aired during the election. This organization was sponsored by the Annenberg Public Policy Center of the University of Pennsylvania. If you compare their assessments of the positive and negative ads aired by Bush and Kerry, the patterns are pretty clear. Of the negative ads, only 88% of the fact checks made reference to the ad being misleading, an exaggeration, deceptive, and so on.[36] Among positive ads, 58% had such references—a thirty-percentage point drop from the negative commercials. Now, of course, one could argue that the negative ads were more misleading. But that interpretation misses the whole point. Negative ads are more often labeled as misleading because they used more evidence, opening themselves up to this charge. It is this basic point that often escapes those who have sought to evaluate these spots. This argument becomes clearer when we consider the other side of this coin. FactCheck.org, when evaluating commercials, talked about claims that were "matters of opinion," such as a Bush ad stating the Kerry would "weaken" the Patriot Act. This is a vague claim that might be true and was treated by FactCheck.org as a "matter of opinion." Only 13% of the fact checks on negative ads mentioned that the spot contained a reference to a matter of opinion. For positive ads, the proportion soars to 58%. This gap underscores that positive commercials are vague and contain less evidence than negative ads.

It is important to realize that there is no such thing as *the* truth. Yet because observers often make that assumption, they will penalize negative ads for using evidence that best bolsters their argument. This is a serious problem. In a sense, campaigns offer two sets of truth. In 2004, both Kerry and Bush were both putting their best spin on the available data.

One side marshaled evidence that the economy was slipping, the other that it was surging. Both sought to support their claims. These truths clashed, with the public serving as the final arbiter of which side made the best case. Journalists need, in short, to understand more about the content of advertising and the realities of propaganda. Once they do, the news media will be much better able to interpret elections and assess the merits of the messages candidates send during the campaign. Until that point, they will continue to exaggerate what transpires "between combatants fighting under hostile banners."

CHAPTER SEVEN

Negativity, Democracy, and the Political System

The arguments and evidence presented in this book offer a unique perspective on negativity. Rather than concluding that negativity undermines the quality of debate in presidential campaigns, which is the conventional wisdom, I have demonstrated the opposite—attack advertising can *enrich* the information environment available to citizens. If we want voters to have access to more discussion about important issues presented with specificity and evidence to support candidates' appeals, then negative information has clear advantages over positive information. Scholars have long argued that campaigns would be better able to perform their democratic functions if voters had access to such information (see Kelley 1960; Thompson 1970). Political observers have largely assumed that positive advertisements, which tended to make the public feel good, were more likely to achieve these ideals. This book turns such conclusions on their head.

There are, as I have argued, real and substantial democratic payoffs to negativity. This is a strong conclusion that surely will not go unchallenged. To put it in terms familiar to this book, these claims will face their own kind of negativity. Because I believe this general line of argument is important, this concluding chapter seeks to extend it further. Over the last six chapters I have dissected and assessed negative appeals in presidential advertising. My task now is to step back and discuss negativity in more general terms. My effort to speak to broader issues will be pursued on four fronts.

First, I will consider the rise of negativity in light of other important trends in American politics, such as declining voter turnout, lower faith in elections, and shrinking trust in government. Second, I will offer an explanation for the rise of negativity. The third task will be to discuss negativity's relationship to democracy and accountability. Finally, I will conclude with a discussion about civility and negativity.

NEGATIVITY'S IMPACT ON THE ELECTORAL SYSTEM

Observers worry that negativity in campaigns undermines the public's faith in the political process. Richard Fenno (1996, 75), a keen observer of politicians and the political process, worries that "negative campaign advertising can distort" the representation links between politicians and the public. Thomas Hollihan (2001, 224) also expresses concern, noting that "the public responds to negative campaigning by becoming more cynical about politicians and political institutions." Richard Gephardt agrees, worrying that the electoral process is being destroyed "with negative advertising, which is giving everybody cynical attitudes about politics."[1]

There is little doubt from survey data that the public does not like negativity and views it as one of the major problems facing our electoral system (see Brooks 2000a; Freedman and Lawton 1999). Disagreements, as reflected in negative advertising, make voters feel uncomfortable and may well lead them to lessen their support of the broader electoral system (see Hibbing and Theiss-Morse 1995, 2002). The battling, fights, and disagreements between candidates during campaigns could lead voters to lose faith in elections and have less trust in government overall. On the surface, one can easily imagine that after hearing time and time again that a candidate will free criminals to roam the streets or pursue policies that will wreck our children's future, that the public might become less committed to the political system. If that happened, it would dramatically undermine the evidence and arguments I have marshaled in this book.

Of course, as someone who sees merit in negativity, I would posit that there is not a causal connection between the rise of negativity and the decline in trust and turnout we have witnessed over the last forty-five years. Even so, I understand the logic of those who fear the adverse effects of attack politics. Not only does the public not like fights, but the rate of negativity has been increasing (recall figure 2.1). Perhaps the amount of negativity in campaigns is excessive. I have yet to test explicitly for such an effect. If true, such attacks could have a corrosive effect on the political system. However in the broader sweep of history this amount of political attack is not unprecedented. Recall that my small sample of newspaper ads from 1916 to 1956 suggests that negativity has remained about the same—attacks constitute one-third of the appeals presidential candidates make to the public. Even when one looks back further, the exchanges of today seem modest by comparison. Sapiro (1999, 12–13) reminds us that politics in the first half of the nineteenth century was "fractious, noisy, rude, often physically dangerous." No historian paints a picture of that period as anything but highly negative, especially by today's standards (McGerr 1987; Silbey 1999; Altschuler and Blumin 2000). Recall, Riker's (1996) compelling data about the negativity involved in the debate over the Constitution—about 90% of the claims by the Anti-Federalists were attacks on the new rules for government. Such a rate makes the 2004 presidential campaign look quite tame.

While negativity is unlikely to have corrosive effects on the political system, I do *not* hypothesize that negativity strengthens the public's ties to the electoral process. The public's dislike of negative advertising gives one little reason to believe such an effect could take hold. It seems to me that broader, structural forces are far more likely to be driving these trends. Negative ads influence the public, but they are not so powerful as to help reshape the political landscape. The work by Holbrook (1996) and Finkel (1993) show that presidential campaigns influence voters, but structural features such as the economy, peace, and partisan balance are more important (see also Zaller, 2004). In the end, this is an empirical matter that requires evidence to render an informed judgment.

With that in mind, I will focus on three of the most visible trends involving the public's attitude toward the electoral process that might plausibly be tied to increasing negativity. The first is the public's "faith in elections." This attitude seems especially appropriate because it captures whether the public views elections as promoting democratic ends. The second trend involves the public's "trust in government." A key ingredient to a successful democracy involves the electorate's confidence in government. It is well known that this trust has waned over the last forty years (e.g., Hetherington 1998; 2004), making this trend an obvious area of inquiry. Finally, I will examine turnout in presidential elections. There has been a great deal of work examining the link between participation and negativity (e.g., Ansolabehere and Iyengar 1995; Finkel and Geer 1998; Lau et al. 1999; Clinton and Lapinski 2004). I will take each of these in turn.[2]

Faith in Elections

When estimating the public's "faith" in elections, I rely on the postelection survey question that the National Election Studies (NES) has asked a national sample of citizens since 1964: "How much do you feel that having elections makes government pay attention to what people think—a good deal, some, or not much?" This question taps directly into whether citizens believe elections make government responsive. As Bartels (2002) notes, this question "has the virtue of focusing squarely on the key function assigned to elections in democratic theory: ensuring the responsiveness of public officials to the preferences of ordinary citizens." Observers often comment that negativity undermines the process because voters see candidates tearing each other down rather than advancing their own plans for government.

Bartels has developed a revised measure of "faith in elections" that better captures trends over time.[3] As one might guess, there has been a decline between 1964 and 1996 (see Bartels 2002). About 81% of the public felt that elections made government responsive to their wishes. It had dipped about fifteen percentage points by 1988 and has rebounded slightly since then, standing at about 73% in 1996. Note that these data are from 1964 to 1996, since there is no revised estimate available for 2000.[4]

At this point, we have two trends that are working in the directions feared by the critics of negativity—increasing rates of attacks and lower levels of faith in elections. However as figure 7.1 shows, there is no relationship between the two trends. With only nine data points, one has to be cautious in drawing any firm conclusions from these results. Even so, the near random pattern offers little comfort to those who worry that increased negativity undermines the public's belief that elections generate responsiveness to their views. The data are highly aggregated, so it is quite possible there are significant individual level effects. But the focus here is whether there has been an adverse effect of negativity on the

Figure 7.1. Negativity and Faith in Elections, 1964–96

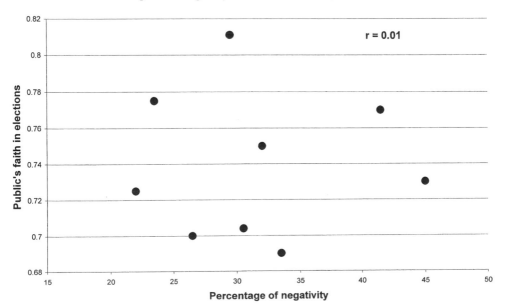

electorate's evaluation of the electoral system. This snapshot suggests that there is no connection.

Trust in Government

Political theorists view trust as an important component of democracy. Yet the public might lose faith in government when they hear more and more about the mistakes the other side has made and how their policies will lead to disaster. If the public tends to learn about the problems rather than the successes, such information might well weaken its trust in government. Certainly, the work of Hibbing and Theiss-Morse (1995, 2002) would predict such a causal connection.

Marc Hetherington (2004) and others have studied this trend and it is clear—the public has less faith in the government's ability to handle problems. There has been a steady decline in political trust between 1964, the first year we have good measures of it, and 2004 (see Hetherington 2004).[5] While the details of the measure are available in his book, I will provide a brief overview. Political trust, according to Hetherington, is the "degree to which people expect government will produce outcomes consistent with their expectations" (2004, 9). The measure employs a 0 to 1 scale built from the four key questions asked in the NES post election survey:

> Trust: How much of the time do you think you can trust the government in Washington to do what is right—just about always, most of the time, or only some of the time?
>
> Waste: Do you think that people in government waste a lot of the money we pay in taxes, waste some of it, or don't waste very much of it?
>
> Interest: Would you say the government is pretty much run by a few big interests looking out for themselves or that it is run for the benefit of all the people?
>
> Crooked: Do you think that quite a few of the people running the government are crooked, not very many are, or do you think hardly any of them are crooked?

Figure 7.2 provides a visual display of the relationship between negativity and Hetherington's measure of political trust.[6] As one can see, there is not a strong link. Even so, a modest statistical connection exists (the simple correlation is −0.24), hinting that perhaps more negativity does yield slightly lower levels of trust. In an upcoming section, I will explore this statistical relationship more systematically, providing explicit estimates of the impact of negativity on trust. For the time being, figure 7.2 does not give much reason to fear a substantial link between these two forces.

Figure 7.2. Negativity and Trust, 1964–2004

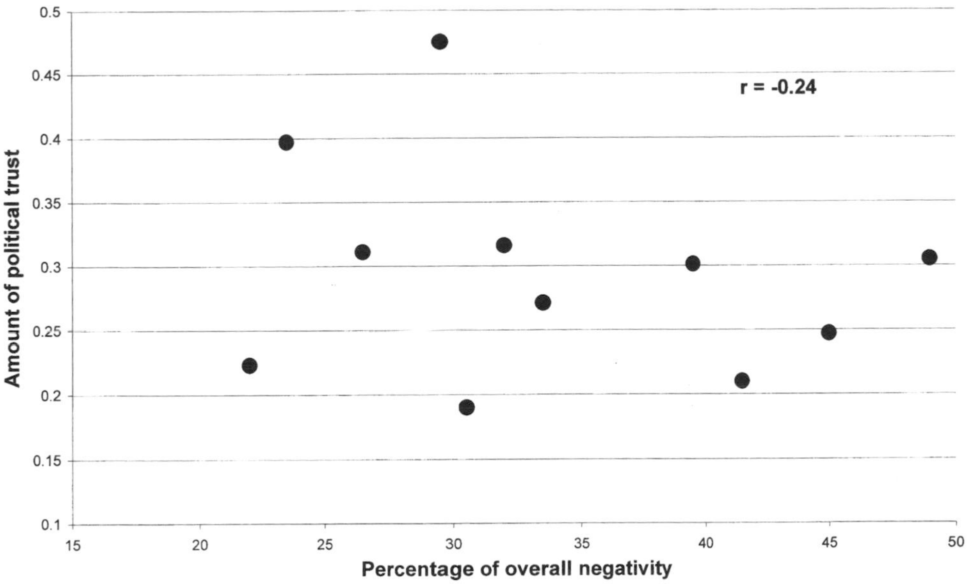

Turnout in Presidential Elections

Turnout is perhaps the most widely talked about measure of the health of our political system. A great deal of research has been undertaken to explain the decline in turnout (e.g., Brody 1978; Miller 1992; Teixiera 1992; Patterson 2002). The most recent twist in this debate has been presented by McDonald and Popkin (2001). They argue, in effect, that the cause of the decline in turnout (at least since 1972) lies in the denominator. That is, we have been overestimating the number of eligible voters (due to increasing numbers of illegal immigrants, growing prison population, etc.), which has artificially deflated turnout rates. Figure 7.3 compares the commonly used Voting Age Population (VAP) with the McDonald-Popkin (2001) Voting Eligible Population (VEP).[7] The VAP measure reports a general decline in turnout, at about one percentage point per election.[8] The VEP tells a different tale. The decline is far more modest—just one half a percentage point per election over the last forty-four years.[9] Even more to the point, VEP turnout has been *flat* since 1972.

As noted earlier, there has been over the last decade a serious and engaging debate concerning the so-called demobilization hypothesis. The idea, which was developed most convincingly by Ansolabehere and Iyengar (1995), is that negative advertising alienates voters and leads to

Figure 7.3. Rate of Turnout in Presidential Elections, 1960–2004

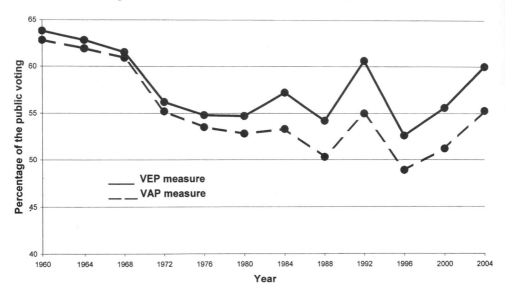

less participation (see also Ansolabehere et al. 1994 and Ansolabehere, Iyengar, and Simon 1999). These scholars argue that this relationship is strong enough to be a real concern to democratic government and perhaps significant enough to consider reforms that would lessen the amount of attack advertising in campaigns.

Ansolabehere and Iyengar's work sparked much interest in the scholarly community (see Lau and Pomper [2004] for a review). The emerging consensus of this second wave of research is that negativity does *not* lower turnout (Lau et al. 1999; Lau and Pomper 2004; Clinton and Lapinski 2004). We may be able to find such effects in some cases and under some conditions, but, in general, there is no clear connection between turnout and negativity in political campaigns. The reason is that while attacks turn off some voters, they engage others. As Finkel and Geer (1998, 577) point out, negativity could "augment turnout by arousing the voter's enthusiasm for his or her preferred candidates or by increasing the degree to which a voter cares about the outcome of the election." In addition, people like a good fight and negativity is a product of the often fierce competition between the two parties. On the surface, the 2004 presidential election confirms these counterhypotheses. As noted earlier, 2004 was the most negative election in recent memory, yet turnout increased dramatically from 2000.

As a first cut, figure 7.4 appears to offer some support to the demobilization hypothesis. Using the VAP measure, more negativity seems to depress turnout a bit. Yet this potential relationship weakens further

Figure 7.4. Negativity and Turnout, 1960–2004

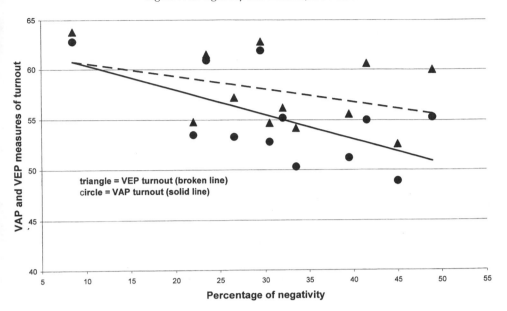

when looking at the revised VEP measure. In fact, if one adopts the McDonald-Popkin estimate, the whole debate loses steam, since, as noted earlier, turnout has not been declining over the last thirty years.[10] Yet it is during this time when we have seen the biggest increase in negativity. I do not want to claim that the McDonald-Popkin measure is superior. That would be a bit too self-serving. Instead, I recommend interpreting these various results against the backdrop of the vast array of recent work that calls into question the demobilization hypothesis of Ansolahebere et al. (see Lau and Pomper 2004). In fact, Brooks (2000b, 2004) calls into question some of the original results presented by Ansolabehere and Iyengar (1995). She uses their original aggregate level data and finds, once correcting for some errors, that turnout does not decrease with greater levels of negativity.

But even so, the bivariate relationships presented in figure 7.4 warrant more investigation. In what follows, I will take a more systematic look at the possible impact that negativity has on turnout and the two previous trends that I just examined.

A More Systematic Look

Table 7.1 presents an array of coefficients. There are two things I must mention before discussing what they mean. First, I have expanded my empirical

Table 7.1. Impact of Negativity on Trust, Faith, and Turnout

	Political Trust	Faith in Elections	VAP[1]	VEP[2]
Overall Negativity	0.000*	0.001	−0.009*	0.006*
	(0.002)	(0.002)	(0.14)	(0.13)
Issue Negativity	0.001	0.001	−0.22	−0.18
	(0.003)	(0.002)	(0.14)	(0.15)
Trait Negativity	−0.006	0.003	0.17	0.16
	(0.004)	(0.003)	(0.31)	(0.34)

Notes: These estimates all come from a simple multivariate model that seeks to explain the dependent variable (the top row of the table) by a measure of issue, trait, or overall negativity and a lagged dependent variable. The text explains the reasons for this choice.

* These three estimates include data from 2004. Estimates in parentheses are the standard errors for these coefficients.

[1] VAP uses the usual estimate of the voting age population to estimate the rate of turnout in presidential elections.

[2] VEP uses the Popkin-McDonald revised measure of voting age population that corrects for the number of illegal immigrants, prisoners, and other errors in the count.

examination beyond my overall measure of negativity, including separate analyses for trait and issue negativity. It is quite possible that personal attacks (i.e., trait negativity) might have more pernicious effects on the political system. We know that the public is far more bothered by personal attack than issue-based criticism. Hence, it makes sense to pull the overall measure apart and consider differential effects. Second, the regressions I report include a lagged dependent variable as a control, taking account of the autocorrelation that may be present in these time series data.[11]

For starters, in no case is any coefficient of interest close to statistical significance. With so few data points, that is not a big surprise. Even if one ignores the standard errors, the coefficients for trust and faith in elections suggest a modest *positive* relationship in four of the six estimates—the opposite effect feared by the critics of negativity. In one of the other two estimates, overall negativity has no effect on the public's trust. Only one of the six estimates even yields a negatively signed coefficient. The story for turnout is a bit different in that the coefficients are larger. Yet only one half of the estimates for turnout suggest that negativity might decrease rates of participation. The VAP measure, for example, suggests that a 10% increase in overall negativity would drop turnout by 0.9%. Not only is that a modest effect, the standard error is large enough to keep anyone from placing much faith in it. Moreover, the VEP measure is a coefficient in the opposite direction, although also accompanied by a hefty standard error. It is also worth noting that increased trait negativity actually yields a positive coefficient—the direction is opposite to what we would expect from the fallout usually associated with personal attacks.

Overall, the results in table 7.1 and the accompanying graphs do not suggest that negativity has had strong, adverse effects on the political system.

EXPLAINING THE RISE OF NEGATIVITY

I have spent a great deal of time assessing negativity and developing ways to better understand attack politics in presidential campaigns. I have, however, ignored one question that merits attention, especially as this book comes to a close. Why has negativity been on the rise in presidential elections? In what follows, I will sketch out an answer to this question—an answer that is quite consistent with the core argument of this book. Attacks reflect real political disagreements—candidates do not fabricate their criticisms—and we simply have more political disagreements between the two major parties now than we did thirty years ago. That change has helped to generate the increased rate of negativity we have witnessed in presidential advertising.

A first step in seeking an explanation to this increase in negativity is to recall that it is *not* tied to more personal attacks, but attributable to greater criticisms over issues. This point was already made in chapter 5 (figure 5.1). The rate of personal attacks is basically flat over the entire period, where as for issues it follows the same upward trend as my overall measure. The rate of overall negativity increased on average 2.5% each election between 1960 and 2000.[12] The rate of issue negativity grew 2.2% each election over those forty years. By contrast, the amount of trait negativity increased just 0.6% each election.[13]

These contrasting patterns are quite important, since it suggests that the rise of negativity is tied to the business of governing. It is not about undermining people's character. Personal attacks take place but they are not on the rise in any significant way. The fact that candidates are attacking each other more on issues shapes the kind of explanation we should pursue. The rise of negativity is not likely to be found in an explanation tied to a greater willingness by candidates to make personal attacks. Prior to examining the trends in the last graph, such an explanation would have been quite plausible. There have been a host of critics of news media, arguing that journalists have been overly concerned with personal scandal of visible political figures (Sabato 2000; Fallows 1997; Kalb 2001). It would make sense that this personalization of politics would have worked its way into presidential advertising, but the data simply do not support the hypothesis.

There are, of course, other hypotheses that could easily explain this rise. For example, political consultants may have become more skilled at creating effective attack ads and that might account for the rise. While this is possible, negativity has always been part of politics. I mentioned earlier that the rate of negativity in newspapers from 1916 to 1956 mirrors what I found in TV ads from 1960 to 2000. Recall the Truman campaign in 1948 and its harsh attacks on the Republican party. Perhaps it took time for candidates to understand TV as a new mode of communication, making them hesitant to go on the attack for fear of a backlash. As political operatives learned how to master TV, they became more comfortable with attack advertising. Yet it appears that 1956 had quite a few negative ads. Jamieson (1996) reports a sizable number of attack ads in this contest. West (2001), in examining Jamieson's commentary on that contest, estimates that 1956 had about the same rate of negativity as 1972 or 1976. And, of course, the 1964 election serious poses problems for this thesis. The LBJ campaign was among the most negative in the forty years under study. Campaign consultants seemed to understand the value of attack advertising even when TV was still a relatively new medium.

A better and more systematic test of whether attack advertising is on the rise due to changes in the norms of consultants or the belief that attacks simply work better than positive spots would involve examining data from other elections that map changes in share of negativity over time. There are some data on Senate campaigns, but they are either sporadic (Kern 1989; Joslyn 1980) or simply do not cover enough elections for my purposes (e.g., Kahn and Kenney 1999; Lau and Pomper 2004). There are only a handful of systematic studies about House or gubernatorial elections, which limits opportunities for scholars to examine the frequency of attack over time in these contests. Fortunately, I do have one time series from 1980 to 2000 that cover ads aired during presidential primaries.[14]

Figure 7.5 reports the average share of negativity in each of these six election years.[15] There is *no* increase in negativity in nomination battles over these twenty years. It is that same period of time where we witness a sizable increase in attacks during the general elections. These data, although limited, cast doubt on the general claim that negativity is on the rise in all elections, which we would expect in light of the previous hypothesis.

What structural features of American politics might account for this rise in negativity? To put it another way, what might explain the increasing rate of criticism between presidential candidates? One hypothesis involves the polarization of the parties over the recent past (Bond and Fleisher 2000; Stonecash, Brewer, and Mariani 2002; Layman and Carsey 2002; Poole and Rosenthal 1996). Polarization means, among other things, a growing gap between the parties' views on issues and, therefore, more reasons to attack the other side. Polarization offers a

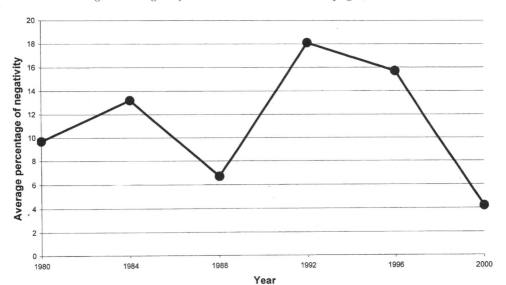

Figure 7.5. Negativity in Presidential Nomination Campaigns, 1980–2000

theoretically compelling explanation for the rise of negativity. If the parties are close together on the issues, there are fewer disagreements and less incentive to attack. The reasoning is at least twofold. First, parties off the median position are more open to criticism from each other. To criticize any action of the other side, there needs to be some difference in opinion. As the gap between the parties grows, so do the differences and, therefore, so do the opportunities for attack. Second, disagreements are more likely to be heated, because losing the election has more policy consequences in a polarized system than a nonpolarized one. If parties are battling over the "median" position, the loser will not see a big change in governmental policy. Each side wants to win, but the policy consequences simply are not as great. In short, the stakes of the election should increase along with polarization, providing more incentive to attack. Or as John McCann observed prior to the start of the 2004 campaign, this election will probably be "the nastiest we've ever seen from both side because of the polarization that exists in politics today."[16]

It is possible to draw the causal arrow in the other direction. Ansolabehere and Iyengar (1995, 113) make exactly that case, contending that "negative advertising is . . . fueling the polarization of American politics." They argue that negativity is driving the independent voter from the polls, generating a more partisan and hence more polarized electorate. That increasingly divided electorate, in turn, is giving rise to the polarization between the parties. While an interesting argument, there are at least three problems with it. First, they are assuming a model of party change that relies on a bottom up approach. That is, the changes in the electorate drive changes in the parties. That model is not widely supported in political science. Scholars, such as Carmines and Stimson (1989) or Aldrich (1995), view parties as elite driven, not mass driven. Geoffrey Layman (2001) examines with great care the role of religious attitudes in party politics and shows convincingly that Christian right activists led the process of mass political change. The second problem with this causal connection is that the literature, as noted earlier, shows little support for the demobilization hypothesis, which is so central to their argument. It is no longer credible to argue that negative advertising has this pernicious effect on the voting intentions of the electorate. The third problem is that this causal argument gives tremendous influence to the impact of advertising on the public. Spots do influence the public in many ways, but their impact is not so strong as to reshape the political landscape.

How can I test the hypothesis that increased polarization is giving rise to more and more attack advertising? Clearly, the most visible measure of party polarization comes from the work of Keith Poole and Howard Rosenthal (1996). As Nolan McCarty, Poole, and Rosenthal (2003) observe, this "polarization measure reflects the average difference between the parties on a liberal-conservative scale." This scale relies upon the roll call voting records of members of Congress. Poole and Rosenthal offer a number of different ways to measure polarization, but each indicator correlates very strongly with each other.[17]

I have constructed a graph that illustrates the hypothesized relationship between polarization and negativity. I then present some simple correlations to augment this picture. These data test three interrelated hypotheses. First, greater polarization will yield greater negativity. Second, this relationship should be strongest when only looking at negative issue appeals. If my contention is correct that growing disagreement between the parties on issues is the engine that drives negativity, we should see an even stronger relationship when looking only at issues. The corollary (the third hypothesis) is that this relationship should weaken when examining just trait negativity.

Figure 7.6 provides a simple scatter plot summarizing the relationship between polarization and overall negativity. There is a compelling correspondence, as represented by the tight pattern of data points.[18] It is, frankly, an impressive relationship, especially with so few cases, strongly confirming the first hypothesis. If one pulls apart the overall measure of negativity into a dimension for traits and for issues, I can assess my followup hypotheses that this relationship should be even stronger for issues than for traits. This is an important test, given my underlying argument

Figure 7.6. Polarization and Negativity, 1960–2004

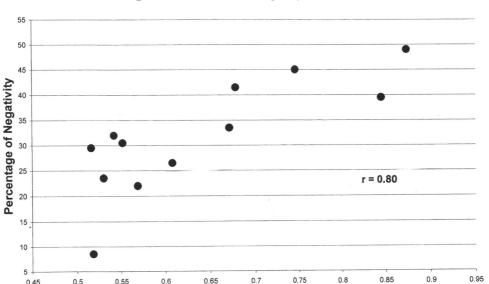

that it is policy differences between the parties that are driving negativity. The results confirm my suspicions. Polarization corresponds more closely with the issue negativity (r = 0.81) than trait negativity (r = 0.31).[19]

Table 7.2 offers a more systematic test of this relationship, since I introduce a lagged dependent variable to control for statistical problems that crop up when correlating two time series variables. The findings reinforce the patterns suggested in the bivariate tests. Polarization is a

Table 7.2. Impact of Party Polarization on Negativity

	Overall negativity 1960–2004	Issue negativity 1960–2000	Trait negativity 1960–2000
Poole's measure of polarization	79.1*	68.9**	10.9
	(20.8)	(27.1)	(13.8)
R^2	0.75	0.67	0.10

Notes: These estimates all come from a simple multivariate model that seeks to explain the dependent variable (the top row of the table) by a measure of polarization and a lagged dependent variable. Estimates in parentheses are the standard errors for these coefficients.

*significant at 0.01

**significant at 0.05

powerful explanation for "overall" and "issue" negativity—even with the lagged measure of negativity on the right-hand side of the equation. If the parties continue to polarize at a rate comparable to 1996–2004, we should see another ten-percentage point jump in overall negativity and about a nine-point rise in issue negativity. There should be, given these estimates, little or no affect on the share of character attacks.

One potential criticism of this analysis is that my focus should not be on *party* polarization, but on the differences between the particular candidates. There are both methodological and theoretical reasons for employing the Poole-Rosenthal measures. First, presidential nominees may like to distance themselves from the party, but they are a product of that party and its platform. There is much talk of "candidate-centered" elections (Wattenberg 1991). The reality, however, is that the Republican nominees tend to be vulnerable to attacks about Social Security while their Democratic counterparts are subject to criticism about their willingness to raise taxes. The nominee is tied to the party and its views.

The second reason why I adopted this measurement strategy is methodological. Most efforts to measure where the candidates stand on the issues are endogenous to the campaign. Candidates will paint themselves as moderate in their quest for votes, making a content analysis of their own statements, such as in their acceptance speeches, questionable indicators of their policy views. It would also suggest that the candidates agree far more on the issues than they really do. By contrast, the Poole-Rosenthal measures I employ come from the Congress prior to the presidential election. Hence, this variable is exogenous to the campaign under study, making it an attractive alternative.

To provide additional faith in this measure's applicability to presidential elections, I sought to examine whether the amount of polarization helps explain the frequency of "ordered" appeals in battles for the White House. Recall from chapter 5 that I developed a way to estimate how often candidates presented issues in a position or valence frame (see Stokes 1963). The hypothesis I am testing here is that as polarization increases we should see a corresponding increase in candidates' use of ordered appeals. The starker differences between candidates on an ideological dimension should help fuel this difference at the presidential level, if the polarization measure works as I suggest.

Figure 7.7 provides a graphical presentation of the data. The results support the hypothesis. There is a clear positive relationship between the two variables (correlation = 0.78). The relationship holds even if you control for the amount of negativity in the campaign. As noted in an earlier chapter, negativity encourages candidates to be more specific in their issue appeals. Hence, one could argue that this simple bivariate relationship is

Figure 7.7. Polarization and Position Appeals, 1960–2000

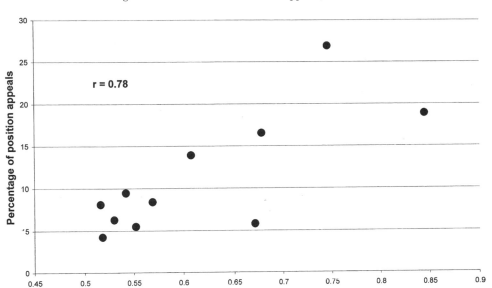

spurious due to the intervening force of rising negativity. However, when controlling for negativity, the core relationship remains strongly positive.[20]

While I find much merit in party polarization measures, I have nonetheless expanded the analysis to include a measure of candidate differences. These measures were created by John Zaller. He created a scale to judge the position of presidential candidates from 1948 to 2000 using a mix of data.[21] This measure has face validity. For example, the three elections with the most polarized set of candidates from 1960 to 2000 were 1964, 1972, and 1984.

Table 7.3 shows the results of these new regressions.[22] The coefficient for the candidate polarization score suggests that if you move from the least polarized candidates (Kennedy-Nixon) to the most polarized (McGovern-Nixon), you will have about 10% more in negativity. If you shift among extremes within the Poole-Rosenthal measure, there is about a twenty-four percentage point rise in negativity. So while both variables influence the amount of negativity, the party polarization measure remains the more powerful force in this process.[23] This difference speaks to my point earlier that it is difficult to get a true measure of the potential for attack from the candidate's own statements. They want to downplay differences, while when on the attack one would want to expand differences.

As I have said previously, the small number of data points urges caution before accepting these empirical claims. The real story, however, lies

Table 7.3. Impact of Party Polarization and Candidate Polarization on Negativity

	Overall negativity[1] 1960–2004	Issue negativity 1960–2000	Trait negativity 1960–2000
Poole's measure of Polarization	65.6*	64.9*	11.6
	(15.1)	(11.9)	(12.5)
Zaller's measure of candidate differences	11.7***	11.5**	1.1
	(6.0)	(4.0)	(4.2)
R^2	0.75	0.82	0.10

[1] I did not include the lag of negativity, since I lose two degrees of freedom—one due to the lag and the other due to the addition of a third variable. With only 12 cases at best, these constraints pose serious problems for the estimation. The coefficients are pretty stable. It is the standard errors that become larger.
Estimates in parentheses are standard errors.
*significant at 0.01
**significant at 0.05
***significant at 0.10

in the theoretical argument. This argument has been implicit or explicit in nearly all facets of this project: negativity reflects real world problems. Candidates are constrained by the context they face. And if candidates, when attacking, go beyond what the evidence will support, the attacks fall flat and are often counterproductive.

So as disagreement between the parties increases, so will attacks. When considered in this light, the rate of negativity Riker (1996) reports in the founding period makes even more sense. The stakes were extremely high and the disagreement fundamental, yielding lots of incentives to attack. The Anti-Federalists were waging a battle to stop a major change in the rules of the game that would move power from the states to the national government. It was more than disagreements about which policy to adopt; it was a disagreement about what institutions should exist to create policy.

If this basic argument is sound, we should also expect negativity to increase during times of realignment when disagreement between parties is at a peak and for it to decline once the party system stabilizes. Unfortunately, I do not have enough data about negativity in campaigns prior to 1960 to test for such possibilities. However, the full time series of the Poole-Rosenthal polarization data provide a better context to judge the potential for attacks in campaigns in the future. While 2003 witnessed a very polarized debate between the parties, the parties were even more polarized in the late 1800s. If you add more disagreements between the parties and between the candidates themselves, the upper limit of negativity is probably about 68% or so.[24]

The polarization of the country continues and shows little sign of ebbing. With the so-called blue and red states and the close partisan split in the electorate, there is little reason to think negativity will decline. Bush, who claimed to be a uniter not a divider, ran a very negative campaign. Over 50% of his spots were attacks on Kerry. He had real differences with Kerry on a number of issues and he made sure the public learned about those differences. Kerry too attacked Bush. He ran fewer negative ads than Bush (31%), turning more heavily to contrast ads (43%).[25] There were a lot of differences and negativity was higher than at any time in the last five decades.

The 2008 presidential election may well break more modern day records. Just imagine the response if Hillary Clinton was the Democratic nominee and with Bill Frist leading the GOP. There would be many reasons to go on the attack. These additional doses of negative advertising would surely provide the pundits something to talk about, but the nation will not be on the verge of collapse. In fact, if one believes the argument I have advanced in these pages, it should be viewed as a sign that the public has had the opportunity to take advantage of an information environment rich with discussion about issues in a clearer fashion backed with more evidence than if candidates only aired positive, feel-good ads.

While I view negativity as part and parcel of the democratic process, I would not want to see negativity to reach its maximum point—all attacks and no positive appeals. Such an outcome strikes me as a problem for government. If a candidate only attacks, any mandate that he or she would receive from an election outcome would be difficult, if not impossible, to infer. Richard Fenno (1996, 265) makes a similar point when he observes that after a negative campaign the "winning candidate will have earned the legal right to represent a constituency, but the constituents are left without a clue as to how [he or she] would go about doing it." Fortunately, we are not even close to such a scenario. And if one views elections as retrospective undertakings where the public renders a decision on the incumbent, an entirely negative campaign by a challenger would still produce an acceptable, although messy, outcome. The next section will talk about negativity's role within retrospective and prospective views of democracy.

DEMOCRACY, ACCOUNTABILITY, AND NEGATIVITY

A central argument of this book has been that negativity advances the cause of democracy by informing the public of important issues and concerns. I want, however, to take a closer look at this basic claim. I do so in part because democracy itself is a broad concept with many meanings to many different people. For my purposes, I will borrow a well-worn and well-developed distinction between retrospective and prospective democracy (see, for example, Key 1966; Fiorina 1980; Przeworski, Stokes, and Manin 1999; Manin 1997; Powell 2000). In a retrospective world, voters hold incumbents accountable for past actions. This mechanism provides a strong incentive for office holders to do a good job, assuming they want to remain in power. Elections are designed to evaluate the performance of the incumbent party. The opposition, under this framework, "must monitor the performance of the government and inform citizens" (Przeworski, Stokes, and Manin 1999, 48). In a prospective world, candidates make proposals about future policy and the public renders a judgment on those competing visions for government. Here, "the focus is not only on the incumbents," according to Powell (2000, 12), "but on the opposition party and the policy alternatives presented by both."

There are attractive features to both views and scholars have argued over the years about their respective merits. There is much appeal, for example, to the idea that elections are about competing parties offering different visions for the future direction of government. The public has a more direct role in shaping the course of policy and candidates need to lay out their plans for the public to judge. The attraction of the retrospective model is that it demands far less of the citizenry (Powell 2000; Riker 1982; Fiorina 1980). The public only needs to know whether the incumbent party has done a good enough job in office to warrant another term. This may not be the ideal form of democracy, but the ability of citizens to punish ineffective leaders provides at least some control in steering the course of government.

Attack politics can advance the prospects of democratic government, but in a limited way. Negativity tends to focus on the past, not the future, since attacks often involve the record of the incumbent (or challenger). Where have they failed? What have they done wrong? The reason for this retrospective focus to negativity is twofold. First, the need for evidence, which I talk about throughout this book, posits that candidates will pour over the *past* actions of the opposition for weaknesses. For example, the out-party looks for evidence to document problems with the in-party's record.[26] In 2004, Kerry took aim at the loss of jobs during George Bush's first term and questioned the growing budget deficit. In 1980, Ronald Reagan attacked Carter on his handling of inflation or inability to deal with the Soviet Union. The second reason for this focus is that candidates tend to be vague about their promises. Their plans for government will be harder to criticize, especially since they are likely to be framed as a valence appeal. Clinton in 1992 promised "to grow the economy." Could President Bush attack that claim? Hardly. In 2004, Senator Kerry talked about improving our education system. Again, Bush did not have much basis to attack Kerry, given how vague these pledges were worded. However, President Bush did criticize various votes Kerry made as a Senator in regards to education, casting the appeal retrospectively. In the same way, Walter Mondale could point to the huge deficits President Reagan oversaw during his first four years in office.

So, when I argue that negativity advances democratic governance, I have a particular form of democracy in mind—one where retrospective assessments lie at the center.

Fortunately, I can do more than speculate about whether negativity promotes retrospective concerns more than prospective one. I coded each ad for whether it was retrospective, prospective, or contained elements of both, allowing me to test my argument.[27] Figure 7.8 presents the results. It is clear: negative ads are much more likely to be retrospective than prospective in nature—three times more likely. The opposite is true for positive ads—38% were prospective and only 17% were retrospective. Interestingly, over two-thirds of contrast ads contain elements of both prospective and retrospective appeals—a finding that nicely confirms my hypothesis.

The data mentioned above examine all ads, but we should see a differential pattern among incumbents and challengers. Challengers should be especially prone to attack using retrospective ads, since they must raise doubts about the incumbents' record. By contrast, incumbents will have incentive to air retrospective *positive* ads—spots that stress their accomplishments in office. For instance, Clinton in 1996 could talk about

Figure 7.8. Distribution of Retrospective and Prospective Ads

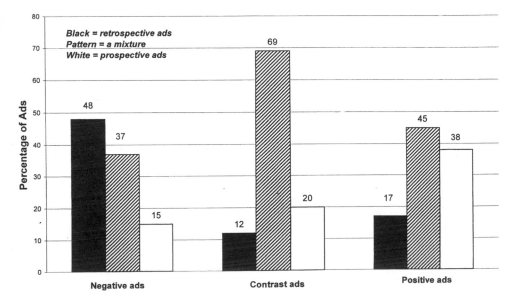

putting 100,000 more police on the streets. Or Nixon in 1972 could stress his efforts to make peace with China and the Soviet Union. The evidence strongly supports these hypotheses as well (see figure 7.9). The challenger's negative ads are five times more likely to be retrospective than prospective. The positive spots of the out-party mirror that image—50% of them are prospective and only 8% are retrospective. For the incumbent party, positive ads are just as likely to be prospective as retrospective. The negative ads of the in-party are still more likely to be retrospective than prospective, but that gap is just twelve percentage points as opposed to the forty-six-point gap among challengers.

These data strongly confirm that attack politics tends to be retrospective in nature, especially for the out-party. For those who want campaigns to be about assessments of what the parties *will* do in office, negativity has far less appeal. Consider David Gergen's comment in 2000 on *The News Hour with Jim Lehrer*: "When negative campaigning becomes the dominating campaign, it wipes out the capacity to talk about the future [and] lowers the quality of discourse in an election."[28] Gergen's criticism has appeal if we accept that assumption that elections should be prospective affairs. Yet there is good reason to want elections to be retrospective undertakings, as noted earlier. The public renders a judgment on whether the current occupant of the Oval Office has done a good job or not. It is a judgment that can be informed and advanced by negative advertising.

Figure 7.9. Challengers' and Incumbents' Retrospective and Prospective Ads

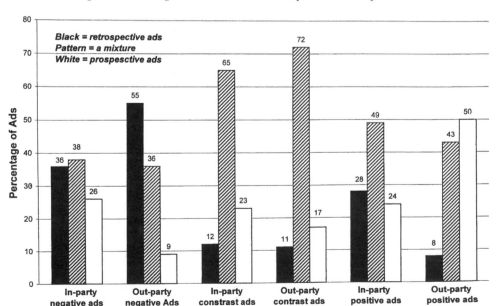

Without such attacks the public will be less aware of the problems with the current administration. One can be sure that, as the data above suggest, the sitting president will also be telling the public about what good they have accomplished. This exchange of information comes close to the kind of system espoused by those who advocate responsible parties (see Epstein 1986; Schattschneider 1942, 1960; Ranney 1962). In short, the potential for negativity to advance democratic government will hinge in large part on how one defines this thorny concept. However, if one thinks of elections as referendums on the past, then negative advertising has much to recommend itself.

CIVILITY AND NEGATIVITY

I have discussed a number of reasons why negative advertising has so many detractors. While I have tried to confront these concerns with evidence, there is an even broader underlying worry about negativity that I have not discussed. That is, negativity breeds incivility and incivility undermines democratic politics (Gutmann and Thompson 1996; Carter 1998). Competing parties in a democracy need to conduct the business of government in a fashion that allows for disagreements to take place within a spirit of mutual respect. There is a fear that if mutual respect fades and incivility intervenes, then the glue of democratic government weakens as both sides let disagreements spin out of control until the whole fabric of society is torn apart.

This focus on civility is partly responsible for the outcry against negativity. There is a fear that excessive attacks will have serious repercussions for democratic government. Stephen Carter (1998, 120), for example, posits a causal connection between negativity and a decline in civility in the U.S. He argues that "when candidates treat each other so badly" during a campaign, "it is folly to suppose that they will readily kiss and make up when the election is over." Attack advertising, in particular, and negativity, in general, makes it hard for both sides to govern together. And in a system that gives the minority a substantial say in the policy-making process, such a development is quite troubling. Carter is not alone in this assessment. Thomas Hollihan (2001) titles his book on modern political campaigns: *Uncivil Wars: Political Campaigns in a Media Age*, worrying about how negativity undermines "the health and vitality of the American political system" (iii).

This assumption of a causal link where negativity breeds incivility is hasty, if not outright wrong. There may well be a correlation between the two, since these forces are both by-products of the growing disagreement between our political parties. That is, the decline in civility, which has been documented in a number of quarters (e.g., Loomis 2000; Sinopoli 1995; Uslaner 1993; Carter 1998; Sapiro 1999; Marks 1996; Pohlman

2003), is a consequence of the polarization of American politics. As noted earlier, the stakes of whether Democrats or Republicans win elections are now higher, since they have increasingly different plans for government. When there were a lot of conservative Democrats and liberal Republicans in government, the parties overlapped more on matters of policy. That is no longer the case. The homogenization of the parties has helped to breed more fighting between the two combatants. The rise in incivility speaks, therefore, to the structural changes in the political system, not the increase of negativity in campaigns.

It is also not clear how serious is the problem of incivility for democratic government. While civility is a norm worthy of attention, it is also a norm that usually lacks a clear or precise definition (see Sinopoli 1995). Although simplistic, my basic view of civility involves respect for the opposition. Bob Dole, as he accepted the Republican nomination for president in 1996, made such a reference when he pointed out that the Democrats were "opponents, not enemies." Oftentimes people associate civility with being polite and of course that is part of this general concept. The key, however, is to realize that it is possible to be civil when criticizing the other side. Civility does not preclude disagreement. It simply prescribes the degree of the attack. During Ronald Reagan's funeral in June 2004, commentators made frequent mention of the fact that he had many disagreements with his political opponents, but he never let it get personal. These journalistic characterizations cast the former president as someone who practiced civility as he governed.

The problem with all this discussion about civility is that politics is about disagreement. As Schattschneider (1960, 2) reminds us, "at the root of all politics is the universal language of conflict." If disagreements widen, the stakes grow. The winners gain more and losers lose more. With increasing stakes and more differences, we should expect harsher conflict. We should expect, in other words, incivility. Shouldn't the tone of our disagreement correspond to the importance of that disagreement? If we disagree deeply on some matter, is it better to try to sweep those disparities under the rug or work them out in the political arena? Should the public not learn about the differences between the parties so they understand the stakes involved? As Lau and Pomper (2004) remind us, "Elections are about choice, not courtesy."

There is another aspect of civility that does not get sufficient attention from political observers. It strikes me that *elite to elite* discourse profits from increased civility since politicians and policy-makers are trying to work together to solve problems. Loomis (2000) makes this point in reference to the U.S. Senate (see also Uslaner 1993). There is a payoff, therefore, in the long run from civility in such institutions, since the two parties will be more likely to work together in their effort to forge legislation. But what about *elite-mass* discourse? What about discourse when one side (i.e., the public) is not engaged very much and does not have the incentive to be fully engaged? Might it pay to make strong statements to get their attention? Elites are more able to read between the lines and understand subtle differences. But what about a less engaged and poorly informed public? If there are important differences might it now pay to raise those differences in strong terms so as to catch the attention of the public?

Consider the campaign of Howard Dean. Dean was the first Democrat seeking the presidency in 2004 who decided to attack President Bush. There was widespread unhappiness with the president's actions in Iraq and with the economy. But most Democrats feared attacking him harshly would backfire. They did not want to be accused on being, in effect, uncivil (or worse, unpatriotic). Dean did not let such concerns constrain his rhetoric. He attacked Bush's actions in Iraq and the public responded, or at least Democratic voters responded. While Dean's quest for the nomination fell short,[29] he showed other Democratic contenders that attacks could work and that votes could be secured through such rhetoric.

I do not think the country is worse off because of Howard Dean. Frankly, I think he set in motion key forces that led many segments of the public to reconsider their support for President Bush and the Iraq war. Of course, other citizens became even stronger supporters of the president, rejecting the criticisms of Dean and other Democrats. But by increasing the volume and tone of the attacks, there was a more thorough discussion of this important issue. If a group is inattentive, it may take some yelling to get their attention. This process may bother people who want politics to be tidy and neat. But democratic politics is not and we need these heated exchanges to engage the citizenry in the debates over the proper course for government.

I am not, as one might have guessed by now, overly concerned with civility in political campaigns. The public needs to know about the good and bad of the candidates and negative appeals help provide important pieces of information. I also believe that emphasis on civility tends to favor the status quo. If those in power are not doing a good job, it is the responsibility of the opposition to attack and raise doubts about incumbents. If we argue that such attacks must be civil and not harsh, will the public be able to understand that we need a change? Could not one argue that President Bush and his administration associated criticism with being unpatriotic? Didn't such claims discourage key players from going on the attack? Yet, might not the country have been better off if we had had a more open (and yes, harsher) debate over the merits of invading Iraq prior to sending our troops over there? We can only guess. But by muting the level of attack on key issues, we may well be lessening the chances for those on the outside to raise serious doubts about those in power and the merit of important policies.[30]

An obvious response to this argument is that the public dislikes negativity and incivility. They want campaigns to be positive, not negative. It is clear that the public favors civil exchanges in campaigns (Brooks 2000a; Bartels et al. 1998). The public also wants the process of governing to be positive, not combative. The electorate's unfavorable reactions to Congress appear to be a product of the partisan fighting among members (Hibbing and Theiss-Morse 1995, 2002). Given these kinds of findings, there is even more reason, one could argue, for less negativity, because the process of governing will be better received by the public. As Hibbing and Theiss-Morse (2002) note, however, just because people do not like the messiness of politics does not mean we should devise a system that is consistent with those preferences. The key question, then, is whether the public will be engaged by an adversarial process or whether greater congeniality will foster more involvement by the public. We cannot be sure, but the recent the 2004 presidential campaign gives us reason to think that harsh attacks do not disengage the American public from participating.

Whichever side one comes down on this debate, the findings of this book show that any effort to lessen negative advertising will lessen the quality of information available to the public. Even though the public is not fond of these attacks, they do appear to have substantial payoffs and any effort to lessen the frequency of attack ads seems misplaced. Actually, the best way, according to my results, to forge a decline in negativity would be to lessen the polarization between the parties. And that undertaking is beyond the power of the best designed reforms. This structural feature of American politics will surely over the years ebb and flow along with the broader tides of society.

There is, however, one thing we might be able to do about negativity, especially the public's adverse reaction to attack politics. We need to find ways to encourage the news media to provide a more accurate account of negative campaigning. As we know from chapter 6, the news media are drawn to the negativity and give it lots of coverage (see also Patterson 1993). Recall in chapter 6 the graph that showed the media's sudden fascination with negativity in 1988 and how that interest has continued. Yet, there were plenty of negative ads prior to 1988. Currently, if a fight breaks out on the airwaves during a campaign, journalists are likely to give it lots of coverage. I do not think it likely that journalists will suddenly start covering the feel good positive ads or any "civil" exchanges between the candidates. Even so, I do believe that if journalists can learn more about how negativity works and see that there are positives to the negatives, perhaps they could frame that coverage differently. If the news media knew that negative appeals are more about issues than positive appeals and that the former are more likely to have documentation attached to them than the latter, perhaps that might alter how they cover and interpret these spots. Such a change in coverage might then be absorbed by the public, providing them a more complete story about attack politics. This kind of change is more likely and potentially beneficial to the electoral process.

A FINAL WORD

At the very start of this book, I began with a quotation from John Stuart Mill. In *On Liberty*, he observed that "truth . . . has to be made by the rough process of a struggle between combatants fighting under hostile banners."[31] Mill never thought about negative advertising on television, but he did understand that disagreement and criticism provides decision makers of all stripes with a chance to learn more about what is the best course of action. Any opinion, according to Mill, gains in value if it faces criticism. The competitive battle, or what Mill refers to as the "collision with error," over the best course of action strengthens the political process. "Truth," in short, becomes the outcome of political struggles, as competing sides make their case. It is not something that can be determined by vigilant members of the news media or even pundits with best intentions. The world can be viewed from many angles and there is not a single truth—there are many.

Negative advertising is usually not thought of as a process that helps shape and mold the course of government. Instead, we tend to think of it as simply misleading, frivolous, nasty, and counterproductive. The findings and arguments in these pages call into question those assumptions. It is important to realize that negativity, whether in the form of ads, speeches, or debates, can in fact inform the public. With a political system that seems to be increasingly prone to disagreement, we are not likely to see any decline in the attacks in political campaigns (or during the process of governing). Perhaps we can begin to think of negativity as an important part of democratic politics. Certainly, our founders understood its role. Thomas Jefferson once observed that

> in every free and deliberating society, there must from the nature of man be opposite parties, and violent dissensions and discords. . . . an association of men who will not quarrel with one another is a thing which never yet existed, from the greatest confederacy of nations down to a town meeting of vestry.[32]

Disagreement goes hand in hand with democracy. We tend to lose sight of that fact, especially as observers seem to want to sweep our disagreements under the rug and avoid the conflicts between our political leaders.

Negativity provides a chance for those competing for power to make a case for why they should be given power and it gives those in power the chance to show the risks associated with the other side. This struggle may not be pretty and at times the rhetoric will cross the line of civility and even be insulting to our collective intelligence. We need, however, to make room for it in our politics and, moreover, we need to appreciate its contributions to the political process. Any effort to curtail negativity is far worse than enduring harsh rhetoric, since it means that the ability of the opposition to hold the other side accountable for their actions would be weakened. If negativity ever happened to disappear from our electoral battles, we can safely assume that so would our freedoms and any chance we have to lay claim to being a democratic nation.

Key Variables from Content Analysis of Presidential Ads, 1960–2000

This short appendix is designed to provide readers more information about the content analysis I conducted. Chapter 2 describes many of the relevant details about these data. Here I sketch the variables gleaned from the data collection. In each case, I provide some sense of the variable and how it was coded. For those who are interested in the actual data or additional details about the coding, please contact me at john.g.geer@vanderbilt.edu. I also have made these data publicly available with a more complete handbook for the data on my website, http://www.vanderbilt.edu/psci/geer/.

Candidates. This variable reports which candidate aired the spot.

Year of Ad. This variable reports the year the spot was aired.

Party. This variable identifies the party of the sponsor, including third-party spots, such as Wallace or Perot.

Length of Ad. This variable reports the length of the ad in seconds.

Date of Production. The date of production of the spot is available for most ads from 1976 to 1996. I also have dates for some of the McGovern spots in 1972. I recorded the day and month of the spot's creation.

Does the Ad Mention the Candidate and/or Opponent? This variable captures explicit references to the candidate or the opposition in the narrative.

Type of Ad. Here I coded whether the ad was about traits, issues, or both and whether the spot was positive, negative, or contrast. I also have information about whether the spot was endorsement spot, and whether it was about the vice presidential candidates. I captured a great deal of detail with this variable, employing over fifty codes.

Central Actors in the Ad. Was the candidate shown? Was the voice of candidate used? Was a narrator used? Was the opponent shown? Was the voice of opponent used? I sought to capture the key figures used in the spot.

Partisanship. I counted the number of mentions of Democratic and Republican party.

Retrospective(Past) or Prospective(Future). Was the ad retrospective in nature? Prospective? Both? No such references?

Ideological Mentions in Ad. I coded the ideological references in the spots, such as mention of being liberal, conservative, too extreme, and so on. Such codes also appear in the issue section discussed later.

Strategic Mentions in Ad. Did candidates discuss strategic themes in the ad? What was said? Did they talk about whether the opposition was going to lose? These codes played a bigger role in spots aired in the nomination process.

References to Values in the Ads. I coded up to twenty different references to values for each spot. There are ninety-nine unique codes for these references. Some examples are as follows: "Greatness/spirit of America/best America/great resources," "rule of the people/government of the people/the government belongs to people," "founding fathers/Jefferson/Washington," "God or some religious connection/faith," "justice/just/right," "future/tomorrow/look ahead," "change," "community/town/village/city/neighborhood/small town," "children/kids/future generations/grandchildren," "get country moving again/move forward/let's take charge of our future/take back America/bold ideas," "the American way/the American dream/American values/dreams," "love/love each other/caring nation/decency."

References to Traits in the Ads. I coded up to twenty references to traits for each spot. There are over 200 unique codes for these references. Some examples are as follows: "active/acts/vigorous," "brave/tested/proven," "untested," "cares/listens/fights for people like you/protects people like you," "common man/humble origins/self-made/one of us," "consistent," "flip-flops/doubletalk," "effective/good record," "ineffective/incompetent," "experienced/prepared," "inexperienced," "ahead of his time," "honest/does not over promise," "dishonest/misleading," "intelligent/smart/wisdom," "military man/veteran," "a politician," "strong/good leader," "weak/not tough," courage/courageous, "integrity/honorable/dignity," "imprudent/not practical," "family man," "corrupt," "controlled by special interests," "fighter," "just talks," "war monger/militaristic," and "can unite nation."

References to Issues in the Ads. I coded up to thirty references to issues for each spot. This part of the content analysis is the most complicated by far. There are nearly 2000 unique codes for issues. I captured as much detail as possible. I will list a sizable number of examples to provide a flavor of the data. The coding system is set up to distinguish between negative and positive appeals. The following are some examples: "stop growth in government," "favors investment," "management of economy," "mismanagement of economy," "candidate will bring good times/prosperity," "opponent will bring bad times," "supports small business," "doesn't support small business," "favors high wage jobs," "stop exporting jobs overseas," "unemployment too high/lost jobs," "inflation cut/under control," "inflation too high," "lowered interest rates," "opposes right to work laws," "increased standard of living" "cut standard of living, "end marriage tax penalty for working families," "favors $500 tax credit per child," "risky tax scheme," "opposed tax cut," "cut red tape/bureaucracy," "seeks to balance budget," "will not balance budget," "growing deficit," "controlled/cut government spending," "excessive government spending," "supports line-item veto," "agricultural policy," "cut support price supports/subsidies for farmers," "supports big government for prescription drugs," "opposes health care for elderly," "cut/opposes federal funding to schools," "cut health care for kids," "supports Medicaid," "supports medical research," "opposes family and medical leave," "create affordable housing," "supports minimum wage," "doesn't support minimum wage," "supports Social Security," "Doesn't support Social Security," "welfare out of control/too many on welfare," "opposed welfare reform," "Civil rights," "affirmative action," "appointed blacks to cabinet," "supports right to abortion/right to choose," "opposed to abortion/right to life," "for capital punishment," "against capital punishment," "tough on crime," "stop drugs from getting into the country/fighting drugs," "for gun control/takes on gun lobby," "against gun control," "opposes Brady Bill," "support ERA/ERA extension," "lessened communism," "soft on communism," "poor handling of Vietnam War," "supports Israel," "favored NAFTA," "opposes SALT treaty," "military preparedness/strong defense," "military not prepared," "for Nuclear Test Ban Treaty," "against Nuclear Test Ban Treaty," "opposes MX missile," "energy policy, "opposes ocean drilling for oil," "lessen pollution/cleaner environment," "cuts to environment/less toxic clean up/protects polluters," "smear campaign," "opposes term limits," "appoints bad judges," and "campaign reform."

Notes

1. The epigraph was quoted in a column by George Will, "The First Amendment on Trial," *Washington Post*, November 29, 2002.

2. *Washington Post*, October 7, 2002.

3. The title of Kamber's book provides another example: *Poison Politics*.

4. The Institute for Global Ethics conducted the poll; see http://www.globalethics.org.

5. Data come from a survey by Pew Research Center, conducted by Princeton Survey Research Associates International, February 11–16, 2004 and based on telephone interviews with a national adult sample of 1,500.

6. Some scholars disagree, questioning these hypothesized ill-effects of attack ads (Finkel and Geer 1998; Lau et al. 1999; Freedman and Goldstein 1999; Freedman, Franz, and Goldstein 2004; Clinton and Lapinski 2004). Some suggest that there is no adverse effect on participation and interest in politics. Others go so far as to claim that there is a small stimulation effect. The basic idea is that negativity stimulates interest in politics, engaging voters in the process. Like a good fight, it fires them up, rather then turns them off. More will be said about this topic.

7. *Time*, September 25, 1964, p.16

8. Nan Robertson (1964), *New York Times*, September 15.

9. Charles Mohr (1964), *New York Times*, October 2.

10. Quoted in Pete Hamill (1964) "When the Client is a Candidate," *New York Times*, September 15.

11. See interview with Tony Schwartz, the ad's creator, from Bill Moyer's PBS special: "The 30 Second President." It is also worth noting that John Kessel's book on the 1964 campaign, which is the most thoughtful account of that contest, is not highly critical of the Daisy spot. Instead, Kessel (1968, 238) notes that "nuclear responsibility" was "one of Goldwater's weakest areas." This assessment is telling, since no one can question whether Kessel, a Republican, held partisan bias against the senator from Arizona.

12. I asked Greg Stevens, the creator of the Tank ad, about the grinding gears in the audio portion of the spot, thinking it was not part of the original footage. He laughed, pointing out that the sound was that of an "eighteen wheeler," not a tank.

13. This passage is drawn directly from the ad itself.

14. Newspaper accounts of the ad offered a mixed verdict on whether the ad was misleading or not. I conducted a search on Lexis-Nexis about reactions to the Tank ad.

15. That claim appeared in a number of Dukakis's spots, such as the one titled New Era. See http://livingroomcandidate.movingimage.us/index.php for a copy of this ad.

16. This quotation comes from a personal interview with Alex Castellanos in January 2003. Alex Castellanos worked as a central media advisor to the Bush-Cheney campaigns in 2000 and 2004.

17. I shall define with a bit more precision what I mean by "information environment" in the next chapter.

18. Such a focus means that I must assume that these short spots that appear on television in a campaign are part of the information environment used by the public. If the public is unmoved by political ads then one could question the importance of this focus. Fortunately, there is a good deal of scholarship that documents their impact on the public; see chapter 3 for a brief account of that research.

19. For the time being, I am going to equate negativity with criticism. Some would argue that negativity is a unique form of criticism—excessively harsh or unfair. I will indeed discuss such concerns. But my goal for the moment is to remind readers that negativity is a form of criticism and therefore may have an important role in democratic politics.

20. Other scholars agree with this need for data and they too have collected valuable evidence that will advance our understanding of this general issue. See the work of Jamieson, Goldstein and Freedman, and Vavreck.

21. The next chapter will spell out in detail the merits of these data and how they compare to the evidence collected by other scholars.

22. Of course, the presidential focus potentially limits the applicability of my findings to elections in general. It is quite possible that the workings of negativity in campaigns for state and local elections may be different. The amount of negativity varies more in local and state elections than in presidential contests (see Kahn and Kenney 2004; Lau and Pomper 2004). With over thirty races for the senate every two years, one can easily imagine some very negative contests and some very positive ones. That same dynamic should be true for the 435 House races, not to mention the contests of state legislature. More will be said about this matter in subsequent chapters.

23. I do hope that my efforts spark additional attempts to provide even better standards to evaluate the tone and content of campaign rhetoric.

24. I must confess that content analyzing the Declaration of Independence is the social scientists' equivalent of breaking one of the Ten Commandments. It seems to me that some documents rise above the crudeness of quick content analysis. But the results are interesting enough that I decided simply to admit my sin as I presented the relevant proportion.

25. See Adam Clymer (2002) "Threats and Reponses," *New York Times*, September 28, p. 25.

26. See, for example, Silbey (1999, xviii).

27. Quoted in Kahn and Kenney (2004, 110).

28. I conducted this search on Lexis-Nexis, examining the full text of news stories by the Associated Press on "negative campaigning" from September 1 to November 1, 1980 and 2000.

29. Officially the act punished only "political criticism if it was 'false, scandalous, and malicious,' and only if the author intended to defame," But the Federalist controlled courts

placed the burden on the authors to prove that they were not in violation of the act, which meant that a "critical statement was presumed to be false unless the defendant could prove it was true in all respects" (Lewis 1991, 58). See Levy (1985) for the most important scholarly account of the development of freedom of the press. For an interesting reassessment of the Federalist position, see Martin (1999).

30. *New York Times vs. Sullivan.* 1964. 372 U.S. 254. See http://www.epic.org/free_speech/nyt_v_sullivan.html, p. 8.

31. Even in campaigns for the presidential nomination, where the electoral viability of a candidate matters a great deal, contenders rarely mention such concerns in their spots (see Geer 1999).

32. For the political junkies among us, you can go to www.cspan.org and look for the program titled: "British House of Commons Prime Minister's Questions." The exchange can often get quite heated and can be quite informative.

33. This quotation came from a personal interview I had with Alex Castellanos on January 17, 2003. This was an open-ended interview that centered on negative advertising and his views on it. I will talk more about these interviews later on.

34. *American Political Science Review* (1950), 44:1–2.

35. See Riker (1996) for a thoughtful theoretical account of negative campaigning. This scenario was inspired by his work.

36. From Madison's *Report on the Virginia Resolutions.* See http://www.jmu.edu/madison/center/main_pages/madison_archives/life/retirement/nullification/va.htm, p. 31.

37. In some sense, the opposite of this view is the concern expressed by Janis about "groupthink," which can be thought of as decision making without the benefit of negativity.

38. Hibbing and Theiss-Morse (1995, 2002) take this point in a slightly different direction, arguing that the public is turned off by political attacks. Citizens do not want candidates fighting among themselves. They see the battles as undermining government and it turns them off from the political process.

39. It is worth noting that recent work by Prior (2002) suggests that voters may be more informed than we typically think, because we have relied too heavily on the written word to test information. Visuals and pictures contain information that have not been as well tapped by scholars, potentially leading us to underestimate how well informed the public is about politics.

CHAPTER TWO

1. When assessing negativity's contribution to the information environment, interest groups play a very significant role. Just consider the role of so called 527 groups in the 2004 campaign. They aired a lot of negative commercials aimed at both Kerry and Bush. Using the ads available through the *National Journal*, 72% of the ads aired by 527s in 2004 were negative, 18% were contrast and just 10% were positive.

2. Radio offers another way for candidates to communicate directly to large number of citizens. But TV reaches a larger audience than radio. Radio does permit targeting of select groups of voters (see Herrnson 2001; Geer and Geer 2003).

3. The ads reported here include ads sponsored by the candidates, their parties, and their allied interest groups, see Goldstein and Freedman (2002, 8).

4. The total was 600 million, if you included 527 and PAC advertising (Sidoti 2004).

5. There have been far fewer efforts to look at more local elections. For notable exceptions, see Krasno (2000), Kahn and Kenney (1999), and Valentino and Hutchings (2003).

6. Of course, there were some earlier attempts to measure the content of presidential ads, see for example Joslyn (1980) and Patterson and McClure (1976).

7. For earlier work using these data, see Geer (1998), Finkel and Geer (1998), Geer (2000), and Geer and Lau (2005).

8. It should be noted that these scholars are speaking to product advertising, not political advertising.

9. CNN.com, March 12, 2004, "Kerry Strikes Back at Bush on Ads."

10. William Mayer (1996) also argues that journalists and pundits rarely define negativity with any clarity.

11. See Bartels et al. (1998, 17) for an account of Jamieson's position.

12. Montague Kern (1989) talks about "hard sell" and "soft sell" negativity. The former uses "dark colors and threatening voices," while the latter might use humor or storytelling to communicate its message (Kern 1989, 94). Bruce Gronbeck (1994) talks about sorting negativity along three dimensions: implicative, comparative, and assault. Richardson (2002) applauds such efforts, arguing that we need to move beyond the "negative-positive taxonomy."

13. In a personal interview, I asked George W. Bush's media advisor, Alex Castellanos, about the conceptual ambiguity associated with the terms "negativity" and "attack." He acknowledged that there was some conceptual slippage and offered his own favorite term for negativity: "hard hitting issue ads about our opponent's record of shame." Frankly, I find his suggestion appealing, but, alas, it is a bit wordy. It is worth noting that unlike the public, which sees negativity as personal attack, Castellanos sees negativity as tied to issues. This is a theme that will become central to this book.

14. I began the original data collection in the early 1990s, using this approach at that point. I did not borrow from any existing work and started largely from scratch.

15. I did supplement my sample with some ads from my own collection. But these were very few in number, probably around ten to fifteen.

16. For data from 2000, I also made use of Stanford University's website and *National Journal's* Hotline. The former supplied some of the late spots not on the CD-ROM. The latter served as a check to see if any ads were missing. In an interview with Al Gore's media advisor in 2000, Carter Eskew confirmed that Gore aired about slightly less than fifty ads—a number that squares nicely with the sample from *In Their Own Words*.

17. There is a CD-ROM available, *The Annenberg/Pew Archive of Presidential Campaign Discourse*.

18. The CD-ROM does not have any spots from the Goldwater campaign in 1964. The Kanter Archive has at least twenty-six, according my count. Vavreck (2001) puts the average number of ads even lower, about seventy-nine, because some of the spots are double counted in the Annenberg collection.

19. Julian Kanter made available to me about 120 ads per election, but this number includes the third party bids of Wallace and Perot. Kaid and Johnston (2001, 40) report the average of 113 that I reference above.

20. Benoit (1999) offers yet another sample of ads. He pulled together all the sources of ads he could buy and then supplemented that sample with the presidential ads available at the Kanter Archive. He reports coding 761 ads from 1960 to 1996, which is nearly 400 fewer than at the University of Oklahoma.

21. This number includes spots from 2000 and the third party candidacies of Wallace, Anderson, and Perot (1992 and 1996).

22. This statement is not entirely true. In the 1960s, some ads ran the odd time of sixty-one or sixty-two seconds. I included them in the analysis. Also, as one may recall, the "Catholic problem" was an important issue in Kennedy's 1960 campaign. In the archive, the only "Catholic ad" was a two-minute spot. Given the importance of this issue, I made an exception for fear of misrepresenting Kennedy's appeals.

23. In recent years, this has meant the sample includes spots that were not formally paid for by the two parties' national committees, but that were authorized by the candidate. In 1972, Nixon had a group called Democrats for Nixon. These spots were included in the sample.

24. This calculation includes a small number of spots that varied from fifty-three seconds to sixty-two seconds in length. If you look only at those ads exactly sixty seconds long, the proportion drops to 67%.

25. See *30 Second Presidency,* a PBS special hosted by Bill Moyers.

26. Sidoti (2004) reports that Kerry and Bush spent about $500 million, while 527 groups spent about $100 million—or 17% of the total.

27. If the change, however, introduced an important new idea, then an effort was made to include that new appeal into my results.

28. See also Subervi-Velez (1999) and Subervi-Velez (1992).

29. See http://nationaljournal.com/pubs/hotline/ for a listing of 2000 ads, as well as *In Their Own Words.* One of the more visible ads aimed at a Latino audience was then Governor Bush's nephew speaking on behalf of his uncle, addressing issues such as education in a mix of English and Spanish.

30. From 1960 to 1996, Benoit (1999, 219–20) reports utilizing 761 ads. Excluding 2000 from the above table, I have 720 ads from the two major parties.

31. There were 832 ads, which included thirty-seven third-party ads. Most of these ads came from Ross Perot's campaigns. For most of the analysis in this book, I examine only the major party spots—795 from 1960 to 2000.

32. I am drawing a distinction between personal traits and issues. There is, of course, overlap between the two. Some issues speak to traits. When George W. Bush talked about being tough on terrorism in 2004, he was also sending a message about his personal traits. I code the explicit references. This general approach is motivated in large part by the work of Stanley Kelley (1983), as he sought to develop a scheme that effective captured the considerations voters brought with them into the polling booth.

33. The data are publicly available and I will provide the codebook upon request.

34. The 91% percent refers to the proportion of agreement across all items in the code sheet. In general, the coding for issues yielded the highest reliability whereas the coding of values was less successful (about 84%).

35. This spot is a classic "man/women" in the street ad where a series of people offer their opinions about the candidates. If the ad does not seem coherent, it is because the transcription does not do justice to the interviews.

36. Kaid and Johnston (2000) address some of the visual aspects of presidential ads. Such efforts are to be applauded. There is also important work being done by Nick Valentino that also pays close attention to the visuals. For example, just simply counting the number of children or women in ads would be of value and something that could be coded easily. Valentino has done that and more, including efforts to record the frequency with which African-Americans appear in spots. There is also work by Prior (2004) that talks about visual versus verbal information.

37. In the few cases where I made this exception, I ran various analyses with and without the visual appeal. In no case, did the findings change. I decided to include ads like the Daisy spot, given its importance to that campaign and its continuing significance today.

38. Castellanos made this observation in a presentation he made to my class on negative campaigning, on February 18, 2004.

39. These twenty-five ads were drawn from those available to me; it is not a random sample of the population.

40. The exception to this general pattern was a 1968 Nixon ad where the visuals were the only message—there was no audio portion to the ad.

41. The average amount of attention race received was about 4% of the candidates' issue appeals from 1960 to 1968.

42. That is not entirely true. Rick Lau and I (2005) have developed a simulation procedure to develop weights for past elections that helps fill in some of the missing data.

43. This proportion comes from adding half of the contrast ads (12%) to all the negative ads (28%).

44. The measure reported in figure 2.1 is calculated as follows. First, I summed all negative appeals in a candidate's campaign and divided that number by the total number of appeals. That yields a proportion for each nominee. I then took the average of those two numbers to estimate the negativity for the campaign.

45. Even if one drops the 1960 campaign from the analysis, the trend remains positive and significant—about 2.2% per election.

46. I looked at negative, positive, and contrast ads from 1988 to 2000, determining the share of negative appeals in each kind of spot. I limited to more recent campaigns under the notion that they should provide a better prediction for what 2004 looks like. I then applied those proportions to weighting the 2004 ads data to generate an estimate of negative appeals for both Kerry and Bush. Bush's ads yielded an estimate that 52% of his appeals were negative. Kerry's stood at 46%. The average of these two proportions is 49%.

47. The data for Benoit (1999, 163) come from his book and pulling together his negativity measures for presidential candidates and then averaging the two estimates across each election. Jamieson et al. (2000) provide their measure of negativity for each presidential campaign. West's (2001) is available in his widely cited book, *Air Wars*. Kaid's data comes from her book with Anne Johnston (2000, 111). In this case, I also averaged the amount of negativity across the two major party nominees.

48. To ensure these correlations were as high as I suggest, I did "difference" the data. That is, I correlated the differences between elections, as opposed to the absolute amount. The correlations remained impressive for Benoit's measure (0.94) and Kaid's (0.82). It dropped for Jamieson's (0.50), largely due to our different estimates for 1964. If you drop that case, it is comparable. The correlation with West's data does drop a lot, but as one shall see that is not a cause for concern.

49. Recall, that this proportion is different from the one reported earlier in two ways. First, here I am only looking at the 1960 to 1996 period. Second, I am averaging across individual campaigns, where earlier I summed appeals across all the campaigns.

50. We do have slightly different samples (761 to 720) for the period between 1960 and 1996. However, given that there is only a difference of forty-one spots and that we both made use of the Kanter Archive, this difference strikes me as unlikely to be part of the explanation.

51. It becomes even more puzzling when we realize that the Annenberg Archive does not have Goldwater's ads from 1964. Goldwater's ads were more positive than Johnson's spots, which should lead Jamieson to overreport negativity in 1964. Yet the opposite takes place. Jamieson et al. (2000) claim to use the Annenberg Archive, but are silent on the Goldwater spots of 1964.

52. There is only a 0.18 correlation between the gap in the presidential vote between the top two contenders with my measure of negativity. I tried other measures and nothing worked. See Sigelman and Buell (2003) for different look at this problem.

53. In 1972, I have data on the date of creation for McGovern's spots, but not Nixon's. In these spots from 1972 to 2000, there was usually a "slate" in front of the actual

spot. That slate usually indicated the date of the ad, the producer, and the campaign it was created for. I always recorded the date of creation, if possible.

54. I tried other cut-off dates and the basic findings do not change.

1. Cited in George Will (2002) "First Amendment Critical," *Washington Post*, November 29.

2. For the time being, I will leave the term "substance" undefined, but I will clarify my meaning later in the chapter.

3. In 2000, Gore's and Bush's number of appeals per commercial dropped back to a more typical rate—about fifteen appeals per spot. I mention these additional data since a counterhypothesis is that Clinton's high rate of appeals per ad were a product of changes in advertising formats, not his interest in policy. These data cast doubt on that interpretation.

4. There is a vast amount of scholarship in this area, see, for example, Pomper (1975); Converse and Markus (1979); Bartels (1986); Aldrich et al (1989); and MacDonald et al. (1995). Using JSTOR, I located 322 articles from 1980 to 2000 in the twenty-six political science journals in the database that addressed the subject of issue voting.

5. In *Benchmark for Better Campaigns*, www.globalethics.org.

6. I will define "relevant" in the upcoming chapters and offer ways to measure this concept.

7. I originally developed this argument in Geer (1998). For a recent and thoughtful treatment of this general issue, see Carsey (2001).

8. There are, of course, rules that might force candidates to stop ducking an issue and tackle it. The news media can ask lots of questions of candidates, forcing them to respond. Debates, of course, are ideal forums for direct exchanges and provide a chance for the kind of dialogue Simon (2002) advocates.

9. It is also a theme raised by Mill in the opening quotation for this book and a theme I shall return to in the conclusion.

10. One could argue that exaggeration might be worse in positive ads in today's campaigns, because they do not usually draw a response. It is the negative ads that always draw a response from the opposition. The potential of a response could provide further incentive for politicians to stay closer to the facts in their negative ads.

11. Castellanos made this point during the course of our conversation in January 2003.

12. The potential importance of this asymmetry can be highlighted by using the framework established long ago by Aristotle in his classic *On Rhetoric*. In that famous treatise, Aristotle argued that the effectiveness of any speech is shaped by three forces: the character (ethos) of the speaker, the audience's state of mind, and the evidence marshaled in support of the proposition. Scholars have studied quite extensively the importance of these forces in shaping the effectiveness of an appeal in persuading the public to change its mind (see Hovland et al. 1953; Sternthal et al. 1978; Lupia and McCubbins 1998; Lupia 2002). We also know from Lau (1982, 1985) that negative information tends to resonate more with the electorate than positive information. A number of explanations have been offered to explain these findings. My argument offers another one—negative appeals have more evidence attached to them and hence are more persuasive.

13. I was able to interview a number of political consultants on negative advertising. I had a set of questions to ask each person, but I decided to allow the conversation to follow its own unique path. I did so, in part, because approaching these interviews with some flexibility would more likely to yield interesting insights and encourage longer conversations.

In each case, I was able to talk to the consultant for at least thirty minutes. I did not see the payoff to being overly formal since I was only planning on talking to a handful of consultants. I was fortunate to be able to speak to the leaders in this field, which made the interviews especially rewarding. As a warm up to these interviews, I talked to Bill Fletcher, founder of Fletcher, Rowley, and Chao. Fletcher has worked for various gubernatorial and senatorial candidates in the South and has much insight to offer about negative advertising. This initial conversation helped me better approach my subsequent interviews. I conducted a telephone interview with Carter Eskew, Gore's media advisor in 2000, on March 18, 2002. On January 17, 2003, I interviewed Alex Castellanos (and had two follow-up conversations). I conducted a phone interview with Greg Stevens, the founder of Stevens Reed Curcio and Potholm on May 21, 2003. On December 15, 2003, I interviewed Mike Murphy, a Republican consultant for numerous candidates, including Lamar Alexander and Arnold Schwarzenegger. Finally, on March 21, 2003, I was able to have a personal interview with Jennifer Tierney, who has worked on local campaigns in California. This conversation was far more wide ranging that my other interviews, making it very helpful. I thank each of these people for the generous time. I also want to thank David Bader, Anne Duke, Paul Freedman, Roy Neel, and Vin Weber for helping me secure these interviews.

14. Each side also prepares for anticipated attacks by the other side, combing through evidence that could be used against their candidate.

15. For this analysis, I reexamined 238 ads from these six elections. The number in each election ranged from eighteen in 1964 to fifty-seven in 1988. I want to thank Ken Goldstein, Shanto Iyengar, and Stan Kelley for making some of these ads available to me. This sample was not drawn in a random fashion. It was simply an effort to pull together all possible ads for this new analysis. There is no reason to believe that this sample is not representative of the larger population.

16. Just as a reminder, these thirty-seven spots are ones for which I have copies. It is not the exact same sample as in the full dataset.

17. I want to thank Lynn Vavreck for sharing her data with me. When she collected the data, she had far different purposes than to test for relative sourcing of negative and positive appeals. However, her detailed coding made it possible for me to offer these additional tests.

18. Actually, this pattern likely has deeper historical roots. I have, for instance, a flyer from the 1932 Roosevelt campaign that showed the same basic tendency. Roosevelt notes that during the Republican administration "farm values have fallen over $22,000,000,000 since 1920," "farm products are worth about half as much as in 1929," and "farm taxes have risen from an average of $100 in 1914 to $266 in 1932." By contrast, Roosevelt promises to "lighten tax burdens," "reduce excessive interest rates," and "bring back better times to farmers." The flyer is titled "The Forgotten Farmer."

There were, of course, negative ads on television even as early as 1952 (Jamieson 1996). But it is pretty clear that 1964 was a "negative" campaign, especially on Johnson's side (see Benoit 1999; Kaid and Johnston 2000).

19. Tony Schwartz, the creator of this ad, makes this very point; see Bill Moyer's PBS special *The 30 Second Presidency*.

20. See Bartels (1998, 43).

21. There were no explicit references to the sexuality of the candidates, but the visuals were suggestive. This case is an example of implicit appeals (see Mendelberg 2002).

22. See Joslyn (1980) was among the first to show that presidential spots contain a good deal of discussion about policy. More recently, see West (2001) and Kahn and Kenney (1999).

23. These differences are statistically sound as well. The fact that each of the eleven elections works in the direction posited by the hypothesis is well beyond the normal 0.05

cut off of significance. If you think of each election as a random draw (p = 0.5) and you multiple 0.5 by 0.5 ten times (n − 1), the chances you would get eleven straight draws in the same direction is substantially less than 0.001.

24. I focused only on thirty-second ads, since many sixty-second spots tend to be introductory ads that are heavily about candidates' personal histories. This would add to the share of traits in positive ads. So to control for such forces, I limited my attention to thirty-second spots.

25. I did not include the proportion of values, since it was 1% in both cases. This choice made the graph simpler and easier to read. I should also note that I defined "incumbents" as candidates who were seeking reelection. It is not the incumbent party, such as Gore's in 2000, Nixon's in 1960, or Bush's in 1988.

CHAPTER FOUR

1. U.S. Congress, Senate, Committee on Commerce, Science, and Transportation, *Clean Campaign Act of 1985*: Hearing on S. 1310. Washington: U.S. Government Print Office, 1986, 8. Cited in Brooks (2000b, 10).

2. Kurtz, Howard. (2000) "GOP Goes On Attack In New Ad; Gore Campaign Hits TV Spot as 'Negative,'" *Washington Post*, September 1, A1.

3. Kevin Sack (2000) "The Vice President: in Strategy Shift, Gore Ads Question Bush's Capability," *New York Times*, November 3, A1.

4. See Ellis (2000) for a detailed and fascinating account of the duel.

5. See Peter Fimrite's story in the *San Francisco Chronicle*, November 1, 1996, A25 "Stark Furious over Flyer Challenger Refers to Congressman's 'Whore.'"

6. It is worth noting that Fay was a professor of political science.

7. I reexamined ads I had in my possession and spots available on the web as well. I looked in particular for ads that drew criticism in the news media, which tend to be available via the internet. So in the end, I was able to include nearly all controversial attack ads.

8. I should mention that one of the harder-hitting ads came from 1968—the famous Laughing TV ad by the Democrats that attacked Agnew. A devilishly simple ad; it was a spot with a TV screen picture and the simple question: *Agnew for Vice President?* The audio involved someone laughing at the mere suggestion of Agnew for this position. Was this nasty? No explicit attacks were made. Instead, the ad used humor to raise concerns about Agnew's qualifications for office.

9. The comment was understandable when Goldwater was running for reelection in Arizona, but a year later he was competing against Johnson for control of the White House. Hubert Humphrey, for example, made explicit reference to the statement in speeches around the country.

10. These examples are well documented; see Shi (1996) for a brief account of them.

11. The Jackson case is a very famous one. For a serious scholarly treatment of Jackson, see Remini (1998). For a website that contains some of these claims from 1828, see http://www.wnpt.net/rachel/campaign/mudsling.html.

12. Actually, I have data from 1916, 1928, 1932, 1936, 1948, 1952, and 1956. I had a research assistant identify all ads available in the *New York Times*. These ads were then coded for measures of tone in regards to issues and traits, using the same scheme from the television ads.

13. Here are some details about these last three proportions. There were a total of 1123 appeals in the print ad data from 1916 to 1956. There were 107 trait attacks out of a total of 328 references to character. Of all appeals, 351 were negative.

14. The comparability is really quite amazing. For example, the print ads had the same share of issues as in the TV ads—56%. Traits were slightly more common in the print ad data (29% compared to 25%).

15. The proportions in the graph are a simple average of the two campaigns. So in 1960, the number used was 11.5%.

16. If I add all contrast ads that dealt with character at least in part and negative ads that also had some references to character, it constitutes 21% as reported in table 4.1.

17. Studies of leadership come to similar conclusions (see Geer 1996). Bass (1981), for instance, summarizes the vast amount of previous research on "presidential leadership" that discusses the traits necessary for elected officials to be good public servants. In that review, he also shows that competence often lies at the center of these discussions. For example, he refers to the frequent mention of characteristics such as intelligence, knowledge, insight, and originality—all references to what can be reasonably labeled as competence.

18. This passage comes from *The American Commonwealth*, reprinted by the Liberty Fund, 1995, p. 881.

19. For the exact coding scheme, please contact the author.

20. The correlation across the twenty-two presidential campaigns among these five categories is 0.01 (n = 110). In short, the themes candidates raise to promote themselves have little to do with the grounds upon which they attack their opponents.

21. I experimented with a number of ways to measure this concept. None changed the results. I measured, for example, *relative* experience in the campaign (i.e., who was more experienced). That measure and the one used in this analysis correlate at 0.91. To provide a more concrete sense of the measure, I assigned all sitting presidents a 10 on this scale—the highest rating. A rating of 1 would be for those nominees without any prior political experience, not a likely outcome in presidential elections. I assigned Jimmy Carter (1976) a 2—the lowest of all major party nominees between 1960 and 2000—since he was a one-term governor from Georgia. Carter had the least formal political experience of the twenty-two candidates between 1960 and 2000. George W. Bush was next lowest at 3, having served less than six years in public office. I gave all vice presidents (former and sitting) an 8 on this scale. Bob Dole earned a 7 in light of all his years in Congress—the highest rating for anyone who was not a sitting president or a vice president. John Kennedy netted a 4 on this scale, while Michael Dukakis rated a 5. I tried slightly different ratings of candidates and the results did not change.

22. These findings measure the attention a candidate pays to competence in the following way: all positive (or negative) references to competence are divided by all appeals of that candidate. My goal here is to capture the overall attention paid to this theme in a candidate's advertising. As an example, McGovern did not question Nixon's competence in 1972, yielding a value of 0 in this case. By contrast, Carter attacked Reagan heavily on this dimension, dedicating 10% of all his appeals to this concern. As we will see, I also measured attention to this theme by dividing the number of all positive (or negative) appeals about competence by all positive (or negative) appeals. The results tell a similar story. For instance, my measure and this alternative one correlate at 0.94.

23. I have separate measures for each candidate across the eleven presidential campaigns between 1960 and 2000.

24. It is statistically significant at 0.07, which with just twenty-two cases is acceptable.

25. It is statistically significant at 0.03.

26. The specific regression coefficients are as follows: constant (5.3), slope (−0.45, p = 0.03), and r-squared equals 0.21. If you plug in the value I assigned to Jimmy Carter in 1976 (2), the predicted share of attacks is 4.5% of all appeals. For a sitting president, the results predict attacks on competence constituting 0.9% of all appeals.

27. These findings arise from the following regression: constant (1.2), slope (0.79, p = 0.07), and r-squared (0.15).

28. The actual regression results are as follows: constant (21.3), slope (–1.8, p = 0.03), r-squared (0.22).

29. Please contact author for the exact codes used to generate these estimates.

30. Recall, that respondents, on average, make only two comments about the personality of the presidential candidates. Hence, this range is not surprising given that I am breaking down these comments across the five categories for the traits raised in the likes and dislikes. In addition, these means do not make use of the full sample. I used only respondents who made at least one personality comment. I employed this adjustment simply to look at those respondents who found such concerns salient. If you use the whole sample, the findings are unchanged. The correlation across the two measures is over 0.9.

31. Gore drew a 0.31 from the public on liking him for being competent. Bush received just a 0.17. In regards to disliking his integrity, Gore garnered a 0.30 and Bush just a 0.13.

32. I want to thank Larry Bartels for making this suggestion for how to deal with the issue of endogenity.

33. Technically, the estimated value reflects the start of interviewing. But that usually commences in late August or very early September, which generally signals the beginning of the general election campaign.

34. The means of the two measures are the same: 0.14. The standard deviation is nearly identical: 0.12 for unpurged and 0.13 for purged.

35. This regression excludes the data from the miscellaneous category of other. I do so since those appeals represent a range of themes that get aggregated in a way that makes it difficult to know what any relationship might mean. If you include these data in the regression, the basic results are unchanged, but some precision is lost in the estimates. The details of the regression using the dislikes/attacks is: constant = 10.0 (p = 0.01) and slope =118.3 (p < 0.01). For the likes/positive, the results are: constant = 11.6 (p < 0.01) and slope = 72.6 (p < 0.01).

36. To test explicitly this claim, I ran one regression with the likes-dislikes data, a dummy variable for tone (1 = negative, 0 = positive) and an interaction term multiplying the survey data with the tone variable. The slope for the interaction was 45.6, significant at 0.09.

37. I could, of course, present one regression with a series of dummy variables. The results are the same. I chose this approach simply for ease of presentation and comparison.

38. Howard Kurtz, *Washington Post*, February 20, 2004, A01.

39. Of course, the irony here is that this tendency to attack on matters of integrity only reinforces the public's doubts about the honesty of politicians.

40. These proportions reflect the average of the two candidates on this dimension of attack.

CHAPTER FIVE

1. If you correlate first differences the relationship between change in issue and overall negativity remains high, 0.78.

2. I will spend time later in the chapter spelling out what I mean by "important" and "real" issues.

3. I coded platforms in some earlier work and negative statements about the opposition were infrequent (see Geer 1998).

4. To be clear, I generate this proportion by taking the total number of references to urban matters and dividing it by all references to issues.

5. Dole also raised the issue with frequency in 1996 (14%), attacking Clinton heavily on allowing our children to be exposed to illegal drugs. Because of the importance of this particular issue to these two campaigns, I did include references to drug policy in some of the upcoming analyses.

6. Among Mondale ads, abortion constituted less than 1% of his appeals on issues. For Clinton in 1996, the proportion stood at 1.3%.

7. By "relative attention," I subtracted the attention paid by the Democratic nominees from Republican nominees. So on the issue of inflation, the gap for total attention is 3.9 (5.6 – 1.7).

8. Using in large part Petrocik's (1996) work, I coded the following issues as "owned" by the two parties: GOP: Inflation, taxes, spending, deficit, crime, foreign policy, and defense. The Democrats own the other seven issues.

9. "Bush Claims Credit for Third-quarter Boom," a story on www.cnn.com on October 30, 2003.

10. Over the forty-year time period under study, there were at least thirty-three different issues that Gallup reported as being important to at least a small proportion of the public. The dates of these polls varied over this time frame, ranging from July to October of the election year. It was not always possible to use data from the months just prior to the election. I checked to see if data from October reflected any contamination from the campaign itself. The public's rating of the most important problem is reasonably steady in the short term and largely independent of the campaign. I extended this examination to non-campaign periods to see if stability was present there as well, and again it was. Large changes in what the public rates as important are usually tied to big events, like the 9/11 terrorist attacks or the Oklahoma City bombing.

11. I would like to thank Professor Deborah Brooks of Dartmouth College for help in collecting all these data. She was working for Gallup at the time and was kind enough to pull all the relevant polls into a spreadsheet for me.

12. For example, Gallup lumps Medicare and Social Security together. My earlier analysis treated them separately. For this new analysis, I recoded my ad data to create a match. When working with the Gallup data, I also had to take account of the fact that some polls allowed respondents to mention multiple problems, which meant the proportions did not add up to 100%. I simply standardized the proportions in these cases so as to make them comparable over the eleven elections.

13. These issues are as follows: unemployment, inflation, management of government (i.e., spending, debt, deficit), taxes, Social Security–health care, education, poverty-welfare, race, crime, foreign policy and defense, and crime. There is one issue—drugs—that I started to include in 1972. It was not an issue that mattered to the public or to the candidates prior to 1972, so I did not include it for the first three elections under study.

14. I calculated the specific proportion as follows: the number of attacks by the challenger on that issue divided by the total number attacks by the challenger.

15. In these analyses, an "incumbent" includes all nominees of the party in power. In most cases, that was sitting presidents. But in four cases (Nixon 1960, Humphrey 1968, Bush 1988, Gore 2000) it was the sitting vice president, who had clear ties to the administration in power.

16. The second meaningful number is the intercept (a_i). This estimate shows that when the public does not view the issue as important, how much attention candidates dedicated to it. Ideally, that number should be zero—that is, if the topic is ignored in the campaign, it should not draw any attention by the president. In the equations I estimate,

however, there are a sizable number of control variables that make interpreting this intercept contingent on the values of these other variables. For simplicity, I am focusing on the slope, which is the most important indictor of responsiveness.

17. I included dummy variables for each issue and each year. I also ran models where I dropped all the fixed year effects and the results do not change. The findings reported here include all the fixed effects. The full results are available upon request.

18. Data for unemployment came from the Congressional Information Service, which reports the civilian unemployment rate from 1950 to 2000. The actual source is the Department of Labor, Bureau of Labor Statistics. Data for inflation also came from the Department of Labor, Bureau of Labor Statistics. The data on the state of the economy used Zaller's data set available on his website, which is used in his paper with Bartels (2001). I sought to measure the changing tax burden of the public as another objective indicator, but developing a sound measure is tricky at best. Nominal tax rates are often misleading, since it does not consider deductions. Federal payroll taxes are quite different than the income tax and then one needs to mix in the different state and local tax rates around the country. Larry Bartels provided guidance in the land minds associated with measuring the tax burden.

19. Data on crime rates were secured through the *Sourcebook of Criminal Justice Statistics,* www.albany.edu/sourcebook/.

20. I want to thank Tom Smith of Vanderbilt University for sharing with me his insights about the problems with time series data in the education field.

21. Daniel Press of the University of California–Santa Cruz was helpful in guiding me through the data problems facing the measurement of the state of the U.S. environment over the last forty years.

22. For those who want to see the other figures, please contact me.

23. Recall that my measure of inflation is the change from 1976 to 1980 in inflation rates.

24. For recent work on ambiguity, see Lewis (2000), Meirowitz (2002), and Berinsky and Lewis (2002).

25. The above comment just scratches the surface of this general issue. My purpose here is not to present a formal model, but simply to develop the logic beyond the incentive to be specific when going negative.

26. Upon request, I can supply the actual codes that underlie these categories. When developing the original coding scheme, I had the benefit of talking directly to Donald Stokes about it. He made a number of suggestions that helped improve the coding. I was (and am) very grateful for his kind help in this matter. The actual operationalization of a valence issue includes references to caring about an issue, general mentions of a theme like education with no directional thrust at all (although there is an implicit one), and discussion of concepts like "grow the economy" or other nonobjectionable claims.

27. As shown earlier, the negative appeals within the contrast ads are more positional (35%) than are the positive appeals (29%).

28. One variable I did not include in the analysis was the share of thirty-second spots in a campaign. It turns out that thirty-second ads possess more position appeals than do sixty-second spots (28% to 12%). That fact is due largely to the greater negativity of thirty-second spots than sixty-second spots. However, there are two problems. First, I do not see why theoretically length should have an influence on how valenced a spot is. Second, thirty-second spots have become increasingly important since 1960. So, that proportion in some sense is measuring time and we know that spots have become more negative over time and thus, more positional. Given that this variable has little value added, I did not include it in these results. I did, however, run it to see what happened. The variable does

not reach statistical significance ($p > 0.30$) and the coefficient is very small (one would need a 30% increase in the share of thirty-second spots to generate a two-point increase in position appeals) and it lessens the precision of the other key independent variables (due to the small sample size).

29. To capture possible incumbency effects, I used a three-point scale. A president running for reelection was coded 1. Pure challengers were coded 0. I drew a distinction between pure challengers and sitting vice presidents who were running as the nominee. Between 1960 and 2000, four sitting vice presidents ran as their party's presidential nominees. These contenders were tied to their administrations and had to defend some of those policies. Because this was an in between category, I coded them separately (0.5). I ran the analysis using separate dummy variables. The results were substantively the same, but the standard errors were less precise.

30. I ran a number of different specifications and the estimates associated with the share of negative issues and incumbency was very stable. I also checked the Durbin Watson statistic to make sure autocorrelation was not a problem; it was not.

31. I tried to measure competitiveness in a number of ways. For example, I used just the share of the vote the candidate received in the election. I also used a simple dummy variable measuring whether the race was close or not in case the vote totals were misleading, such as in the case of 1980. Another tactic was to measure whether a candidate was a landslide winner or loser. It did not matter. None of the results suggested any noticeable influence on how specific were a candidate's issue appeals.

32. I did drop the competitiveness variable to see if it changed the estimates from the regression model. The results were the same.

33. I generated this estimate by using the results in table 5.3 and assuming the highest share of attacks on issues (Dole's 67% in 1996), that the candidate is an incumbent, and the largest proportion of contrast ads (Clinton 55% in 1996).

34. Nixon's 1960 campaign had the fewest issue attacks: 7%. So if we plug that value in and assume no contrast ads and the contender is a challenger, the predicted value is zero.

CHAPTER SIX

1. Quoted in Lena Williams, *New York Times*, December 18, 1988, 1.

2. Donald Rheem (1988) "Voters Chide Candidates for Negative Campaigning" *Christian Science Monitor*, November 7, 1988.

3. This survey interviewed 1721 citizens via the telephone from November 1–5, 1988.

4. I conducted a search on iPOLL through the Roper Center to make sure that the question was new at least for the major survey organizations.

5. This poll was conducted from October 28–30, interviewing 1250 likely voters by telephone.

6. These data come from a CBS News/*New York Times* poll conducted from November 1–3. There were 1274 respondents in the sample.

7. I surveyed ten political scientists who responded to an email of mine asking them about the ads they remembered most. Such data are hardly definitive, but they fit nicely into this general narrative. I should also note that eight of ten most mentioned ads were also attack ads.

8. Data come from an ABC News/*Washington Post* poll conducted from January 17–23, 1988.

9. Data come from a *Washington Post* poll conducted from June 15–19, 1988.

10. According to a Gallup poll in November 1988, 57% of the public approved of Reagan's job as president.

11. These data come from an ABC/*Washington Post* poll of 1172 registered voters, see Germond and Witcover (1989, 156).

12. Bush's unfavorable ratings stood at nearly 50%, while his positive ones were around 25% (Germond and Witcover 1989, 160).

13. This discussion of the 1988 campaign is drawn from a number of journalistic accounts, mostly notably Germond and Witcover (1989).

14. The data here represent the number of stories between 1968 and 2000 that dealt with the subject of negative or attack advertising. The archive began its collection in 1968. I want to thank Shana Kushner of Princeton University for collecting these data for me.

15. The actual correlation between my measure of negativity and the news media's attention to negativity was –0.59 during these five elections.

16. You can find the full ad on http://livingroomcandidate.movingimage.us/.

17. There were two questions on the subject during the 1982 midterm elections, according to a search using Roper's iPOLL database.

18. I searched Roper's iPOLL database for questions on gay marriage from 1970 to the present. The first time the topic was raised was 1996. There were eight questions on the subject in 2003.

19. I searched between 1976 and 1988 for the phrase "negative advertising" in the text of articles listed in political science. I conducted the identical search from 1989 to 2001. Of these thirty-six articles, most of them appeared in our very best journals. In fact, fifteen of them appeared in either *American Political Science Review, Journal of Politics*, or *American Journal of Political Science*.

20. Of course, it is possible that it was a *qualitative* shift in the attacks that explain the news media's sudden attention. There is in fact some merit to this assessment, but not exactly along the lines most critics envision. I shall, however, save that discussion for later.

21. I suspect a variation from this claim is that Bush ran more *effective* negative spots. That is, they influenced the views of voters more than Dukakis's negative ads. I have no data to support such a claim, however. But Bush's ads were more memorable and caught the attention of political experts—we still talk about them today. I will have more to say about this subject later.

22. It is worth pointing out that my evidence speaks to the date when the ad was created by consultants. Journalists' reports confirm that its airing was only a few days later, but I just want to clarify this point.

23. Perhaps it was not the tone of the ads, but the lack of "substantive" content (see Buchanan 1991; Patterson 1993). This is slightly off topic, but worth considering briefly since this was a campaign known for candidates visiting flag factories. As before, the content of the 1988 commercials do not seem out of balance with previous elections. Of Dukakis's appeals, 49% dealt with issues, which was higher than Reagan in 1984 (43%) or Carter in 1980 (39%). Bush did talk more about traits than many recent campaigns (46%) and, therefore, less about issues (34%). However, Bush's discussion of issues was pretty specific. One quarter of all his issue appeals were positional—only two campaigns of the other fifteen had a higher share of specific issue appeals.

24. The National Security Political Action Committee officially paid for the airing of this spot.

25. Using Lexis-Nexis, I found thirty-four stories in major newspapers between August 1 and November 1, 1988 when searching for "Willie Horton" in the headlines or lead paragraphs. If you look instead in the text of political stories about Horton during the same time frame, the number increases to 118.

26. In a June 23 memo, Janet Mullins, a Bush aide, raised the issue of the furlough program and it possible use in the campaign. The memo was copied to Bob Teeter. Mary Lukens kindly shared this memo with me.

27. See Thomas Owen, September 8, 1988, p. 3, *Christian Science Monitor*.

28. I conducted the search on January 4, 2005.

29. Most recently, George W. Bush ended one of his attacks ads by asking: "John Kerry and his liberal allies—are they a risk we can afford to take today?"

30. This comes from the text of a Nixon ad aired in 1972, see http://livingroomcandi date.movingimage.us/for a transcript of this spot.

31. Quoted in Lloyd Grove (1988) "Dukakis Counterpunches at Bush's Handlers in Television Spots," *Washington Post*, October 5.

32. See www.livingroomcandidate.com for transcript of Reagan's commercials from 1984.

33. I conducted this search on Lexis-Nexis using the general news category for the major newspapers. I looked for all articles that had "swift boat" in the headline, lead paragraph, or term. It is possible that some of the stories might not have talked about the ads in question, but in skimming through many of the articles, it was clear that the campaign was being discussed.

34. See Romano and VandeHei (2004 A0).

35. Using Lexis-Nexis, I searched for "negative advertising" in the full-text option for general news section for the major papers from August 1 to November 1, 1984. I did an identical search for 2004. I conducted this search on January 9, 2005.

36. Caitlin Sause coded these data for her senior thesis project at Vanderbilt. I am grateful that she shared these data with me. For a fact check to be rated as containing "misleading" information, the document had to refer to any of the following terms: misstatement, misquotes, inflates, deception, missing context, misleading, selective, and exaggeration. Sause counted the number of references. My analysis here recoded that variable to yes or no. I looked at the data a number of ways and the story remains the same.

CHAPTER SEVEN

1. See Kahn and Kenney 2004, 110.

2. I also examined other trends, such as interest in politics and efficacy. These results square with the analyses I am about to present.

3. In 1984, the NES changed the question, which artificially depressed the public's faith in elections. To make the full time series comparable, Bartels reestimated these measures. See Bartels (2002) for a full account of how the time series was revised.

4. According to the uncorrected estimates in 2000, there was only a slight one or two point up-tick in 2000 from 1996. To see if not including 2000 might affect the results, I ran additional regressions using a series of reasonable guesses for what 2000 might have looked like. In no instance did the findings change. Consequently, I am employing the 1964–96 time series for this analysis.

5. I want to thank Marc Hetherington for calculating the amount of trust from the 2004 NES Survey.

6. Given that Hetherington's measure of trust is gathered *after* the election and negativity is measured *prior* to the election, there is an opportunity to detect whether the latter influences the former.

7. See, http://elections.gmu.edu/Voter_Turnout_2004.htm. MacDonald has kindly shared his VAP and VEP estimates for turnout in 2004. I used the estimates available on

December 31, 2004. There may be slight changes as more data become available, but any difference will be marginal.

8. If you regress time on the VAP measure, you get a slope of -0.95, with a standard error of 0.26.

9. When regressing time on the VAP estimate, the slope is -0.51. The standard error is 0.285. This is slightly larger than needed for the 0.05 standard of statistical significance. But with twelve cases, one should not be overly concerned with that standard.

10. In fact, when one runs a simple bivariate regression, the size of the coefficient for the effects of negativity on VEP shrinks by nearly 50% (from -0.243 to -0.126) and goes from being statistically significant for VAP ($p = 0.04$) to insignificant for the revised estimate ($p = 0.23$).

11. Another way to control for autocorrelation is to "difference" the data: cast the variables as capturing change between elections rather than the absolute amount of negativity. The problem with that approach is that theoretically I am interested in the effects of the absolute amount of negativity on the political system, not whether it increased from the last election. Consider that in 1996 negativity reached an all time high, according to my data. In 2000, there was a decline in the amount of attacks. Yet, 2000 still witnessed a large amount of negativity, which would be covered up by differencing the data. I want to thank Brad Palmquist and Geoff Layman for helpful advice on this matter. See Layman (2001, 218-19) for further discussion of the merits of this approach.

12. If you include my estimate for 2004, the coefficient increases to 2.7, which I mentioned in chapter 2.

13. This basic pattern holds even if I drop the 1960 election. Overall and issue negativity increased by an average of 2.0% and "trait" by 0.4%.

14. The details of these data are available upon request. I coded these ads in the same manner as the spots from the general election. See Geer (1999) for a discussion of these data.

15. These proportions reflect the average share of attacks across each candidate's campaign. So, in 1980, I have ads from seven different candidates. Ted Kennedy attacked 32% of the time. By contrast, Reagan did not offer one negative appeal in any of his ads, suggesting he took seriously the eleventh commandment (thou shalt not attack fellow Republicans). I examined only candidates who had produced at least five spots, which eliminated candidates like Fritz Hollings in 1984 and Al Haig in 1988. Buchanan, as a point of information, ran the most negative primary campaign in 1992—50% of his appeals were negative.

16. John McCain made this comment on ABC News' *This Week,* March 7, 2004.

17. See Poole's website for the actual data, http://voteview.com/dwnl.htm. Also, see Burden, Caldeira, and Groseclose (2000) for an assessment of the various measures of polarization. I want to thank Marc Hetherington, who helped me better understand these data on polarization and provided the actual data as well. Keith Poole also provided quick and helpful advice via email.

18. The simple correlation for these twelve cases is 0.80, which is substantial by any standard. Most of the remaining estimates will use only data from 1960 to 2000, since I only have the one estimate for overall negativity in 2004. If you examine this relationship and drop the 2004 election, the correlation drops to 0.73. Given the increase in negativity in 2004 and the widening gap between the parties, the relationships reported here will only strengthen with more data from that campaign.

19. These correlations are for data from 1960 to 2000, since I have not measured trait or issue attacks in 2004. As a result, one cannot compare these correlations to the overall measure that includes 2004.

20. With the share of ordered appeals as the dependent variable and polarization and negativity as the independent variables, the coefficient for polarization is significant at the 0.03 level. The correlation drops from 0.78 to 0.51 when controlling for negativity, which is still a healthy statistical relationship.

21. Zaller uses Rosenstone's data until 1972. From 1972 to 2000, he uses NES data. The NES data are the judgments of high information voters about the candidates' views on issues. He rescales the two scores to make them comparable. See Zaller's website for details: www.sscnet.ucla.edu/polisci/faculty/zaller.

22. I have guessed that the differences on issues for Kerry-Bush fell in between the 1984 and 1988 contest. I tried other variations and the story remains basically unchanged, so I stuck with my first guess.

23. I did include a measure of competitiveness to see if that variable helped explain negativity. One might argue that a more competitive race would yield more criticism. Certainly the work of Kahn and Kenney suggest such a pattern. However, the presidential election is always competitive by the standards employed by congressional scholars and so the lack of a relationship probably speaks more to uniqueness of the presidential case than anything else.

24. That estimate assumes a party polarization score similar to that of the late 1890s and candidate differences that would pit a Goldwater against a McGovern.

25. I want to thank Caitlin Sause for making these data available to me.

26. The incumbent does much the same thing for the challenger, looking for problems with their previous record. My focus, however, here is on the out-party's attacks on the in-party.

27. A fourth category: none. Some ads, especially trait spots, did not contain retrospective or prospective themes. Nearly 20% of the spots fell in this category. The upcoming analysis does not include these spots. The size of the sample is 635; 275 of those ads are from the incumbent party and 360 from the out-party.

28. See http://www.pbs.org/, February 2, 2000.

29. The reasons observers have offered for the demise of the Dean campaign are many. One of the more discussed causes is the harsh attacks Dean faced from his opponents and members of the news media. We will have to wait for a more systematic assessment of Dean's downfall.

30. This argument about the conservative nature of the civility was heavily influenced by Lynn Sander's (1998) wonderful essay questioning the merits of deliberation in democracy. In that case, she notes that deliberation favors those who are more likely to speak out, who have the education to do so. Such a bias works against the interests of minorities and women. I have not talked about deliberation in this book, since thirty-second spots are short one-way mechanisms for politicians to communicate to voters. There is not much of a deliberative dimension to these exchanges.

31. I am using Mill's *On Liberty*, which was reprinted in 1972 by J. M. Dent & Sons Ltd. This passage can be found on p. 107.

32. This passage was draw from Stanley Kelley's *Spirit of Party*.

References

Adatto, Kiku, 1990. "Sound Bite Democracy." Research Paper R-2, Joan Shorenstein Barone Center for Press, Politics, and Public Policy, June.

Aldrich, John. 1995. *Why Parties?* Chicago: University of Chicago Press.

Aldrich, John, John Sullivan, and Eugene Borgida. 1989. "Foreign Affairs and Issue Voting: Do Presidential candidates 'Waltz' Before a Blind Audience?'" *American Political Science Review* 83: 123–41.

Altschuler, Glenn and Stuart Blumin. 2001. *Rude Republic: Americans and Their Politics in the Nineteenth Century.* Princeton: Princeton University Press.

American Political Science Review. 1950. "The Need for Greater Party Responsibility." *American Political Science Review* 44: 1–14.

Ansolabehere, Stephen, and Shanto Iyengar. 1994. "Riding the Wave and Claiming Ownership over Issues: The Joint Effects of Advertising and News Coverage in Campaigns." *Political Opinion Quarterly* 58: 335–57.

_____. 1995. *Going Negative: How Political Advertisements Shrink and Polarize the Electorate.* New York: Free Press.

Ansolabehere, Stephen, Shanto Iyengar, and Adam Simon. 1999. "Replicating Experiments Using Aggregate and Survey Data: The Case of Negative Advertising and Turnouts." *American Political Science Review* 93: 901–9.

Ansolabehere, Stephen, Shanto Iyengar, Adam Simon, and Nicholas Valentino. 1994. "Does Attack Advertising Demobilize the Electorate?" *American Political Science Review* 88: 829–838.

Arnold, R. Douglas. 2004. *Congress, the Press, and Accountability.* Princeton: Princeton University Press.

Bartels, Larry. 1986. "Issue Voting Under Uncertainty: An Empirical Test." *American Journal of Political Science* 30: 705–28,

_____. 1998. "Where the Ducks Are: Voting Power in a Party System," In *Politicians and Party Politics*, edited by John Geer. Baltimore: Johns Hopkins University Press.

_____. 2000. "Campaign Quality: Standards for Evaluation, Benchmarks for Reform." In *Campaign Reform*, edited by Larry Bartels and Lynn Vavreck. Ann Arbor: University of Michigan Press.

_____. 2002. "Question Order and Declining Faith in Elections." *Public Opinion Quarterly* 66: 67–79.

Bartels, Larry, Henry Brady, Bruce Buchanan, Charles Franklin, John Geer, Shanto Iyengar, Kathleen Hall Jamieson, Marion Just, Stanley Kelley, Thomas Mann, Samuel Popkin, Daron Shaw, Lynn Vavreck, and John Zaller. 1998. *Campaign Reform*. Princeton: Woodrow Wilson School.

Bartels, Larry and Wendy Rahn. 2000. "Political Attitudes in the Post-Network Era." Paper Presented at the American Political Science Association Conference, Washington D.C.

Bartels, Larry and John Zaller. 2001. "Presidential Vote Models: A Recount. *PS: Political Science and Politics*. 34: 8–20.

Bass, Bernard. 1981. *Stodgill's Book of Leadership*. New York: Free Press.

Bennett, Lance. 1996. *The Governing Crisis*. New York: St. Martin's Press.

Benoit, William. 1999. *Seeing Spots*. Connecticut: Praeger Publishers.

Berinsky, Adam and Jeffrey Lewis. 2002. "Voter Choice and Candidate Uncertainty." Unpublished manuscript.

Blumenthal, Sidney. 1991. *Pledging Allegiance*. New York: Harper Collins.

Bond, Jon and Richard Fleisher. 2000. *Polarized Politics*. Washington D.C.: CQ Press.

Brader, Ted. 2005. *Campaigning for Hearts and Minds*. Chicago: University of Chicago Press.

Brians, Craig and Martin Wattenberg. 1996. "Campaign Issue Knowledge and Salience: Comparing Reception from TV Commercials, TV News, and Newspapers." *American Journal of Political Science* 40: 172–93.

Broder, David. 2002. "Turned off by Triviality." *Washington Post,* 6 October.

Brody, Richard. 1978. "The Puzzle of Declining Turnout." In *The New American Political System,* edited by Anthony King. Washington: American Enterprise Institution.

Brooks, Deborah. 2000a. "Negative Campaigning Disliked by Most Americans." *Gallup Report,* 17 July.

_____. 2000b. "When Candidates Attack: The Effects of Negative Campaigning on Voter Turnout in Senate Elections." Yale University. Ph.D. dissertation.

_____. 2004. "Replicating Ansolabehere and Iyengar's Demobilization Hypothesis." Unpublished manuscript.

Bryce, James. 1891. *The American Commonwealth*. New York: Macmillan.

Buchanan, Bruce. 1991. *Electing a President*. Texas: University of Texas Press.

_____. 2000. "Regime Support and Campaign Reform." In *Campaign Reform,* edited by Larry Bartels and Lynn Vavreck. Ann Arbor: University of Michigan Press.

_____. 2004. *Presidential Campaign Quality*. New York: Prentice Hall.

Budge, Ian, David Robertson, and Derek Heard. 1987. *Ideology, Strategy and Party Change*. Cambridge: Cambridge University Press.

Burden, Barry, Greg Caldeira, and Timothy Groseclose. 2000. "Measuring the Ideologies of U.S. Senators: The Song Remains the Same." *Legislative Studies Quarterly* 25: 237–58.

Burns, James MacGregor. 1978. *Leadership*. New York: Harper and Row.

Campbell, Angus, Philip Converse, Warren Miller, and Donald Stokes. 1960. *The American Voter*. New York: John Wiley.

Campbell, James. 2000. *The Presidential Campaign*. College Station: Texas A&M University Press.

Carmines, Edward and James Stimson. 1989. *Issue Evolution.* Princeton: Princeton University Press.

Carsey, Thomas M. 2001. *Campaign Dynamics: The Race for Governor.* Ann Arbor: University of Michigan Press.

Carter, Stephen. 1998. *Civility, Manners, Morals and the Etiquette of Democracy.* New York: Harper Collins.

Clinger, J. H. 1987. "The Clean Campaign Act of 1985." *Journal of Law and Politics* 3: 727–48.

Clinton, Joshua and John Lapinski. 2004. "'Targeted' Advertising and Voter Turnout: An Experimental Study of the 2000 Presidential Election." *Journal of Politics* 1: 69–96.

Clymer, Adam. 2002. "Threats and Responses." *New York Times,* September 28.

Cmiel, Kenneth. 1990. *Democratic Eloquence: The Fight over Popular Speech in Nineteenth-Century America.* New York: W. Morrow.

Converse, Philip. 1964. "The Nature of Belief System in Mass Publics." In *Ideology and Discontent,* edited by David Apter. New York: Free Press.

Converse, Philip and Gregory Markus. 1979. "Plus ca change . . . The New CPS Election Study Panel." *American Political Science Review* 73: 32–49.

Dahl, Robert. 1998. *On Democracy.* New Haven: Yale University Press.

Downs, Anthony. 1957. *Economic Theory of Democracy.* New York: Harper.

Ellis, Joseph. 2002. *Founding Brothers.* New York: Vintage.

Epstein, Leon. 1986. *Political Parties in the American Mold.* Madison: University of Wisconsin Press.

Erikson, Robert. 1988. "The Puzzle of Midterm Elections." *Journal of Politics* 50: 1011–29.

Fallows, James. 1997. *Breaking the News.* New York: Vintage Books.

Fair, Ray C. 1988. "The Effect of Economic Events on Votes for President: 1984 Update." *Political Behavior* 10: 168–79.

Farah, Barbara G. and Ethel Klein. 1989. "Public Opinion Trends." In *The Election of 1988,* edited by Gerald M. Pomper, pp. 103–28. Chatham, N.J.: Chatham House Publishers.

Farnsworth, Stephen and S. Robert Lichter. 2003. *The Nightly News Nightmare: Network Television's Coverage of U. S. Presidential Elections, 1988–2000.* New York: Rowman and Littlefield.

Fearon, James. 1999. "Electoral Accountability and the Control of Politicians." In *Democracy, Accountability, and Representation,* edited by Adam Przeworski, Susan Stokes, and Bernard Manin. Cambridge: Cambridge University Press.

Fenno, Richard. 1978. *Home Style.* Boston: Little Brown.

———. 1996. *Senators on the Campaign Trail.* Norman: University of Oklahoma Press.

Fimrite, Peter. 1996. "Stark Furious Over Flyer." *San Francisco Chronicle,* November 1.

Finkel, Steven. 1993. "Reexamining the 'Minimal Effects' Model in Recent Presidential Campaigns." *Journal of Politics* 55: 1–21.

Finkel, Steven and John Geer. 1998. "Spot Check: Casting Doubt on the Demobilizing Effect of Attack Advertising." *American Journal of Political Science* 42: 573–95.

Fiorina, Morris. 1980. *Retrospective Voting in American National Elections.* New Haven: Yale University Press.

Fishkin, James. 1991. *Democracy and Deliberation.* New Haven: Yale University Press.

Freedman, Paul, Michael Franz, and Kenneth Goldstein. 2004. "Campaign Advertising and Democratic Citizenship." *American Journal of Political Science* 48: 723–41.

Freedman, Paul, and Kenneth Goldstein. 1999. "Measuring Media Exposure and the Effects of Negative Campaign Ads." *American Journal of Political Science* 43: 1189–1208.

_____. 2002. "Campaign Advertising and Voter Turnout: New Evidence for Stimulation Effect." *Journal of Politics* 64: 721–40.

Freedman, Paul, W. Wood and Dale Lawton. 1999. "Dos and Don'ts of Negative Ads: What Voters Say." *Campaigns and Elections* 20: 20–25.

Funk, Carolyn. 1999. "Bringing the Candidates into Models of Candidate Evaluation." *Journal of Politics* 61: 700–20.

Geer, John. 1988. "What Do Open-Ended Questions Measure?" *Public Opinion Quarterly* 52: 365–71.

_____. 1991. "Do Open-Ended Questions Measure Salient Issues?" *Public Opinion Quarterly* 55: 360–70.

_____. 1996. *From Tea Leaves to Opinion Polls*. New York: Columbia University Press.

_____. 1998. "Campaigns, Competition, and Political Advertising." In *Politicians and Party Politics,* edited by John Geer. Baltimore: John Hopkins Press.

_____. 1999. "Presidential Advertising in Nomination Battles." Paper presented at Dartmouth College.

_____. 2000. "Assessing Attack Advertising: A Silver Lining." In *Campaign Reform,* edited by Larry Bartels and Lynn Vavreck. Ann Arbor: University of Michigan Press.

Geer, John and James Geer. 2003. "Remembering Attack Ads: An Experimental Investigation of Radio." *Political Behavior* 25: 69–95.

Geer, John and Richard Lau. 2005. "Filling in the Blanks." *British Journal of Political Science.*

Gelman, Andrew, and Gary King. 1993. "Why Are American Presidential Election Polls So Variable When Votes Are so Predictable?" *British Journal of Political Science* 23: 409–51.

Gergen, David R. 2000. *Eyewitness to Power*. New York: Simon and Schuster.

Germond, Jack and Jules Witcover. 1989. The *Trivial Pursuit of the Presidency 1988*. New York: Warner Books.

George, Alexander. 1972. "The Case for Multiple Advocacies in Making Foreign Policy." *American Political Science Review* 65: 751–85.

Goldstein, Ken and Paul Freedman. 2002. "Lessons Learned: Campaign Advertising in the 2000 Elections." *Political Communication* 19: 5–28.

Gronbeck, Bruce. 1994. "Negative Political Ads and American Self-Images." In *Presidential Campaigns and American Self-Images*, edited by A. H. Miller and Bruce Gronbeck. Boulder: Westview.

Grove, Lloyd. 1988. "Dukakis Counterpunches at Bush's Handlers in Television Spots." *Washington Post,* 5 October, p. A1.

Guskind, Robert and Jerry Hagstrom. 1988. "In the Gutter." *National Journal,* November 5, p. 2782.

Guttman, Amy and Dennis Thompson. 1996. *Democracy and Disagreement*. Cambridge: Harvard University Press.

Hagen, Michael and Richard Johnston. 2003. "Advertising and the 2000 Presidential Campaign." Paper delivered at the American Political Science Association Conference, Philadelphia.

Herring, Pendleton. 1940. *Politics of Democracy*, New York: W. W. Norton.

Herrnson, Paul. 2000. *Congressional Election*. 3rd ed. Washington: CQ Press.

_____. 2001. *Playing Hardball: Campaigning for the U.S. Congress*. New Jersey: Prentice Hall.

Hershey, Marjorie. 1989. "The Campaign and the Media." In *The Election of 1988,* edited by Gerald M. Pomper, 95–96. Chatham, N.J.: Chatham House, 1989.

Hetherington, Marc. 1998. "The Political Relevance of Political Trust." *American Political Science Review* 92: 791–808.

_____. 2004. *Why Trust Matters.* Princeton: Princeton University Press.

Hibbing, John and Elizabeth Theiss-Morse. 1995. *Congress as Public Enemy.* Cambridge: Cambridge University Press.

_____. 2002. *Stealth Democracy.* Cambridge: Cambridge University Press.

Holbrook, Alysson, Jon Krosnick, Penny Visser, Wendi Gardner, John Cacioppo. 2001. "Attitudes toward Presidential Candidates and Political Parties: Initial Optimism, Inertial First Impressions, and Focus on Flaws." *American Journal of Political Science* 45: 930–50.

Holbrook, Thomas. 1996. *Do Campaigns Matter?* Thousand Oaks, CA: Sage.

Hollihan, Thomas A. 2001. *Uncivil Wars: Political Campaigns in a Media Age.* New York: Bedford/St Martin's.

Hovland, C. I., I. Janis, and H. H. Kelley. 1953. *Communication and Persuasion: Psychological Studies of Opinion Change.* New Haven: Yale University Press.

Jacobson, Gary. 2003. *Politics of Congressional Elections.* 6th ed. Boston: Addison Wesley.

Jamieson, Kathleen Hall. 1988a. *Eloquence in an Electronic Age.* New York: Oxford University Press.

_____. 1988b. "Our Appalling Politics." *Washington Post.* October 30, C1.

_____. 1992. *Dirty Politics: Deception, Distraction, and Democracy.* Cambridge: Oxford University Press.

_____. 1996. *Packaging the Presidency.* 3rd ed. Cambridge: Oxford University Press.

Jamieson, Kathleen Hall and Paul Waldman. 2002. *The Press Effect Politicians, Journalists, and the Stories That Shape the Political World.* New York: Oxford University Press.

Jamieson, Kathleen Hall, Paul Waldman, and Susan Sheer. 2000. "Eliminate the Negative? Defining and Refining Categories of Analysis for Political Advertisements." In *Crowded Airwaves,* edited by James Thurber, Candice Nelson, and David Dulio. Washington: Brookings Institution Press.

Johnston, Ann and Lynda Lee Kaid. 2002. "Image Ads and U.S. Presidential Advertising: Using Videostyle to Explore Stylistic Differences in Televised Political Ads from 1952–2000." *Journal of Communications* 52: 281–300.

Johnston, Richard, Michael Hagen, and Kathleen Hall Jamieson. 2004. *The 2000 Presidential Elections and the Foundations of Party Politics.* New York: Cambridge University Press.

Joslyn, Mark. 1980. "The Context of Political Ads." *Journalism Quarterly* 57: 92–98.

Just, Marion, Ann Crigler, Dean Alger, Timothy Cook, Montague Kern, Darrell West. 1996. *Crosstalk.* Chicago: University of Chicago Press.

Kahn, Kim Fridkin and Patrick J. Kenney. 1999. *The Spectacle of U.S. Senate Campaigns.* Princeton: Princeton University Press.

_____. 2004. *No Holds Barred: Negativity in U.S. Senate Campaigns.* Upper Saddle River, NJ: Pearson Prentice Hall.

Kaid, Lynda Lee and Anne Johnston. 1991. "Negative Versus Positive TV Advertising in Presidential Campaign, 1960–88." *Journal of Communications* 41: 53–64.

_____. 2000. *Video Style in Presidential Campaigns.* Westport: Praeger.

Kalb, Marvin. 2001. *One Scandalous Story.* New York: Free Press.

Kamber, Victor. 1997. *Poison Politics.* New York: Insight Books.

Karabell, Zachary. 2000. *The Last Campaign*. New York: Vintage.

Keeter, Scott and Michael Delli Carpini. 1996. *What Americans Know About Politics and Why It Matters*. New Haven: Yale University Press.

Keeter, Scott and Cliff Zukin. 1996. *Uninformed Choice*. New York: Praeger.

Kelley, Stanley, Jr. 1956. *Professional Public Relations and Political Power*. Baltimore: Johns Hopkins Press.

————. 1960. *Political Campaigning*. Washington: Brookings Institution.

————. 1983. *Interpreting Elections*. New Jersey: Princeton University Press.

————. 1988. "Democracy and the New Deal Party System." In *Democracy and the Welfare State*, edited by Amy Gutmann. New Jersey: Princeton University Press.

————. 1998. "Politics as Vocation." In *Politicians and Party Politics*, edited by John G. Geer. Baltimore: Johns Hopkins University Press.

————. N.d. *The Spirit of Party*. Unpublished manuscript.

Kern, Montague. 1989. *30-Second Politics: Political Advertising in the Eighties*. New York: Praeger.

Kernell, Samuel. 1977. "Presidential Popularity and Negative Voting." *American Political Science Review* 71: 44–66.

Kessell, John. 1968. *The Goldwater Coalition*. Indianapolis: Bobbs-Merrill Co.

Key, V. O. 1966. *Responsible Electorate*. Cambridge: Harvard University Press.

Kinder, Donald. 1986. "Presidential Character Revisited." In *Political Cognition*, edited by R. Lau and D. Sears. New Jersey: Earlbaum.

Kinder, Donald, M. Peters, R. Abelson, S. Fiske. 1980. "Presidential Prototypes." *Political Behavior* 2: 317–57.

Krasno, Jonathan, and Daniel Seltz. 2000. *Buying Time: Television Advertising in the 1998 Congressional Elections*. New York: NYU School of Law.

Kurtz, Howard. 2000. "GOP Goes on Attack in New Ad: Gore Campaign Hits TV Spot as Negative." *Washington Post*, 1 September.

————. 2004. *Washington Post*, 20 February.

Lau, Richard. 1982. "Negativity in Political Perception." *Political Behavior* 4: 353–77.

————. 1985. "Two Explanations for Negativity Effects in Political Behavior." *American Journal of Political Science* 29:119–35.

Lau, Richard R. and Gerald M. Pomper. 2002. "Effectiveness of Negative Campaigning in U.S. State Elections." *American Journal of Political Science* 46: 47–66.

————. 2004. *Negative Campaigning: An Analysis of U.S. Senate Elections*. New York: Rowman and Littlefield.

Lau, Richard R., David Sears, and Richard Centers. 1979. "The 'Positivity Bias' in Evaluations of Public Figures: Evidence Against Instrument Artifacts." *Public Opinion Quarterly* 43: 347–58.

Lau, Richard R. and Lee Sigelman. 2000. "The Effectiveness of Political Advertising." In *Crowded Airwaves*, edited by James Thurber. Washington D.C.: Brookings Institute.

Lau, Richard R. Lee Sigelman, Caroline Heldman, and Paul Babbitt. 1999. "The Effects of Negative Political Advertising: A Meta-Analytic Assessment." *American Political Science Review* 93: 851–75.

Layman, Geoffrey. 2001. *The Great Divide*. New York: Columbia University Press.

Layman, Geoffrey and Thomas Carsey. 2002. "Party Polarization and 'Conflict Extension' in the American Electorate." *American Journal of Political Science* 46: 786–802.

Levy, Leonard. 1985. *Emergence of Free Press*. New York: Oxford.

Lewis, Anthony. 1991. *Make No Law*. London: Random House.

Lewis, Jeffery. 2000. "Risk Preferences in Spatial Voting Models and the Strategy of Electoral Ambiguity." Unpublished manuscript.

Loomis, Burdett. 2000. "Civility and Deliberation: A Linked Pair?" In *Esteemed Colleagues*, edited by Burdett Loomis. Washington D.C.: Brookings Institution.

Lucas, D. and C. Benson. 1929. "The Historical Trend in Negative Appeals in Advertising." *Journal of Applied Psychology* 13: 346–56.

Luntz, Frank. 1988. *Candidates, Consultants, and Campaigns*. New York: Basil Blackwell.

Lupia, Arthur. 2002. "Who Can Persuade Whom? Implications from the Nexus of Psychology and Rational Choice Theory." In *Thinking About Political Psychology*, edited by James H. Kuklinski. New York: Cambridge University Press.

Lupia, Arthur and Michael McCubbins. 1998. *Elements of Reason, Cognition, Choice, and the Bounds of Rationality*. Cambridge: Cambridge University Press.

MacDonald, Stuart Elaine, George Rabinowitz, and Ola Listshaug. 1995. "Political Sophistication and Models of Issue Voting." *British Journal of Political Science* 25: 453–83.

Macedo, Stephen, ed. 1999. *Deliberative Politics*. New York: Oxford University Press.

Manin, Bernard. 1997. *Principles of Responsible Government*. Cambridge: Cambridge University Press.

Mansbridge, Jane. 1980. *Beyond Adversary Democracy*. New York: Basic Books.

Marcus, George. 2002. *The Sentimental Citizen*. State College: Penn State Press.

Marcus, George and Michael MacKuen. 1993. "Anxiety, Enthusiasm, and the Vote: The Emotional Underpinnings of Learning and Involvement During Presidential Campaigns." *American Political Science Review* 87: 672–85.

Marcus, George, Russell W. Neuman, and Michael MacKuen. 2000. *Affective Intelligence and Political Judgment*. Chicago: University of Chicago Press.

Marks, John. 1996. "The American Uncivil Wars." *U.S. News and World Report*: 67–72.

Mayer, William. 1996. "In Defense of Negative Campaigning." *Political Science Quarterly* 111: 437–55.

McCarty, Nolan, Keith Poole, and Howard Rosenthal. 2003. "Political Polarization and Income Equality." Unpublished manuscript.

McDonald, Michael and Samuel Popkin. 2001. "The Myth of the Vanishing Voter." *American Political Science Review* 95: 963–74.

McGerr, Michael. 1987. *Decline of Popular Politics*. New York: Oxford.

McGinniss, Joe. 1969. *The Selling of the President 1968*. New York: Trident Press.

McWilliams, Wilson Carey. 1989. "The Meaning of the Election." In *The Election of 1988*, edited by Gerald Pomper. New Jersey: Chatham House.

Mendelberg, Tali. 2001. *The Race Card*. Princeton: Princeton University Press.

———. 2002. "The Deliberative Citizen: Theory and Evidence." In *Political Decision-Making, Deliberation, and Participation*, edited by Michael Delli Carpini, Leonie Huddy, and Robert Shapiro. Amsterdam, Boston: JAI Press.

Meirowitz, Adam. 2002. "Informational Party Primaries and Strategic Ambiguity." Unpublished manuscript.

Mill, John Stuart. 1972. *On Liberty*. New York: J. M. Dent & Sons.

Miller, Arthur, M. Wattenberg, and O. Malanchuk. 1986. "Schematic Assessments of Presidential Candidates." *American Political Science Review* 80: 521–40.

Miller, Warren E. 1992. "The Puzzle Transformed." *Political Behavior* 14: 1–43.

Monroe, Alan. D. 1983. "American Party Platforms and Public Opinion." *American Journal of Political Science* 27: 27–42.

Mutz, Diana. 2002. "Cross-Cutting Social Networks: Testing Democratic Theory in Practice." *American Political Science Review* 96: 111–26.

New York Times vs. Sullivan. 1964. 372 U.S. 254.

Neustadt, Richard E. 1990. *Presidential Power and the Modern Presidents.* New York: Free Press.

Page, Benjamin. 1976. *Choices and Echoes.* Chicago: University of Chicago Press.

Patterson, Thomas E. 1993. *Out of Order.* New York: Knopf.

———. 2002. *The Vanishing Voter.* New York: Knopf.

Patterson, Thomas E. and Robert McClure. 1976. *Unseeing Eye.* New York: Putnam.

Petrocik, John. 1996. "Issue Ownership in Presidential Elections, with a 1980 Case Study." *American Journal of Political Science* 40: 825–50.

Pohlman, Dick. 2003. "Americans See Breakdown of Civility." *Kansas City Star,* 17 August.

Pomper, Gerald. 1975. *Voters' Choice: Varieties of American Electoral Behavior.* New York: Dodd, Mead, and Co.

Poole, Keith and Howard Rosenthal. 1996. *Congress: A Political-Economic History of Roll Call Voting.* Oxford: Oxford University Press.

Popkin, Samuel. 1991. *The Reasoning Voter.* Chicago: Chicago University Press.

Powell, G. Bingham. 2000. *Electors and Instruments of Democracy.* New Haven: Yale University Press.

Przeworski, Adam, Susan Stokes, and Bernard Manin, eds. 1999. *Democracy, Accountability, and Representation.* Cambridge: Cambridge University Press.

Prior, Markus. 2001. "Weighted Content Analysis of Political Advertisements." *Political Communication* 18: 335–45.

———. 2002. "Efficient Choices, Inefficient Democracy? The Implications of Cable and Internet Access for Political Knowledge and Voter Turnout." In *Communications Policy and Information Technology*, edited by Lorrie Crasnor and Shane Greenstein. Cambridge, MA: MIT Press.

———. 2003. "Political Implications of Changing Media Environments." Stanford University. Ph.D. dissertation.

———. 2004. *Visual Political Knowledge.* Unpublished manuscript.

———. 2005. "News versus Entertainment." *American Journal of Political Science* 49: 594–609.

Ranney, Austin. 1962. *Essays on the Behavioral Study of Politics.* Urbana-Champaign: University of Illinois Press.

RePass, David. 1971. "Issue Salience and Party Choice." *American Political Science Review* 65: 389–400.

Remini, Robert U. 1998. *Andrew Jackson.* Baltimore: Johns Hopkins University Press.

Rheem, Donald. 1988. "Voters Chide Candidates for Negative Campaigning." *Christian Science Monitor,* 7 November.

Richardson, Glenn. 2002. *Pulp Politics: How Political Advertising Tells the Stories of American Politics.* New York: Rowman and Littlefield.

Riker, William. 1982. *Liberalism Against Populism.* San Francisco: W. H. Freeman.

———. 1996. *The Strategy of Rhetoric.* New Haven: Yale University Press.

Robertson, Andrew W. 1995. *The Language of Democracy.* Ithaca: Cornell University Press.

Robinson, Michael and Margaret Sheehan. 1983. *Over the Wire and on TV.* New York: Russell Sage.

Romano, Luis and J. M. VandeHei. 2004. "Kerry Says Group is a Front for Bush." *Washington Post,* August 8, p. A01.

Runkel, David. 1989. *Campaign for President*. Dover, MA: Auburn House.

Sabato, Larry. 2000. *Feeding Frenzy*. New York: Lanahan Publishing.

Sack, Kevin. 2000. "The Vice President: In Strategy Shift, Gore Ads Question Bush's Capability." *New York Times*, 3 November.

Sanders, Lynn. 1998. "Against Deliberation." *Political Theory* 25: 347–76.

Sapiro, Virginia. 1999. "Considering Political Civility Historically: A Case History of the United States." Paper presented at the Annual Meeting of the International Society for Political Psychology, Netherlands.

Schattschneider, E. E. 1942. *Party Government*. New York: Holt, Rinehart and Winston.

———. 1960. *Semi-Sovereign People*. Hillsdale: Dryden Press.

Schwartz, Tony. 1974. *The Responsive Chord*. New York: Bantam Dell.

Shi, David. 1996. "When Mudslinging was Muddier." *Christian Science Monitor* (17 October).

Sidoti, Liz. 2004. "A Record $600 Million Spent on Presidential-Campaign Ads." *Philadelphia Daily News*, November 1, p. 1.

Sigelman, Lee and Emmett Buell. 2003. "You Take the High Road and I'll Take the Low Road." *Journal of Politics* 65: 518–31.

Sigelman, Lee and Mark Kugler. 2003. "Why Is Research on the Effects of Negative Campaigning So Inconclusive? Understanding Citizens' Perceptions of Negativity." *Journal of Politics* 65: 142–60.

Sigelman, Lee and Eric Voeten. 2004. "Messages Sent, Messages Received? Attacks and Impressions of Negativity in the 2000 Presidential Campaign." Paper presented at the Midwest Political Science Association Conference, Chicago.

Silbey, Joel. 1999. *The American Party Battle*. Cambridge: Harvard University Press.

Simon, Adam. 2002. *The Winning Message*. Cambridge: Cambridge University Press.

Sinopoli, Richard. 1995. "Thick-Skinned Liberalism: Redefining Civility." *American Political Science Review* 89: 612–20.

Spero, Robert. 1980. *The Duping of the American Voter*. New York: Lippincott and Crowell.

Sternthal, Brian, Lynn Philips, and Ruby Dholakia. 1978. "The Persuasive Effect of Source Credibility: A Situational Analysis." *Public Opinion Quarterly* 42: 285–314.

Stevens, Daniel, John Sullivan, Barbara Allen, and Dean Alger. 2003. Paper presented at the American Political Science Association Conference, Philadelphia.

Stokes, Donald. 1963. "Spatial Models of Party Competition." *American Political Science Review* 57: 368–77.

———. 1966. "Spatial Models of Party Competition." In *Elections and the Political Order*, edited by Angus Campbell, Philip Converse, Warren Miller, and Donald Stokes. New York: John Wiley.

———. 1992. "Valence Politics." In *Electoral Politics*, edited by Dennis Kavanagh and David Butler. Oxford: Clarendon Press.

Stolberg, Sheryl. 2003. "The High Costs of Rising Incivility on Capitol Hill." *New York Times*, 30 November.

Stonecash, Jeffery, Mark Brewer, and Mack Mariani. 2002. *Diverging Parties*. Boulder: Westview Press.

Subervi-Velez, Federico, Richard Herrera, and Michael Begay. 1987. "Toward an Understanding of the Role of the Mass Media in Latino Political Life." *Social Science Quarterly* 68: 185–96.

Subervi-Velez, Federico. 1992. "Republican and Democratic Mass Strategies." In *From Rhetoric to Reality*, edited by Rodolfo dela Garza and Louis DeSipio. Boulder: Westview.

_____. 1999. "Targeting the Latino Vote: The Democratic Party's 1996 Mass Strategy." In *Awash in the Mainstream,* edited by Rodolfo dela Garza and Louis DeSipio. Boulder: Westview.

Sundquist, James. 1983. *The Dynamics of the Party System.* Rev. ed. Washington D.C.: Brookings Institution Press.

Swint, Kerwin. 1998. *Political Consultants and Negative Campaigning.* New York: St. Martin's.

Teixeira, Ruy. 1992. *The Disappearing American Voter.* Washington: Brookings.

Thomas, Owen. 1988. "Easy Answer on Prison Furloughs Eludes Dukakis: Public Opinion Makes Bush's Job Easier." *Christian Science Monitor,* 8 September.

Thompson, Dennis. 1970. *Democratic Citizen.* Cambridge: Cambridge University Press.

Toner, Robin. 1988. "Bush, in Enemy Waters, Says Rival Hindered Clean Up of Boston Harbor." *New York Times,* September 2, A16.

Uslaner, Eric. 1993. *Decline of Comity in Congress.* Ann Arbor: University of Michigan Press.

Valentino, Nicholas A., Vincent Hutchings, and Ismail White. 2002 "Cues That Matter." *American Political Science Review* 96:75–90.

Vavreck, Lynn. 2001. "More Than Minimal Effects: Explaining the Differences between Clarifying and Insurgent Presidential Campaigns in Strategy and Effect." University of Rochester. Ph.D. dissertation.

_____. 2003. "Advertising Effectiveness: Experimental v. Observational Tests." Paper presented at American Political Science Association Conference, Philadelphia.

Wattenberg, Martin P. 1991. *Era of Candidate Centered Politics.* Cambridge, MA: Harvard University Press.

Wattenberg, Martin and Craig Brians. 1999. "Negative Campaign Advertising: Demobilizer or Mobilizer?" *American Political Science Review* 93: 891–99.

Weisberger, Bernard. 2000. *America Afire.* New York: William Morrow and Company.

West, Darrell M. 2001. *Air Wars.* 3rd ed. Washington, D.C.: CQ Press.

Will, George. 2002. "The First Amendment on Trial." *Washington Post,* 29 November.

Williams, Lena. 1988. *New York Times,* 12 December.

Wills, Gary. 1988. "Introduction: A Moral Derailing." In *The Winning of the White House,* edited by Donald Morrison. New York: Time, Inc.

Zaller, John. 1999. A Theory of Media Politics. Unpublished manuscript.

_____. 2004. "Floating Voters in U.S. Presidential Elections, 1948–2000." In *Studies in Public Opinion,* edited by Willem Saris and Paul Sniderman, pp. 166–214. Princeton: Princeton University Press.

Zaller, John and Dennis Chu. 1999. "Government's Little Helper: U.S. Press Coverage of Foreign Policy Crises." Unpublished manuscript.

Zhao, Xinshu and Steven Chaffee. 1995. "Campaign Advertisements versus Television News as Sources of Political Issue Information." *Public Opinion Quarterly* 59: 41–65.

Index